# THE SIGNIFICANCE OF SOUNESS

# THE SIGNIFICANCE OF SOUNESS

## RANGERS' JOURNEY BACK TO GLORY

### TOM MILLER

Black&White

Black&White

First published in the UK in 2025 by Black & White Publishing
An imprint of Bonnier Books UK
5th Floor, HYLO, 105 Bunhill Row,
London, EC1Y 8LZ

Copyright © Tom Miller 2025

All rights reserved.
No part of this publication may be reproduced,
stored or transmitted in any form by any means, electronic,
mechanical, photocopying or otherwise, without the
prior written permission of the publisher.

The right of Tom Miller to be identified as Author of this
work has been asserted by him in accordance with the
Copyright, Designs and Patents Act, 1988.

The publisher has made every reasonable effort to contact copyright holders
of images in the picture section. Any errors are inadvertent and anyone who
for any reason has not been contacted is invited to write to the publisher so
that a full acknowledgement can be made in subsequent editions of this work.

A CIP catalogue record for this book is available from the British Library.

ISBN: 978 1 78530 895 6

1 3 5 7 9 10 8 6 4 2

Typeset by Envy Design Ltd
Printed and bound by CPI (UK) Ltd, Croydon CR0 4YY

The authorised representative in the EEA is
Bonnier Books UK (Ireland) Limited.
Registered office address:
Block B, The Crescent Building, Northwood, Santry
Dublin 9, D09 C6X8, Ireland

compliance@bonnierbooks.ie

www.bonnierbooks.co.uk

# DEDICATION

For Patricia – 'Simply the Best'
Thanks to Roddy, Sasha, JJ, Karen, Dave, Ellie,
Lenny and so many more for welcoming Pat and
myself into your community.

Hugo's, Brodies, MoHo and Ariete –
you put the magic in Moffat.

For my big pal Ronnie. We were at Pittodrie on that
momentous day in 1987 – it was indeed champagne fitba!

Thanks to the best big sis – Irene – who answered
the late SOS on the final edit.

To all who contributed to *TSoS*, sincere thanks –
you delivered some wonderful memories.

Can't forget the professionals – David S. and all at
Black & White Publishing who made it all possible.
Thank you.

# CONTENTS

*Foreword by Richard Gough*     1
*Prologue*     5
*Mission accomplished!*     7

1. Holmes at the helm     9
2. Necessity for change     18
3. Send for Souness     27
4. Who is Graeme Souness?     36
5. Friday on my mind     48
6. Ibrox reacts     55
7. Football reacts     63
8. Viva Mexico     68
9. New manager, new squad: 1986–87     77
10. Easter Road: The big kick-off     86
11. Grinding out results     93
12. A Christmas gift to the fans     102
13. Prize day at Pittodrie     108
14. Season one, 1986–87: Cups and Europe     117
15. The players, 1986–87     122
16. Time for reinforcements, 1987–88     124

| | |
|---|---|
| 17. The shame game | 131 |
| 18. High five | 141 |
| 19. Season two, 1987–88: Dethroned but determined | 147 |
| 20. The players, 1987–88 | 153 |
| 21. New faces, 1988–89 | 155 |
| 22. Murray-time | 162 |
| 23. Season three, 1988–89: Get set for nine in a row | 167 |
| 24. The players, 1988–89 | 173 |
| 25. Blue & white dynamite | 175 |
| 26. July 1989: Break the mould, MoJo | 183 |
| 27. Season four, 1989–90 | 190 |
| 28. Terry's all gold | 193 |
| 29. The players, 1989–90 | 201 |
| 30. Squad changes, 1990–91 | 203 |
| 31. Season five, 1990–91 | 207 |
| 32. Departure and last-day drama | 210 |
| 33. The players, 1990–91 | 219 |
| 34. The revolving door – the transfers | 221 |
| 35. The lure of Liverpool | 236 |
| 36. The madness of management | 246 |
| 37. Bounce back at Blackburn | 255 |
| 38. North to Newcastle | 263 |
| 39. Media, health & charity | 272 |
| 40. Phil B – Mr Reliable | 278 |
| 41. Memories, legacy and the significance of Souness | 281 |

| | |
|---|---|
| *Addendum: Honours* | 292 |
| *The last word by Ally McCoist* | 295 |
| *Acknowledgements* | 296 |

# FOREWORD

I remember my first call-up for Scotland; I was 19 or 20. My dad told me, when you go into a team for the first time, pick a good example and follow his lead. I chose Graeme Souness, and there was not a better role model. Kenny Dalglish was also in the squad, and what a player he was, but Graeme was the skipper. On my first game he said to me: 'If you are in trouble just give me the ball.' It's something I picked up on, and years later and by then the senior player, I would say the same to youngsters; although if I'm being honest, I was more likely to send a hopeful ball up the park rather than find a special pass to keep possession the way Graeme would. It was a real comfort to me that Graeme Souness was there for me, and I hope young players in my team felt I was there for them.

Graeme was my hero. He had a massive impact on my career, and while he was Scotland captain, I made my mind up that one day I wanted to emulate that, and it was a very proud occasion when I did.

Not long after Graeme had taken over at Ibrox, we played them and we won 3–2, with Coisty scoring both Rangers goals and Kevin Gallacher getting two for Dundee United. I think former Rangers man Ian Redford got the late winner. Rangers may have been beaten, but it was so obvious something special was happening and I wanted to be a part of it. My grandfather and my dad, Charlie, who had played with Charlton, were both Rangers men, and I wanted to do them proud in a Rangers shirt. But Jim McLean was United's manager then, and he wasn't entertaining any approach that Rangers made for me. Remember too, it hadn't been that long since Dundee United were champions and they were expected to continue to improve and challenge at home and in Europe, which they did, so Jim wasn't in the business of selling players to weaken his side and strengthen opponents.

Graeme had just come back from Italy, where he had picked up so many good habits, and they were pretty much all in evidence again now he was Rangers' manager. He was a winner, and he was filling his dressing room with like-minded players who were strong and tough mentally and ready to take the club forwards. I wanted to be one of his winners!

Rangers again tried to sign me from Dundee United, but again Jim blocked the move. This time, however, Spurs also came in for me, and when Jim's valuation was met I was soon on my way to White Hart Lane. I enjoyed my time at Spurs, and captained the side in the FA Cup Final, but I still had a hankering for Rangers, especially after the title had been won in Graeme's first season in charge. He had also made some incredible signings in Terry Butcher and Graham Roberts. Graham got his move because, like Dundee United, Spurs were also quick to reject another approach from Rangers to take me to Ibrox. I was settled in London, but Spurs weren't Rangers, and that's where I was determined to be.

# FOREWORD

Fourteen months after I joined Spurs, they finally accepted that my heart was at Ibrox and they agreed to sell me to Rangers. Spurs made a hefty profit on what they paid for me and Rangers broke the bank to get me. The determination and tenacity of Graeme Souness to make my dreams come true is something I will never forget. I could have made more money staying with Tottenham, but this was the move that meant so much to me. It was a massive fee to pay for a central defender, and at the media conference the press were making a big thing of the 1.5m transfer value. Graeme, in his usual authoritative style, batted the negative away and just said: 'Look, I know Richard Gough will play at this club for ten years, and if you take that into consideration, the transfer fee will prove to be a bargain!' Graeme actually got that one wrong – I played for the club for 11 years! To be fair, Graeme's comments took a lot of pressure off me and avoided the constant reference to my transfer value.

Graeme did so many good things for me. It was the best time of my career, and when you think of the club's history over the last 150 years plus, the nine-in-a-row period is up there with anything they've achieved. When I joined Rangers, it was the perfect time for me, as I had matured and come back to Scotland a better player for my experience down south. Rangers had the cream of the crop, with Graeme bringing in Ray Wilkins, Gary Stevens and, later, Trevor Steven. The approach to training and games that these guys brought to the club, in the image that Graeme wanted, was sensational.

Ahead of games, Graeme wasn't big on tactics; it was maybe the Liverpool way from when he played there. He would say: 'You are here because you are good players – go and show it.'

# THE SIGNIFICANCE OF SOUNESS

For some games, though, such as the Old Firm, he would sit us down and remind us of our responsibilities to the club and the supporters in a very motivational way. Of course, Walter was there too, and he would give us our game plan finesse, but together they were some team. No wonder Graeme still says his best-ever signing was Walter Smith.

It was the most rewarding and enjoyable 11 years of my career. I was very honoured to pull on a Rangers jersey, and I was very honoured to play under Graeme Souness. He had a huge impact on me, all the way back to my Scotland squad days as a youngster, making my way in the game. To this day, I still call Graeme Souness 'gaffer'.

I always will.

Richard Gough, iconic Rangers<br>nine-in-a-row-winning captain

# PROLOGUE

In late May 2025, a consortium headed by Andrew Cavenagh and Paraag Marathe took a controlling interest in Rangers Football Club.

Cavenagh would take on the role of chairman while Marathe would support him in the position of vice chairman. Paraag Marathe remains a vastly experienced business leader, including carrying the title of President of 49ers Enterprises, a sports investment operation with San Francisco 49ers CEO Jed York. World-class sports brands are Cavenagh and Marathe's bread and butter.

No time was wasted, and a new board of directors was soon in place with the vision to prioritise Rangers' on-pitch performance while ensuring long-term financial sustainability.

An immediate investment of £20 million was also committed.

It's another epic new era for Rangers, with the incoming hierarchy determined to build something supporters can be proud of for years to come.

Within a week of taking over, the new board appointed Russell Martin as head coach to take the team forwards on the park. Unfortunately, results under Russell Martin proved not to be favourable and he was relieved of his duties on 5 October 2025.

Martin previously managed MK Dons and Swansea, and most recently had secured promotion back to England's top flight with Southampton.

There are clear parallels to the boardroom and football management changes of almost 40 years previous when David Holmes swept into power at Ibrox and shook the football world to the core by making Graeme Souness the new Rangers boss, even though he had no previous experience as a football manager.

It's too early yet to make further comparisons on what success may look like for the new Rangers–49ers alliance, but if they go about their business in a similar fashion to David Holmes and his team, who delivered trophies as Rangers were restored to the pinnacle of the Scottish game, it will be a quite terrific period for Rangers and their massive global support.

We wish them well in everything they do!

# MISSION ACCOMPLISHED!

### 2 May 1987

When David Holmes appointed Graeme Souness as Rangers player–manager in April 1986, his primary target was to secure the Scottish Premier Division title.

Rangers hadn't been champions since the 1977–78 season, as Celtic, Aberdeen and Dundee United dominated the domestic game.

It was the Light Blues' 38th Scottish title, finishing with 69 points from a demanding 44-game campaign. Celtic were runners-up on 63 points, while the New Firm – Dundee United and Aberdeen – finished third and fourth with 60 and 58 points respectively.

The scenes of joy will live long in the memory, as Rangers fans swamped the track and Pittodrie playing surface to celebrate. It may have been only a 1–1 draw against Aberdeen, but with Celtic losing to Falkirk on the same day it was enough to see Rangers crowned as champions.

The Souness influence was almost immeasurable – despite Souness playing only 32 matches across all competitions that season – and his presence alongside, allied to his ability to influence his young midfielders Derek Ferguson and Ian Durrant, was massive. Remember, too, the parts played by his cross-border recruits who came and immediately embraced the demands of being a Ranger. Take a bow Terry Butcher, Chris Woods and Graham Roberts, in particular.

David Holmes enjoyed the moment from his position in the Pittodrie directors' box, and understandably stood back to reflect on the achievement of a job well done. However, it was only the beginning, and a terrific platform was now in place to take the club further forwards.

We now look at the backstory that delivered the title on that momentous day in 1987. The significance of Souness!

# CHAPTER 1:

# HOLMES AT THE HELM

Rangers were in a mess both on and off the park.

In early 1986, John Lawrence Ltd completed the purchase of almost two-thirds of the shareholding of Rangers FC, effectively giving them control of the famous club. Chairman of the John Lawrence Group was Lawrence Marlborough, whose grandfather John Lawrence founded the business and had been a successful Rangers chairman over many years, including on the occasion when the European Cup Winners' Cup was secured in Barcelona in 1972. Marlborough was domiciled in Nevada, partly as a tax exile, and partly as he wanted to take a slight step back from the day-to-day responsibilities of the various group companies, of which Rangers was now a serious contributor.

David Holmes, who was already on the Lawrence Group payroll, was the man Marlborough empowered to review the whole Ibrox operation and report his findings and proposals.

Holmes wasn't a Rangers man, and since his schooldays in Bonnybridge, he had supported his local team, Falkirk, and watched them at their old Brockville stadium as often as he could. While the dark blue of the Bairns was where David's heart lay, his older brother, Danny, was a Rangers fanatic. While at Denny High School, David's PE teacher was the legendary Rangers and Scotland goalkeeper Bobby Brown. They would meet again under vastly different circumstances, when Holmes became chairman of Rangers and Brown as a former player was a regular visitor to games at Ibrox. David Holmes was quite a capable footballer himself and played junior football with both Dunipace FC and Broxburn Athletic. While football was a bit of a passion, the ambitious Holmes decided he wanted to embark on a teaching career. After qualifying, he worked at Graeme High School in Falkirk. His teaching experience stood him in good stead when he joined the Lawrence Group as a training officer. It was a time of change, and his diligence and commitment caught the eye of Lawrence Marlborough. Marlborough saw something in David Holmes and quickly broadened his responsibilities as his stature grew in the business. In the late 1970s, David Holmes had been elevated to director level within Lawrence Construction, and not long after, he was actively involved with almost all the group companies. These experiences made Holmes the perfect man to get under the surface at Rangers to determine just why they were underperforming on the pitch, and as a business as well.

After David Holmes had spent time at Ibrox, and at the first suitable meeting of the Lawrence Group directors, Marlborough invited David Holmes to offer his report on where Rangers were at that time. Rangers chairman, John Paton, whose original group responsibility was with his Taggarts car company, wasn't overly pleased as Marlborough's man took centre stage. David Holmes had been appointed to the Rangers board a matter of months before. However, while new to the Rangers boardroom, Holmes was a trusted lieutenant in the Marlborough hierarchy and had been given a clear mandate by his US-based boss to put things right at Ibrox.

Later, David Holmes was reported to have said: 'Rangers had been run by what could be best described as a committee while lacking direction and purpose, and that was coming from the top.'

There had been quite a number of revolutionary boardroom shake ups in 1983, especially following John Greig resigning as manager. Paton and vice chair Jack Gillespie, who had a Vauxhall dealership based in Lenzie, were joined by two new directors: Tom Dawson, who was also in the motor trade and based in Helensburgh, and Jim Robinson, who ran a successful scrap metal business. Rae Simpson had stepped down from the chairman's role, and this allowed John Paton to take on the main position in the new-look board of directors. Gillespie, however, still retained the second largest shareholding in the club, and that was to later make an influential impact on controlling interests in Rangers.

The directors enjoyed the gravitas and stature that came with the blazer, but it was Holmes who had the vision and drive to make the major changes needed if Rangers were to get back to the top. David Holmes had to achieve this against a backdrop of suspicion and fear from the old guard that they were more than likely on the way out. Fortunately, Holmes had the fortitude, resilience and strength of character to face any obstacles in his way, as he looked to deliver against the biggest challenge he faced since joining the Lawrence empire.

Jock Wallace was the man the directors turned to as the

replacement for John Greig, with perhaps the successes of Wallace's first spell in charge still relatively fresh in the memory. Jock Wallace had delivered three league titles, three Scottish Cups and two League Cups first time round, but had left his position in controversial circumstances in 1978, with Wallace maintaining silence for his reasons for leaving right up until his death in 1996. Speculation suggested Wallace was frustrated by a lack of transfer funds, and a belief that he was undervalued and underpaid, while also facing a breakdown in his relationship with Willie Waddell, who he had replaced as manager after Rangers' European triumph in 1972.

Wallace had gone on to manage Leicester City and Motherwell, before answering the call to come back to Ibrox in 1983.

It was reported Alex Ferguson at Aberdeen and Jim McLean at Dundee United both turned down the opportunity to replace John Greig as Rangers manager, before Wallace took up the challenge.

Success on the field second time round was proving hard to come by but Wallace did win two League Cups; however, it really wasn't enough and crowds were dwindling fast. Rangers had lost their way. Something had to be done.

David Holmes had a plan, and before he pulled the trigger to sack Wallace in April 1986, discussions with Graeme Souness to succeed him were at an advanced stage.

Wallace left Rangers on 7 April 1986 after a crowd of just over 12,500 watched Rangers lose 2–0 in a friendly to Spurs at Ibrox. The fixture had been arranged to fill a gap in the schedule created by an early exit from the Scottish Cup.

Before Holmes struck the deal with Souness, he put

Lawrence Marlborough on the spot by asking for a copy of Rangers' business plan. Marlborough responded that he didn't believe they actually had one, nor to his knowledge had they ever had one! Holmes formulated his own business plan and immediately went about activating it. A big part of that plan was to have Rangers competing in Europe, with the UEFA Cup a prime target in the first instance. David Holmes recruited an experienced campaigner to support his boardroom presentations when he invited Willie Waddell to join him, despite Waddell having left the board a couple of years previously. Thereafter, players were playing for their very future, while the dinosaur directors were also feeling the pressure. David Holmes may have been a fan of Falkirk Football Club, but now Rangers was the only game in town for him! As well as a major overhaul and displacement of the club's accountants, bankers and lawyers, Holmes left no stone unturned to get Rangers off their knees. His business plan was presented to Lawrence Marlborough and it included the appointment of a new manager. The man he put forwards was beyond high profile – it was of course Graeme Souness, who was still playing with Sampdoria. When Marlborough gave the OK it signalled the end for Wallace, and Scottish football was about to be changed, and how!

On 8 April 1986 and on his 51st birthday, David Holmes welcomed Graeme Souness to Ibrox and introduced him to the assembled media pack as Rangers' new player–manager. Souness was 32 years of age and captain of the Scottish national side about to head off to Mexico for the World Cup. On the same day, it was confirmed Jock Wallace had left the club.

Graeme Souness became only the eighth man to manage

# THE SIGNIFICANCE OF SOUNESS

Rangers in their 114-year history and he put pen to paper on a five-year contract.

The appointment captured the imagination of not just Rangers fans, but all of those interested in British football, and immediately the demand for season tickets at Ibrox just went crazy!

Ticket-office manager at the time was Jim Hannah: 'We could hardly cope with demand for tickets. Graeme Souness just being in the building gave everyone a real shot in the arm and energised every department, not just the football side of things. David Holmes too was a terrific leader and very quickly everybody was behind his plans to take the club forwards. The new signings helped, no doubt about that, but there was a real clamber to get season tickets. The Premiere Club was rolled out and sold out in the Govan Rear and Govan Front. Tickets were then released for both Upper and Lower Copland Road stands followed by the main stand then East Enclosure. Every week the numbers were just increasing and we very soon had close to 34,000 at every home game. It was unprecedented.'

Other aspects of the club David Holmes was keen to develop were the advertising sponsorship and commercial opportunities. His timing was spot on, as was John Gilligan's in 1987, when a deal was struck with Scottish & Newcastle Breweries Ltd to have the McEwan's Lager brand emblazoned on Rangers shirts. John was making his way up the corporate ladder and remembers: 'It was a dream come true; as a diehard Rangers fan, to be part of it was just awesome. McEwan's became only the second-ever Rangers shirt sponsor, succeeding CR Smith who had previously balanced their Rangers commitment with the same deal with Celtic. We again offered the same package we had agreed with Rangers to Celtic, but they chose to stick with the glazing company. We were conscious there may have been some negatives, with potential for our brand to be linked with only one side of the Old Firm divide, but it was Celtic's decision not to change. It was exciting times for Rangers' commercial operations, and in the early days [there was] the McPhail Suite, named after legendary forward Bob McPhail, who played at Rangers for 12 years, scoring 230 league goals, which was a record that stood for 50 years before being broken by Ally McCoist. This facility was a popular venue for sponsors and their guests on match days, under commercial boss Bob Reilly, who was so far ahead of his time and vital to David Holmes's plan to bring added finance into the club. Later, the McPhail Suite changed to the Chairman's Club, as it still is today, and it's still a sell-out at every game.' Later, John Gilligan would work closely with Sandy Jardine, when he was in a commercial role at Rangers, while of course, John would have his own part to play in 2015, when along with Paul Murray and Dave King they wrestled boardroom control away from Mike Ashley and his consortium. John would also step in as interim chairman when John Bennett stepped down in September 2024 through ill health.

John looks back on the job David Holmes did: 'Not only did David Holmes get Rangers back profitable and challenging, he did it in double-quick time. His vision to get Graeme Souness on board was a master stroke.'

Previously, David Holmes had confirmed his shortlist to replace Jock Wallace was very short indeed. The only candidate

## THE SIGNIFICANCE OF SOUNESS

was Graeme Souness. It had taken since mid-February to get the deal in place, but David Holmes had his man.

Winning a cup and league double in that first season made David Holmes a very proud man.

David Holmes was empowered by Lawrence Marlborough to take Rangers forwards as he saw fit, and Holmes, who served the club originally as a director and then as chairman after a tryst between Marlborough and Jack Gillespie, gave the Nevada-based grandson of John Lawrence controlling interest in Rangers. It's believed to have incentivised Gillespie to get behind the Marlborough and Holmes plans, including selling his shares to the Lawrence Group for around £1 million. Gillespie was assured that his place on the board was not in jeopardy. Rangers official historian David Mason looks back to those days of change: 'Make no mistake, David Holmes was a colossus for Rangers, a workaholic who was driven, committed and determined beyond belief to restore Rangers to the pinnacle of the Scottish game. David would be at his desk at five in the morning, every morning, and would usually be last to leave of an evening. David Holmes made things happen. By appointing Graeme Souness he was delivering box office, and every aspect of the club was immediately on an upwards trajectory. The huge increase in season ticket sales protected the club financially, with a massively improved income stream. David Holmes got Freddie Fletcher and Bob Reilly on board to take the commercial activities to new levels. Demand for the then limited hospitality facilities was unprecedented. It was the interest in Graeme Souness and his new players that had people clambering to get to Ibrox. As for Graeme himself, when he walked into a room, he owned it. Tanned, immaculately dressed and he carried himself like a film star. David Holmes knew exactly how Graeme would make his aspirations for Rangers a reality, and he was happy to back his judgement in the transfer market to further accelerate it. Our previous big signings had been Cammy Fraser and Iain Ferguson from Dundee, and while they were good players alright, David Holmes sanctioning the signings of Chris Woods and Terry Butcher was from an entirely different script. The fans were flooding back, and David Holmes was very quickly on track to deliver what he had promised Lawrence Marlborough he could achieve.'

Lawrence Marlborough's decision to give David Holmes the keys to Ibrox must be up there, and equal to, David Holmes's own call to install Graeme Souness as Rangers manager. Both have made huge contributions to the history of the football club.

David Holmes stayed at Rangers through the sale to David Murray in November 1988, and continued as chairman until being succeeded by Murray himself in June 1989.

After a break from football, David Holmes had a short spell on the board of his home town team, Falkirk, and later joined Dundee FC as managing director.

## CHAPTER 2:
# NECESSITY FOR CHANGE

The 1977–78 season was momentous for Rangers. Jock Wallace masterminded the club's fourth clean sweep of the major domestic honours. It was the second treble the Light Blues achieved in three years. Some visionary transfer business had been conducted through the summer close season, with Davie Cooper coming in from Clydebank, Gordon Smith swapping the blue of Kilmarnock for Rangers, while a young man stepped out of the junior ranks to become an immediate hero for Rangers fans – Bobby Russell was a midfielder who was so elegant and creative that it's hard to believe his previous club was Shettleston Juniors!

So, with two clean sweeps in three seasons, Rangers fans could be forgiven for thinking that an extended period of dominance was on the cards. However, nobody foresaw that manager Jock Wallace would walk away within a couple of weeks of completing the historic treble, with a 2–1 Scottish Cup Final win over Aberdeen.

Likewise, nobody would have believed it would take another nine years before the league flag again flew over

# NECESSITY FOR CHANGE

Ibrox, with Graeme Souness in charge, but that's exactly how things panned out.

Wallace's departure remains a curious one that the man himself refused to elaborate on, and he effectively took the reasons to his grave with him 18 years later. Even during his second spell as Rangers boss between 1983 and 1986 it was not a topic he chose to develop.

With Wallace away, Rangers wasted no time in elevating retiring captain John Greig to the manager's office. It was a bold move, and a massive challenge for the man who would much later be awarded the accolade of 'the greatest ever Ranger', and undoubtably it was 'big boots' to fill for a vastly experienced player but an untried manager. Greig's previous teammates were all good players, but it was a huge gulf to cross, from playing to being the man in charge. He did inherit a fluid side, with Derek Johnstone scoring 38 goals in all competitions the previous season, while new man Gordon Smith pitched in with 27 goals. Others may suggest some of the squad had peaked and were the wrong side of 30, but guys like Peter McCloy, Sandy Jardine, Tommy McLean and Alex MacDonald, who had all experienced the European Cup Winners' Cup success of 1972, still delivered for their former skipper.

The season began badly for Greig and they failed to win any of their first six league matches. That horrible start pretty much handed the initiative to Celtic; however, Rangers showed their strong desire to retain the domestic cups and were successful in beating Hibernian, although it took two replays to do so, as the Scottish Cup returned to Ibrox. The League Cup was also back in the trophy room after getting the better of Aberdeen in the final.

The league campaign was disappointing, finishing second with 45 points, winning only 18 games, drawing nine, while also losing nine.

In Europe, too, Rangers looked a different proposition, with memorable wins against Juventus and UEFA Cup holders PSV Eindhoven. Rangers exited the European Cup at the quarter-final stage of the tournament despite a heroic one-all draw with Cologne at Ibrox, having lost the first leg 1–0 away; it was the German giants who booked their place in the last four.

Inside Ibrox there were concerns about dropping numbers, particularly for league games. In April, only 12,000 turned out to see a 3–0 win over Motherwell. Against the same opponents in the previous September, 26,000 came through the gates to see Rangers take the points in a 4–1 win.

For a first season under Greig it certainly had some highs, but there were some obvious lows as well.

It all went wrong the following season as Rangers struggled to find any kind of consistency. In the league, Rangers finished a distant fifth behind champions Aberdeen, who had Greig's ex-teammate Alex Ferguson at the helm. Aberdeen also ended Rangers' interest in the League Cup, while the Scottish Cup was adorned with green and white ribbons as the Light Blues lost out to a deflected goal from George McCluskey, which was enough to give Celtic the cup. By the end of April 1980, fans had already started to, again, vote with their feet, as only 7,655 were at Ibrox for a 1–0 win over Kilmarnock. One week previously, 8,504 – almost 1,000 more spectators – were inside Rugby Park as that 1–0 scoreline was reversed and Killie took the spoils.

# NECESSITY FOR CHANGE

The European adventure was over before Christmas, going out to Valencia. Rangers came back from Spain with a very creditable 1–1 draw, but went down 3–1 at Ibrox.

One memory from the season was the 3–1 Drybrough Cup Final win over Celtic. It heralded the most astonishing goal from Davie Cooper as he effectively played keepy-uppy inside the Celtic 18-yard box, lofting the ball over a series of defenders before dispatching the ball into the net. The late Sandy Jardine also scored an incredible solo goal, which he himself described as the best of his career, while young John MacDonald claimed his first Old Firm goal, and as he left the field to celebrate he was promptly sick, as adrenaline and emotion took over. But that early promise from the victory over Celtic in August 1979 had gone by the time the business stage of the season came round in the spring of 1980.

The 1980–81 season didn't deliver much joy either.

John Greig refreshed his squad by bringing in Jim Bett from Lokeren in Belgium, and Colin McAdam joined from Partick Thistle with his transfer fee of £150k determined by a tribunal.

The season started so well as Rangers went on an unbeaten run of 15 matches, including two Old Firm victories. However, through November and December form deserted them, and Celtic were ultimately crowned champions with Rangers finishing third, a full 12 points behind their biggest rivals.

Some consolation was taken when the Light Blues lifted the Scottish Cup, beating Dundee United 4–1 in a Hampden replay after a flat and uninspiring 0–0 draw first time round. In the League Cup, ambitions ended in September, going down to Aberdeen in a sectional mini-league format.

Crowds remained a concern, with a particular low point

## THE SIGNIFICANCE OF SOUNESS

being a home match against Morton on 1 April 1981, when only 7,202 attended.

It wasn't a new phenomenon, fans voting with their feet and not attending matches. In the last season of Jock Stein being in charge at Celtic, despite the incredible success he had previously delivered, as a resurgent Rangers swept the boards winning every major domestic competition, crowds at Celtic Park fell to as low as 5,000, long before the league was officially lost.

John Greig's fourth season in charge, again, ended without the league championship being delivered. The League Cup was small consolation and the only trophy won that season. Rangers finished third in the table as Celtic were again crowned champions. Aberdeen ran out comfortable winners in the Scottish Cup Final despite Greig's side opening the scoring on the day; it finished 4–1 in favour of the Dons. Analysis shows Rangers won only 16 of their 36 games in the league campaign.

For the 1982–83 season, Greig's judgement in the transfer market was backed by chairman Rae Simpson and his board of directors. Dave MacKinnon was recruited from Partick Thistle; Hibernian captain Craig Paterson swapped Edinburgh for Glasgow; while European Cup finalist Robert Prytz, whose Malmö side had lost out to Nottingham Forest, was to be the driving force in a new-look midfield. Former Airdrie favourite Sandy Clark came back north after a spell at West Ham United.

Despite what looked like a fiercely competitive rebuild of the playing squad, the big prize of the title still eluded them. It proved to be a barren season for Rangers. The previous season's 16 league wins was reduced to only 13 this time around, and

# NECESSITY FOR CHANGE

a fourth place finish in the table was as much as John Greig's squad could muster. They managed to be runners-up again in the Scottish Cup, with Aberdeen lifting the silverware just ten days after they had won the European Cup Winners' Cup against Real Madrid in Gothenburg. In December, the League Cup Final was also lost. This time it was Celtic who took the honours. Rangers had used 27 players throughout the season but fluidity and consistency were sadly absent. As far as the league went, it was the unfancied Dundee United who claimed the title for the first and only time in their history.

A new low of only 5,342 were inside Ibrox for a comfortable 6–0 League Cup quarter-final tie against Kilmarnock in October 1982. Financially, the lack of paying fans was surely becoming a genuine concern to the board of directors and stakeholders alike.

The following season, 1983–84, started with John Greig still in the hot seat, with Tommy McLean his assistant. Again, the league campaign started badly with one point only from the first four league games. The League Cup, however, would bring some respite, as they won nine of their home and away ties and drew 1–1 at Tannadice Park to progress to the final against Celtic. It was a thrilling encounter, with Ally McCoist scoring a hat-trick in front of a crowd of 66,369 in the national stadium. McCoist had been snapped up by John Greig from Sunderland, who had signed the young striker two years previously from St Johnstone.

Unfortunately, the signing of McCoist wasn't enough to save John Greig's job. Five months before that League Cup success, Greig had resigned. Before leaving the club, Rangers under Greig had racked up a record-breaking 18–0 aggregate win over Maltese champions Valletta, but it was the lack of league success that ultimately influenced his departure. The pressure proved too much even for a genuine true-blue hero. On 28 October 1983, the Rangers board accepted John Greig's resignation.

Jock Wallace would take over on 10 November, but despite an obvious lift being evident in the dressing room, and the fans believing that the man who had won two trebles in his first spell could now get the club back on track, the season finished with Rangers in fourth place. However, that old habit of League Cup success and the goalscoring prowess of McCoist were the two bright spots that would give the club a platform to go forwards in the 1984–85 season, when old-school pre-season training, including a trip to the infamous murder hill at Gullane Beach, would be high on Jock Wallace's agenda. Wrestling the league title back in the face of the fiercest of competition, in the form of Dundee United, Aberdeen and biggest rivals Celtic, would be his absolute priority.

Hopes and aspirations for success under the returning hero were high. Wallace had done it all before and there was no reason to suggest he couldn't do it again.

It would prove to be tight at the top of the table in the first half of the season, but New Year's Day, 1985, and defeat to Celtic saw the club's form totally implode, and only four more league victories were enjoyed to the end of the season. That awful run of form saw Rangers end the season a massive 21 points adrift of champions Aberdeen. Like Greig the season before, Wallace had been given significant funds to strengthen the squad. Cammy Fraser and Iain Ferguson arrived in a double signing from Dundee, the unpredictable but adventurous Ted

# NECESSITY FOR CHANGE

McMinn joined from Queen of the South, while Wallace coaxed Derek Johnstone to leave Chelsea for a second spell at Ibrox. The Scottish Cup brought no rewards, but again Wallace's ability to bring the League Cup home was evident, with new signing Iain Ferguson scoring the only goal of the game against Dundee United. Ferguson would actually sign for United when he left Rangers.

Another Ferguson was making a bit of a name for himself as a midfield player in Wallace's squad. Derek Ferguson had been given game time as a 15-year-old in Tom Forsyth's testimonial match, and then made his competitive debut aged 16 years and 24 days, a record that stands to this day. As an aside, Derek's son, Lewis, who starred with Hamilton and Aberdeen, before moving to Italy with Bologna, has followed in some famous footsteps. In May 2025, Lewis captained his side to Coppa Italia success in a stunning win over Milan.

Young Ferguson became only the second Scot to lift that particular trophy – Graeme Souness being the other. Many say Rangers should have signed Ferguson because of the family links, but it just didn't happen. His father, however, was an excellent player for the club and really thrived after Souness replaced Wallace.

Again, Rangers completed the league campaign finishing a hugely disappointing fourth. Rangers fans were beyond disillusioned, while the board must surely have been thinking that they should really have pushed the boat out and replaced John Greig with one of the New Firm managers: Alex Ferguson at Aberdeen or Jim McLean at Dundee United. For the last home league game of the season a crowd of only 7,149 were there to see Rangers lose 1–0 to Hibernian.

## THE SIGNIFICANCE OF SOUNESS

One man who was getting more and more frustrated by Rangers' failures was Lawrence Marlborough, who decided changes were essential.

Marlborough, representing the Lawrence Group of companies, set about acquiring shares to gain a majority status, which would allow him to install his own man at Ibrox and drive the club forwards to meet his objectives.

Already a big player in the Lawrence boardroom, David Holmes was tasked by Marlborough to 'make Rangers great again!'

# CHAPTER 3:

# SEND FOR SOUNESS

It was a proud moment when Graeme Souness climbed the marble staircase before entering the Blue Room to be unveiled as Rangers' new player–manager. David Holmes was also a proud man, as Souness had been his one and only target for the job. It was bold, innovative and imaginative, and a radical change of direction for a major club like Rangers to appoint an untried rookie gaffer. But Holmes just knew that everything about getting Souness on board was the real deal, and in their many conversations it became apparent very quickly that Souness was beyond excited at the prospect of restoring Rangers to their former glory. David Holmes consulted a very close-knit number of confidants to discuss Rangers' next potential manager. One trusted associate was Alan Ferguson, who was a director of public relations outfit, Proscot. Holmes had brought Freddie Fletcher into the Rangers inner sanctum in a commercial role; Freddie was with another Lawrence Group company, Treeby Office Supplies. Fletcher was the man who had previous business collaboration with Ferguson. Alan Ferguson remained on call in a consultancy capacity as Holmes's plans were pushed into action, but the thorny issue of a new manager had still to be resolved.

Crowds for home games at Ibrox were continuing to fall, with an average of under 20,000 for most games. On the field the team were far from competitive. The incoming manager had to excite the fans, carry the charisma to reignite the club and have a contacts book that he would use to entice quality players. Holmes felt it wasn't really going to be a gamble to put Souness into office, but it was complicated as Graeme was still under a playing contract at Sampdoria. David Holmes had no previous history with the Scotland star, so making the first and most important contact was going to be a difficult one, and David was cautious about involving intermediaries to at least determine if his plan had legs before it got into the public domain. David was encouraged to take respected sports writer Ken Gallacher into his trust, and see if Ken, who had published many Rangers books over an extended period, could assist. Remember, this was at a time before mobile phones, but Gallacher came up trumps with Graeme's home number in Genoa. Now the chase could be accelerated. The deal with Gallacher, who at the time was chief football writer with the *Scottish Sun*, was that were he to fully respect Rangers' position he would be rewarded with the first exclusive if a deal could be struck. Gallacher agreed that he would hold off until progress was made one way or another. Ken Gallacher was as good as his word and he got his story when the time was right – it was a massive scoop that frustrated every other journalist, but he'd earned his headline.

David Holmes made the call, but Souness was still at training. However, his wife Danielle took the message and promised that her husband would return David's call. When Graeme returned from training and was told of the call – he was intrigued. Graeme phoned back, and that persuasive manner of David Holmes had all but won Souness over within a matter of minutes. Graeme was more than interested, but he had to weigh up all the factors that were all too obvious: still under contract at Sampdoria where he was enjoying his football, the Genoa lifestyle, the money was better than good, his family was settled and there was a summer World Cup coming up that Graeme was keen to be a part of. Management hadn't really been on his agenda, yet. Souness also held the belief that with a bit of investment in key areas of the squad, Sampdoria could build on their Coppa Italia success and actually challenge for Serie A. However, even after the limited conversations Graeme held with David Holmes, he felt comfortable and that he could trust and work with him. A meeting was arranged to flesh out more details of the opportunity. Neutral territory, the Mayfair Hotel in London, was the venue, and it was there that the deal was agreed, subject to Graeme's wife being fully behind the move. That was a conversation that had its own pressures, as Danielle had her own tax implications to face were she to return to the UK as a resident. After some soul-searching it was agreed that Graeme would move to Glasgow himself for the first 12 months, with Danielle and the kids moving to Majorca where she already had family based there. A second follow-up meeting then took place in Milan that saw David Holmes jet in and out on the same day as the i's were dotted and the t's crossed. It was a relatively easy task to finalise the agreement as it was two like-minded professionals committed to the project and a bond between the two was already evident.

The contract was based on a three-year playing agreement and a five-year management package. As for the salary, well, it would prove to be the highest remuneration ever for any player or manager in the history of Scottish football. Graeme was earning serious money in Italy, which at the time was considered to be the world hotbed of high pay in football, and David Holmes knew he had to go the extra financial mile to get his man. But this was about more than money – the key to the relationship was ambition and both men were ready for the challenge.

Next up was the question of an assistant. While Souness could be described as a rookie with limited experience and understanding of the Scottish game, Holmes felt it was vital to get the right support to complement Graeme's presence and style. When Walter Smith was suggested as the perfect man for the job, David Holmes was on board with the idea and immediately set the ball in motion to prise Jim McLean's right-hand man away from Tannadice.

Dundee United were enjoying a hugely successful period for a provincial club, and McLean himself had turned down the opportunity to manage Rangers less than three years before. Walter Smith, who was brought up in a Rangers-minded family, was bitterly disappointed then that Jim McLean had vetoed his chances of working at his boyhood heroes. However, Smith's stock was high and in September 1985 he coupled his Dundee United workload with the role of assistant manager of the Scottish national team under Alex Ferguson.

Ferguson had taken charge of the Scotland side following the sudden and untimely death of Jock Stein at the end of the World Cup qualifier against Wales in Cardiff. The death of Jock Stein was taken badly by Graeme Souness. On that fateful September night in Wales, Souness was suspended, so not available for selection. As Stein took unwell, Graeme was one of the first on the scene when the Scotland boss was taken to the Ninian Park medical room for attention, and again, Graeme was one of the first to be aware that Jock Stein had passed despite the best efforts of all to save him. Graeme Souness was grief-stricken. He was Jock Stein's captain and his respect for the former Celtic boss was immeasurable.

Scotland would go on to make the World Cup Finals and travel to Mexico. Jock Stein had played his part to get Scotland there, but now Alex Ferguson and Walter Smith were tasked with making the national team a force to be reckoned with when the action got underway.

But back to the remodelling of the Rangers management team, and while Walter Smith was the man both David Holmes and Graeme Souness wanted in their corner, the job of striking a bargain with Dundee United for his services wasn't going to be an easy one. Jim McLean was sure to play hardball but perhaps United chairman George Fox could be more amenable.

Smith was also perhaps perceived as a fall-back option should the Souness experiment go sideways. As it was, that was never really a consideration once the pair got to work. Next up for David Holmes was another cloak-and-dagger meeting, this time to secure his first lieutenant for the incoming manager.

When the approach was made, with Alan Ferguson again an influence, Walter Smith was keen right away, so much so a handshake between he and David Holmes sealed the deal at that first meeting. Rangers had a game later that Sunday, and when Holmes took his seat in the directors' box his decision was made that it was the end of the road for Jock Wallace, in the knowledge his dream management team was pretty much in place. The only things still to be established were the timings, again confused by both Graeme and Walter having commitments with the national squad. Holmes now had two major tasks on his radar, firstly to strike an agreement with Dundee United, which he promptly achieved, and then it was to advise Jock Wallace that his time at the club had come to an end. That message was clear and delivered in a cold but calculated business-like fashion when Holmes met Wallace in a car park off the M74, 24 hours after striking the agreement with Walter Smith. While Holmes was making things happen, Jim White, then chief sports reporter with Scottish Television, had got wind that Souness was Ibrox-bound. Perhaps it was serendipity that in an interview with Graeme Souness in Genoa, broadcast on the BBC in their *Only a Game?* series, Souness had flippantly suggested that one day, maybe, he could manage Glasgow Rangers. As a preview to the World Cup, White, too, had gone to Italy for a sit-down with Souness and they established a fairly good relationship.

Indeed, many years later they would work closely together on talkSPORT radio. Perhaps that throwaway line stuck with Jim White, and now that innocent remark was turning into reality. White had done his homework and suggestions are he remained in contact with the Sampdoria media and PR people, who updated him when things advanced between Rangers and Graeme. Of course, being on the case of a massive scoop, he had no intentions of delaying going public with his exclusive news.

With White hovering, David Holmes had to accelerate his plan, ensuring the club were first to break the news that Graeme Souness was to be Rangers' next manager and spoil what would have been White's exclusive.

It all meant a more-than-hectic 48 hours for David Holmes, but as ever he met the challenges head on and got things done.

An exit agreement for Graeme was struck with Sampdoria's president Paolo Mantovani, with a caveat that Souness would continue to play while Sampdoria had a chance of securing a UEFA Cup place for the following season. As it was, the Genoa side lost to Roma in their next fixture and their European ambitions were thwarted. It was now a clear pathway for Rangers to make the crucial announcement.

When the media assembled, it was secretary and director Campbell Ogilvie who read from a prepared statement that had two huge messages. Firstly, it was confirmed that Jock Wallace had left the club, which was viewed only as confirmation by the press as big Jock had already imparted the facts to his favoured journalist pals, but when Campbell moved on to the second part of his statement that Graeme Souness was to be Wallace's replacement, in a player–manager role, you could have heard a pin drop in the Blue Room as the news was met by dropping jaws and looks of incredulity. What a coup for Rangers. What a coup for David Holmes. Graeme Souness then held court with the press pack in a confident and professional manner, as everyone started to think ahead to when he would actually take over the managerial role and what further changes could be expected. Campbell Ogilvie was quoted as saying: 'It was mind-blowing.' Nothing had been leaked; of course, fortunately, in those days there was no such thing as social media. I'm quite sure no one was expecting it, as the looks on the faces of the journalists confirmed.

Graeme Souness then headed back to Sampdoria to fulfil his obligations there, meaning former assistant to Jock Wallace, Alex Totten, was left in charge. Totten was left in no doubt of what was expected by way of results in the final fixtures of the season. Finishing in the European places was crucial to David Holmes's business plan. The cash from UEFA Cup football the following season was central to Rangers' financial plans. Immediate results didn't go favourably and Totten was discharged from his duties. Holmes was decisive as ever. Walter Smith's appointment was to be brought forwards, with considerable compensation to be paid to Dundee United. Smith was in charge for the next match that saw Rangers again lose, this time to St Mirren. Next up, it was another away fixture, but this time Rangers shared the points in a 1–1 draw with Aberdeen. As Rangers were drawing nearest contenders for the coveted Euro place Dundee were going down 2–0 at Celtic Park. To bring the curtain down on a very disappointing campaign, Rangers beat Motherwell 2–0 at Ibrox, meaning the Light Blues finished fifth in the table and European football was assured for the following season. For the record, there was fewer than 22,000 inside Ibrox for that one and celebrations were muted to say the least. The crowd was bigger than previous meetings with Motherwell that season but would be well behind the numbers who took in the same fixture the following season.

Conversely, the emotions of both David Holmes and Graeme

Souness were a mixture of relief and happiness that they could now make their plans with the European finance to be factored in.

The World Cup Finals in Mexico were getting closer, but at least while on Scotland duty Walter and Graeme could hopefully find time to talk Rangers, albeit over 5,000 miles away from Ibrox, which would be a new home for both very soon indeed.

# CHAPTER 4:

# WHO IS GRAEME SOUNESS?

Graeme Souness is widely remembered as a tough-tackling, no-nonsense midfielder who captained Liverpool in the early 1980s. One of only five captains to lift the European Cup for Liverpool, his hardman image and fearless commitment sometimes disguised a player of touch, vision and ability.

This is the introductory profile of Graeme Souness when he was inducted into the National Football Hall of Fame as a player in 2007:

> Souness was presented with his award by his first footballing hero, Dave Mackay. Mackay himself was one of the Hall of Fame inaugural inductees. It couldn't have been more fitting. Both Souness and Mackay had been born and bred in Edinburgh, midfielders with amazing commitment and a will to win that really set them apart from many. In fact, they attended the same school in Edinburgh, and as Souness was growing up in his post-war prefab house, where he spent such a long time with his grandmother, the young Graeme had posters of Mackay on his wall. As Mackay starred at Hearts before

## WHO IS GRAEME SOUNESS?

moving south it made Souness become a Hearts fan, but he always had an interest in Rangers who pretty much dominated the Scottish game at that time.

Souness began his career as an apprentice at Tottenham Hotspur, but frustrated by the lack of first-team opportunities, despite being a teenager at such a massive club, he demanded that legendary Spurs boss Bill Nicholson play him or sell him. Perhaps this mindset gives you an indication of the supreme confidence the young Souness had in his ability, a confidence that stood him in good stead wherever he went in his career thereafter.

Souness got his move and joined Middlesbrough in 1972, and in his six years at the club he secured promotion to England's top flight in the 1973–74 season under the management of World Cup winner Jack Charlton. His mentor in that Ayresome Park midfield was Celtic Lisbon Lions icon Bobby Murdoch, and the young Graeme was quick to highlight the influence Murdoch had on his development.

Tottenham legend Steve Perryman, who played an incredible 866 games for the club between 1969 and 1986, built a friendship with Graeme Souness when they were teenagers together in the Spurs youth team, all the way back to 1970. They remain firm friends to this day.

Steve remembers how Graeme's move to London came about: 'It was England v Scotland schoolboys in 1968 and the game was played at White Hart Lane. Dave Mackay tipped off Spurs boss Bill Nicholson that a young midfielder who went to the same school as he had up in Edinburgh was playing for Scotland. It was of course

## THE SIGNIFICANCE OF SOUNESS

Graeme! Nicholson liked what he saw and ordered club scout Charlie Falconer to follow things up. Also in the Scotland squad was John Robertson, who would later win the European Cup with Nottingham Forest, but it was Souness that caught the eye of the manager.

'When Graeme then joined as an apprentice I was one year ahead of him but we struck up a good relationship immediately. He wasn't overawed coming down from Edinburgh but there again Tottenham wasn't the West End, it was much more working class but not the flashiest part of London. Very quickly you could see Graeme had talent and outstanding technical ability but that fiery streak was evident even back then I remember he was sent off in the FA Youth Cup Final for finally retaliating after he had been kicked up and down the park by a host of Coventry City players with Dennis Mortimer, who won the European Cup when he moved on to Villa, the leader in chief!

Graeme had arrogance but he wasn't flash with it. He knew how good he was and when I got my chance in the first team at 17, Graeme was straight to the manager's door asking why he wasn't playing in his top team. Bill Nicholson told him it would happen but Graeme wasn't big on patience. To be fair, Graeme was doing well but how could he displace guys like Allan Mullery and Martin Peters, who were keystones of the Spurs side at that time? When the chance came for him to move to Middlesborough, he grabbed it and it was a good fit for him.

'Working with Jack Charlton and Bobby Murdoch

added something to his game. He had the swagger, he could drop a shoulder and beat a man but what was evident after his move was, he had developed the spice of competitiveness! The gifts he had all came together with that will to win and he became a great player. He became even greater when he went to Liverpool, which was the perfect upgrade for him.

'We went head-to-head at Wembley in the 1982 Football League Cup Final in front of a hundred thousand spectators. I captained Spurs and Graeme led out Liverpool. Through great respect for each other we avoided having a kick at each other but our great friendship was parked for the duration of the game. It was to be Liverpool's day as they won 3–1. Keith Burkinshaw was in charge of Spurs by then, but I do know that on many occasions Bill Nicholson used to say he regretted allowing the young confident Souness to leave when he did. I too wonder how things would have shaped up had he stayed. How good would a midfield of Perryman, Souness and Hoddle have been?

'It was a pleasure to train and play with Graeme all those years ago and I'm so proud today that we are still good pals. He wasn't just a special footballer, he is a very special man.'

Souness's consistent performances saw Liverpool take an interest, and in January 1978 he was snapped up by Anfield boss Bob Paisley. It took a club-record fee of £350k to secure his services.

It is at Liverpool that his playing career is probably best remembered, as he won five league championships and three European Cups along the way. Souness was given the captaincy for the start of the 1981–82 season and the club flourished under his leadership.

The 1983–84 season brought triple success: a fourth European Cup with victory over Roma, a fifth and final league title, and a League Cup win in the first ever all-Merseyside cup final.

Souness had a hankering to experience a different style of football, a different lifestyle, too, and Sampdoria gave him that opportunity in 1984. When Graeme left Liverpool he had made 358 appearances and scored 56 goals.

In his first season in Italy, Sampdoria won the Coppa Italia for the first time in their history. The significance of Souness!

Souness's reign in Italy would prove to be relatively short as he answered the call from the new Rangers man at the top, David Holmes, to become the Ibrox club's first ever player–manager. It was a left-field appointment, but one that Graeme Souness felt formed part of his destiny. Seventy-three appearances later and with Rangers' status replenished as Scotland's top team, Souness hung up his boots.

The changes Souness initiated at Rangers were many, and some were radical, but that focused winning mentality permeated through the dressing room, and if players didn't commit, they were gone. Just like his on-field performances, Souness took no prisoners, while from a manager's viewpoint, he carried no passengers. When Graeme Souness left Rangers in 1991, when the

## WHO IS GRAEME SOUNESS?

lure of Liverpool tugged at his heartstrings, he not only left a massive and lasting legacy, but gave the supporters a million memories, with three league titles and four League Cup triumphs to look back on.

With hindsight, Graeme has admitted that perhaps the Liverpool move was the right one but the timing was wrong, and success second time round was much harder to deliver as a manager than it had been as a player.

Graeme Souness managed eight different clubs, taking him to Galatasaray in Turkey, Torino in Italy and Benfica in Portugal. He also managed Southampton, Blackburn Rovers and Newcastle United.

However, it's clear the Edinburgh boy made his biggest management mark in Glasgow when he transformed a dormant Rangers and set them off for a record nine titles in nine successive seasons.

Graeme Souness is a worthy member of Rangers Hall of Fame, to match his inclusions in the English and Scottish Football Halls of Fame.

Graeme is still a regular visitor to Ibrox and retains such a huge affinity to the football club. He is revered by the Rangers fanbase young and old, many of whom may be too young to remember his time at the club, but his legend lives on with tales of the Souness revolution handed down from generation to generation.

His contribution to the rich tapestry of Rangers Football Club will never be forgotten.

Stevie Nicol was a rising star of the Scottish game and a fixture in an Ayr United side while still just 17 years of age. It was a very talented Somerset Park outfit, with other youngsters including Robert Connor who would later star with Dundee and Aberdeen, and Alan McInally who proved a sensational signing for Celtic, before a pioneering move to Bayern Munich further developed his unique powerful style. All three, Nicol, Connor and McInally would later prove their qualities in the Scottish national side.

Nicol was constantly tipped for a move to Rangers, but the Ibrox side were perhaps looking to use the young defender's affinity to the Light Blues to get him on as low a transfer fee as possible. While Rangers prevaricated, Liverpool under the wily Bob Paisley nipped in to take him to Anfield for a fee of £300k, and that proved to be an astonishing bargain as Nicol went on to play 468 games for Liverpool, scoring 46 goals.

He won every honour available to him, including a host of league titles, FA Cups, Charity Shields, League Cups, and the big one, the European Cup, in the 1983–84 season. Graeme Souness was captain of Liverpool for that final in Stadio Olimpico, Rome, a final that went all the way to a penalty shoot-out to determine a winner. In fact, Nicol, who had come off the bench for Craig Johnston in the second half, missed the first spot kick, but Phil Neal, Ian Rush, Alan Kennedy and Souness himself made no mistakes from 12 yards, while Bruce Grobbelaar, in the Liverpool goal, performed heroics to deny Bruno Conti and Francesco Graziani for Roma, ensuring the giant silver trophy was heading back to Anfield.

Souness knew all about Stevie Nicol's qualities and versatility, as both were part of the Scotland squad for the 1986 World Cup in Mexico. Of course, by the time Scotland travelled to the tournament it had been confirmed that

# WHO IS GRAEME SOUNESS?

Graeme Souness was heading to Ibrox for his first managerial appointment. Nicol was a player Souness admired, and he was keen to bring him north to join his new-look Rangers side. Stevie Nicol himself recalls: 'Graeme going to Rangers was the perfect fit for them both [Graeme and the club]. Graeme was driven for sure, but he still managed to "park it" to prioritise the Scottish World Cup campaign. I was tempted for sure, but at 24 I was settled at Liverpool and Phil Neal hadn't long moved on, which gave me an opportunity to find a settled position in the side, as previously I had played in both full back positions, midfield and even in central defence. Liverpool was the dominant team in English football, and that continued when Kenny Dalglish took over from Joe Fagan in a player–manager role. Kenny wanted me to be a big part of his team, as did Graeme with his desire to take me to Glasgow; it really was a win-win situation for me because there was never any doubt that Graeme was going to be anything but a phenomenal success at Rangers. Looking back, with guys like Terry Butcher and Graham Roberts becoming genuine Rangers legends, maybe I did miss out on pulling on the colours of my boyhood heroes, but much as I had a great affinity with Graeme, my loyalty to Liverpool was just too strong. What a job Graeme did, though; Rangers was the first result I looked for as soon as our own game was over on a Saturday!'

Stevie Nicol's decision to stay on Merseyside was fully vindicated, when you consider he was a first-team player in a number of top-notch Liverpool sides for 13 years before he left for Notts County in January 1995. Nicol, who is now a commentator with ESPN in the USA, still takes a regular interest in what's happening at Rangers from his home across

## THE SIGNIFICANCE OF SOUNESS

the Atlantic.

Broadcaster Clive Tyldesley knows Graeme Souness well; a relationship that has stood the test of time since they first met when Clive was a young radio reporter. Clive was ITV's senior football commentator from 1998 to 2020. In his time with ITV, Clive covered five World Cups, five European Championships, 17 Champions League Finals and nine FA Cup Finals.

Tyldesley's broadcasting career started at Nottingham's Radio Trent in 1975, before moving on in 1977 to Radio City in Liverpool. Four of those European Cup Finals, previously mentioned, featured Liverpool. It's fair to say he built strong relationships with players at both Liverpool and Everton, but it was more than football with Graeme Souness. They would regularly go out for dinner with their respective partners and often be joined by Graeme's Anfield teammate, the late Michael Robinson and his wife.

Clive was far from surprised when Souness took up the challenge of player–manager at Ibrox. Clive's face lights up when you start to discuss Graeme Souness or 'Champagne Charlie' as he was nicknamed during his Liverpool playing days: 'As a player, Graeme was a leader, and was always destined to further his career in management. I don't recall being aware of any other player who had such a strong influence over the other 21 men on a football field. I am happy to call "Souey" a friend of over 40 years – I would hate to have him as an enemy! At his peak he was quite simply the best midfielder in Britain. He was a cool-hand gunslinger with a menacing on-pitch presence, but he could play. He had it all.

'Even now, professional standards echo as loudly in every word he speaks in the television studio as they did through just about everything he did as a player or manager (OK, there was the occasional "don't watch alone" challenge or two), but standards were so important to the Edinburgh-born footballing genius. To Graeme, the result of every match he was involved in was important – more important than anything else happening anywhere in the world during that particular 90 minutes.

'Do you know what? I think back to Graeme returning to Anfield as manager after a seven-year sabbatical in Genoa and Glasgow, and Graeme, who normally kept quite strict dividing lines between his football business and social pleasures, was now a football nut! He would happily talk football for hours in any company.

'Graeme Souness was a leader, and he knew the value of leaders and winners in his dressing room, hence the presence of like-minded standard-bearers at Ibrox, including Richard Gough, Terry Butcher and Ray Wilkins. It had been nine years since Rangers celebrated a title win before Graeme took office, but everyone bought into the new deal, aspirations and standards he brought to Rangers.'

As previously mentioned, Graeme was known as 'Champagne Charlie', with Clive confirming: 'Make no mistake, Graeme richly deserved every glass of bubbles he earned in his time at Rangers, and they had so many successes to celebrate – he made Rangers great again!'

Tom Cowan was a Graeme Souness signing for Rangers for £100,000 from Clyde in February 1989. Cowan had offers from Nottingham Forest and Tottenham Hotspur, but when he had that first conversation with Graeme Souness it was only ever going to be Rangers for him: 'I could have had a higher

## THE SIGNIFICANCE OF SOUNESS

salary elsewhere, but when Graeme Souness entered the room to meet me for the first time, I was awestruck. We had spoken briefly on the phone, but this was real; he had such a presence and he had everyone's respect immediately. As a player he was world-class. As a manager he was magnificent; sure, he could fire teacups across the dressing room and he could give you the hairdryer treatment, but you took it because you knew he was right. He made me a better player, but then again, playing with better players helped too. He gave me my chance to play for my team; he gave me my career. I'll never forget that. Many years after I had left Rangers and was playing with Sheffield United, I was leaving Bramall Lane one day after training and Graeme Souness was crossing the car park about 100 yards away. He had been called to an FA disciplinary hearing that was being hosted at my club. He was still manager of Liverpool at the time. I didn't know whether to approach him or not – would he remember me? I should have had no fears; when he saw me, he said, "Tommy, alright pal?", then gave me the biggest of bear hugs ever. That was the mark of the man. A football genius with a hardman image, but he had a heart of gold at times too. To remember me, having played so few games for him, and considering the superstars he played with and signed, it meant the world to me. To this day, he's the only boss I've ever had that I still call "gaffer", and now in my role with the Fire & Rescue Service in South Yorkshire, there are many bosses and many are termed "gaffer", but not by me – Graeme Souness is "THE GAFFER!"'

John Gibson is a staff reporter for the *Chronicle* and has been their Newcastle United newshound since 1966 – an incredible period that continues right into 2025, and he knows a different style to Graeme Souness that others may not be aware of: 'When Graeme came to Newcastle as manager, we picked up where we had left off, from the days when he had been at Middlesbrough, although we had some regular contact in between when Graeme's former Liverpool teammate Ray Kennedy had been diagnosed with Parkinson's disease and had moved back to his native north-east. Ray settled in New Hartley near Whitley Bay. Graeme made a point of having Ray as his regular guest at games, and even training. As Ray's condition deteriorated and he was using a wheelchair, Graeme remained undeterred, and made sure Ray could still get out and about as best he could, and he personally paid to have Ray's home converted to allow wheelchair access, while he also had the bathroom refitted to allow a suitable shower to be installed. Graeme didn't do this for publicity or gain; I have so much respect for him for that. This was a side of Graeme Souness that the public didn't see.'

## CHAPTER 5:

# FRIDAY ON MY MIND

By beating Motherwell and securing the lucrative Euro slot, Rangers would bring the curtain down on a momentous season ending in massive change, by taking on newly crowned champions Celtic in the Glasgow Cup Final. With Graeme Souness now officially in charge, his Sampdoria contract ended, it would afford some players an opportunity to prove they should be part of the new gaffer's plans for the next season and beyond. Graeme Souness would be heading off to Mexico on World Cup duty with Scotland, but this match would give him a real gauge as to what lay ahead when he returned. Souness tried to avoid taking centre stage for that Friday-night fixture, but when he turned up in the finest black Italian leather jacket and a black roll-neck sweater underneath, he looked as if he had just stepped off the catwalk in Milan. The media cameras were flashing!

Everyone wanted to see the new man in person. He was box office. It was three days after Souness had celebrated his 33rd birthday.

He was suntanned, fit and carrying an air of confidence to confirm he was ready to take his first steps in football management.

# FRIDAY ON MY MIND

The reason the game was arranged for the Friday was to avoid clashing with Aberdeen and Hearts who would contest the Scottish Cup Final the next day. The significance of Souness played a part in enhancing the attendance, as did the fact that Celtic fans wanted to acknowledge their title-winning heroes. So much so a crowd of 40,741 took their seats to witness an extremely competitive game that needed extra-time to determine a winner. It was Rangers who lifted the cup, with Ally McCoist scoring a hat-trick in a 3–2 thriller.

Futures would be determined that Friday night.

Six of the players who started against Celtic on the evening of 9 May would also be given starting jerseys for the big league kick-off at Easter Road three months later on 9 August. For Dave MacKinnon, the Glasgow final signalled the end of his time at Rangers. Also released was Barcelona hero Derek Johnstone, who had played 546 times for the club and scored 210 goals. Youngster Billy Davies who had made his debut as a 17-year-old against Brechin City back in 1981, was also free to go. Despite such early promise, Davies had failed to develop enough to claim a regular slot in the first-team squad. Another young front man allowed to leave was Eric Ferguson, as was goalkeeper Andy Bruce. Former Aberdeen midfielder Dougie Bell was made available for transfer; so too was John MacDonald, who like Davies, had come through the Ibrox youth ranks. Others such as Iain Ferguson, whose goal had won the League Cup, was out of the scheme of things despite also scoring regularly for the second 11. One-time captain Craig Paterson, Hugh Burns and Bobby Williamson all had work to do to convince the new management team they were players Souness would want as part of his squad.

## THE SIGNIFICANCE OF SOUNESS

Dave MacKinnon was a player Souness admired, but a serious knee injury was restricting his ability to play as often as he would like. MacKinnon was an all-action energetic operator who never shirked a tackle and would have run through brick walls for the cause. Having overcome the loss of a kidney following a back injury while with Partick Thistle, 'Diamond Dave' had the heart of a lion and was given the job of captaining Rangers in his final game on that Old Firm Friday night. Souness had been delighted with the way MacKinnon had gone about his business to help Rangers qualify for Europe. To make the contribution MacKinnon did was quite remarkable, as earlier in the season he had gone under the surgeon's knife for cartilage problems, but then was back playing in a remarkable Old Firm showdown within ten days of the operation! That game ended 4–4 and had taken place only a couple of weeks before Souness was appointed. Being captain was fitting recognition for a player who loved his time at Rangers. Dave recalls the build up to that Glasgow Cup Final: 'I knew I was moving on and Graeme couldn't have been straighter with me. He pulled no punches, and without giving anything away he hinted that the players coming in would be big players with big reputations and probably arriving with big transfer fees being paid to get them on board. He was being totally honest, and he also wanted to make sure I knew my time at Rangers had been valued by everyone at the club. It could have been so different, as originally Graeme wanted me to go to Italy to have my knee reconstructed by the best in the business, but following closer inspection from club doctor, Donald Cruickshank, it would have been unlikely to be successful. Graeme had said a new contract would have been on the table for me as he wanted my experience to assist in the development of Ian Durrant and Derek Ferguson. To do so, my knee needed to be up to it. Sadly it wasn't.'

To the game itself, it gave Rangers their second win against Celtic for the season. Two other fixtures had ended in draws, while Celtic claimed their only win at their home ground Parkhead on New Year's Day, 1986.

Ally McCoist's hat-trick that Friday night saw him finish top scorer for the season, with 27 goals in all competitions, as he led the line with Davie Cooper and Ted McMinn on the flanks. Cammy Fraser and Ian Durrant were the key men in midfield. Nicky Walker was in goal, with Hugh Burns, Dave McPherson, Ally Dawson and Stuart Munro in defence.

Dave MacKinnon was deployed as the holding midfielder with instructions to protect the back four. Celtic lined up with Peter Latchford, Peter Grant, Danny McGrain, Roy Aitken, Paul McGugan, Murdo Macleod (Dave MacKinnon's full cousin), Brian McClair, Paul McStay, Maurice Johnston (more on him later), Tommy Burns and Mark McGhee. Celtic certainly fielded what was probably their best starting 11. Traditionally, the Glasgow Cup would have been pretty much a low-key, modest tournament, until Souness was on board for his first game in charge. The cup itself is a very special, ornate trophy and one of the oldest in world football. A quick look at the official team lines confirmed both were taking this one seriously. Rangers were looking to prove they could compete with new champions Celtic, while they themselves were looking to lay down a marker and make a statement that Souness's appointment wasn't going to change their dominant status. Rangers were in front twice, but twice

## THE SIGNIFICANCE OF SOUNESS

Celtic dragged themselves back into the contest, but when McCoist claimed his third goal in extra-time, Davie Hay's men could not find another equaliser. It was now 11 Old Firm goals for McCoist in 13 matches since joining Rangers in June 1983 from Sunderland. McCoist seemed to thrive in the Old Firm environment.

The Rangers players celebrated and the Light Blue fans were delighted. They now had optimism and a vision of the potential that could see Rangers mount a genuine challenge the following season. Graeme Souness had got off to the dream start in his first match against his Glasgow rivals.

Back in the dressing room Souness didn't hold back, as he went round his victorious players one by one. As he assessed their performances, he gave them a clear indication as to what was expected and where some would fit into his plans. Others were shocked when the ruthless new gaffer let them know their futures probably lay elsewhere. It was an emotional night for Dave MacKinnon as he had kept the news to himself that he would be moving on. MacKinnon was last to leave the Ibrox playing field at the full-time whistle, as he took in the magnificence of Ibrox as a Rangers player for the last time. Later, as he headed to the exit door he bundled up his number 4 shirt as a final memento of his time at Rangers, but it took a bit of persuasion to keep it as the physio gave chase and demanded the shirt back as he didn't want a good set of strips to be missing a number! Two weeks' wages was the final pay-off for David. Fair play to MacKinnon, as after that emotional night he worked on his fitness and built up his knee to go on and forge out a terrific playing career with Kilmarnock and Airdrie. Dave later stayed in the game after hanging up his boots, showing his business acumen and adaptability as he went on to work with some blue-chip companies before also serving Dundee FC and later Kilmarnock as chief executive officer.

To perhaps give an indication of just how ruthless, cold and calculating Graeme Souness would prove to be as a manager, we can quote Derek Johnstone, a true Rangers hero who scored so many goals for the club: 'On the night of that Friday game, incoming boss Graeme Souness terminated my Rangers career with three words, "You are freed!" – nothing more, nothing less! We may have previously been international teammates, but there was no emotion, no acknowledgement of my time at the club where I made over 500 appearances; that was it. It was all over without any further conversation. I don't mind admitting it, I left Ibrox that night fighting back tears, but when I got home I could hold them back no longer, and I was very emotional as I realised my time at the club I had been at since I was a kid was now consigned to history. I loved the club dearly and still do; I probably suspected it was coming but it was still hard to face when the time came.' Derek Johnstone went on to have a terrific career in the media after a brief spell in management with Partick Thistle. Derek remains a regular visitor to Ibrox, and is a very popular guest when he meets and greets fans in the various hospitality lounges.

The retained Rangers squad could head off on their summer break after the Celtic victory, but there would be very little rest for Souness and Smith as they had to get new faces in and both still had responsibilities to Scotland with the Mexico World Cup looming large on the horizon. David Holmes would be

## THE SIGNIFICANCE OF SOUNESS

equally busy, finding the funds to make Graeme Souness's ambitious transfer targets a reality.

To assist with pre-season, and with Walter and Graeme in Mexico, Donald Mackay joined the back-room staff. Mackay, a goalkeeper by trade, had been a teammate of Walter Smith at Dundee United. It was a wise choice as he had previously cut his management teeth in Denmark, before taking on the main job at Dundee, then Coventry City. Mackay would later take on the responsibilities of the Rangers Reserve team and work closely with Peter McCloy, who in 1970 had been then-manager Willie Waddell's first signing, coming from Motherwell in exchange for Brian Heron and Bobby Watson, and had been in goal when Rangers won the Cup Winners' Cup two years later. Apart from reserve team work, Peter would dedicate himself to, and set aside time for, specialist coaching of the goalkeepers. That was a fairly innovative move at the time.

That Friday night was the start of a new era. It gave the Rangers fans a sneak peek into the future, but it was obvious recruitment would be vital if Graeme Souness was to restore Rangers back to the top of the Scottish game. The hunger for success from Souness was obvious, and it was matched by the expectation of the massive Light Blue support. They were in for an interesting summer, as transfer speculation mounted as to who Souness would entice to Ibrox. It wasn't long until the fans forgot about those who were moving on and focused on the big-name players who were coming in to replace them.

# CHAPTER 6:

# IBROX REACTS

Alex Totten was a casualty of the Rangers management changes.

He was assistant 'boss' under Jock Wallace, and in the style of when 'Big' Jock replaced Willie Waddell, Alex was being groomed to take over when it was likely that Wallace would move 'upstairs'.

Alex knew his time was up when Souness was appointed: 'I was obviously disappointed, and while results hadn't been favourable, I think Jock and I could have turned it round if we'd had a bit of investment for new players. After all, our budget, compared to the money made available to Graeme, was night and day. I was tasked with taking the team against Clydebank, after Jock was away, and before Graeme came in. We had lost to Hearts the week before, and things didn't get any better when we went to New Kilbowie Park and lost 2–1. That was the end for me; even if we had won, I don't think there was a place for me as Graeme would be bringing in his own back-room team; I did the same when I took over at Falkirk and made Gregor Abel my assistant. Although I was out the door, I made a point of catching up with Souness before I left to wish him all the best and remind him of what a special club Rangers is.'

Alex Totten went on to have a hugely successful career in football management, particularly at St Johnstone, Kilmarnock and Falkirk. He was granted a testimonial by Falkirk in 2007. Walter Smith sent a very strong Rangers side to recognise the man he succeeded as assistant manager at Ibrox.

Dave MacKinnon, former Rangers captain, recalls: 'Most of the players had enjoyed working with 'Big' Jock [Wallace] and were sad to see him go; he was a real Rangers man. But when news filtered through that Graeme Souness was the new man in charge, it was met with a bit of a mixed reaction in the Ibrox dressing room. The first response was one of euphoria that this was a genuine top-class operator coming to our club; he's sure to improve things. This was quickly followed by a few pensive thoughts in relation to what does this mean for me? Yes, it soon became a case of what will the future look like? Will he fancy me? Will he make radical changes in the team, on the training ground, and most importantly, will he be buying players for my position? Everyone knew just how ambitious Graeme was. The dressing room had a definitive atmosphere of uncertainty, and that was evident from the most experienced to the youngest guys in the squad.'

Rangers had standards and traditions that went back to the regimental ways of Bill Struth, and these had been upheld since then by Scot Symon and all his successors thereafter. A key part of the tradition was that players travel to training wearing a suit, shirt and tie, even on the warmest of days.

Dave MacKinnon remembers the first day Graeme Souness arrived at Ibrox as manager: 'We were all in our shirts and ties as usual, when Graeme appeared in reception in a casual polo shirt. He also had a moustache and the start of an obvious full beard. Facial hair was taboo at the club! He had commandeered the referee's room as his own changing room, and as we headed to the old Albion to get training underway he crossed the road in a slight jog bordering on a confident strut. He had presence, that's for sure. Our normal warm-up was running round the track, but Souness got us all in the middle to introduce how we would go forwards. Running was out – stretching, squats and bending were in – as Graeme demonstrated how they did things in Italy. It was brilliant. It lasted 20 minutes or so and was all about ensuring we were nimble. After this new routine, parks were marked out for eight-a-side games, which would last around an hour, or until Graeme's team were winning if they were behind! We were encouraged to express ourselves in possession, win the ball back as quickly as possible when you lost it, but most importantly, enjoy it! Everyone did. It was such a change from slogging round the track. Souness's training mantra was "get the ball and play – get the ball and play!"'

Most of the squad wanted to be in the manager's eight, but in those early days there was one young player who wasn't, and on the opposition, and he wanted to make an impression with his commitment and aggression. Dave MacKinnon remembers what happened like yesterday: 'Shuggie [Hugh] Burns loved a tackle, and he decided he wasn't going to hold back in what looked like a 50-50 challenge with the boss. Shuggie caught Souness on the shin and immediately blood appeared, as the manager had his socks rolled down and hadn't bothered with shin guards. Walter stopped the game with a blast on

# THE SIGNIFICANCE OF SOUNESS

his whistle, with everyone waiting for a reaction. There was absolute silence as the squad looked on. After around 30 seconds Souness wiped the blood away, before instructing Walter to get the game underway again. Within a couple of minutes of the restart, Graeme caught Shuggie with a thigh-high challenge that poleaxed our young full back. As Shuggie went down the manager shouted to Walter to blow for time-up. Game over! No drama, no toys out the pram, but a lesson that if you are prepared to dish it out, you must be ready to receive it. That lesson was taken on board by everyone else on the training ground in those early days. Fair play to Hugh Burns – he knew the score and didn't change his wholehearted style. Soon after, he moved to Hamilton on loan before joining Heart of Midlothian on a permanent deal.'

For the first couple of seasons in Iain Ferguson's Rangers career, things were pretty good and he scored some big goals, including the winner in the 1984 League Cup Final against Dundee United. A few days after that glory strike, Ferguson would produce two tremendous goals against Inter Milan, but it wasn't enough to avoid Rangers being eliminated from Europe with a 4–3 aggregate scoreline falling in favour of the Italian giants.

By the time Graeme Souness was appointed Iain had fallen out of favour, despite scoring goals regularly in the second 11. Iain remembers when the news of Souness joining Rangers broke: 'There was a massive buzz at the club when it was confirmed that the Scotland skipper was to be the new boss. Fans were absolutely enthralled by the concept too. For my own part, I was hoping for a new beginning, especially as I had a good relationship with Walter Smith, but we all knew as players we had to up our game. It was very quickly obvious Souness was going to clear the ship, and as it was, I was first to be sold! In search of first-team football I went on loan to Dundee, where it had all started for me, and that was despite me rejecting two offers to join their neighbours across the road at Tannadice. Maybe I harboured thoughts that I could still do a job *for* Rangers! At Dundee [United], I scored two goals in two games, and when Jim McLean came calling for a third time, and as Rangers were signing big names for every position, it was probably time to go in a move that was best for everybody. Things weren't so bad at Tannadice, and I played in the 1987 UEFA Cup Final and scored the winner in the Camp Nou against Barcelona, and got the opener in the semi-final as we beat Borussia Mönchengladbach to book our place in the final against IFK Göteborg. Could I have scored in big games under Graeme Souness? I believe I would have, but when you think back, even Ally McCoist wasn't guaranteed a regular starting jersey at that time!'

Iain Ferguson still has great affection for Rangers and is a regular on the club TV channel. Iain is often seen around the Ibrox lounges too, in his role in hospitality with a host of other former players.

In the run-in to the end of the 1985–86 season, Ian Durrant and Derek Ferguson were regulars in the Rangers engine room, often joined by the more experienced Dave MacKinnon to bring drive and defensive cover to support the youthful zest and adventurous side of the youngsters. Ferguson had made his debut against Queen of the South in a 4–0 League Cup tie a matter of days after his 16th birthday. Meanwhile, Ian Durrant had been given his first taste of top-flight football when Jock

Wallace handed him a starting jersey for a trip to Morton 12 months before the arrival of Graeme Souness.

Both were terrific talents, and while they were great teammates on the park, they were also best friends off it.

Ian remembers the day he found out Souness was coming: 'My first thought was, *he's not keeping me out the team*, and I said to Derek, "that will be your place he's after; you are heading to the bench!" We were young, living the dream, and had no real thoughts about how the club would be managed. We just wanted to play, and we were both really excited to get the chance to play alongside a guy who had just been playing in Serie A. We had watched him on the telly and seen him play for Scotland. He had a real swagger, and when we met him at Ibrox on his first day that confidence was intoxicating.' Derek Ferguson picks it up: 'Durranty was trying to wind me up, but it did make you think, *he's picking the team so it's likely he'll pick himself first*. I was thinking, *I can and will learn from him*; he could tackle, pass and score with either foot – he was just an all-round natural talent. He had won everything to win at Liverpool, so we naturally thought he would turn us into winners, too.'

The records show Ian Durrant had a wonderful Rangers career, despite it being blighted with the most horrific knee injury that cost him three seasons of the 14 years he was at the club as a player. He was rewarded with a testimonial in April 1998 in an emotional evening at Ibrox, with Sheffield Wednesday providing the opposition.

For Derek Ferguson, who had a habit of testing Souness's patience, some off-field exploits arguably stifled his development. It was suggested, too, that Souness saw a lot of himself in Ferguson and was frustrated that he didn't have the application that would really have made him a fixture in the side. Eventually, Graeme Souness lost what patience he had left, and after a brief loan spell at Dundee, Derek joined Heart of Midlothian for a fee of £750,000. He would later play with Sunderland and Dunfermline (where he would play against his younger brother Barry, who had by then broken into the Rangers' team), before moving on to Falkirk and finishing up at Clydebank.

Both guys remain diehard Rangers fans and are as passionate about their club today as they were the first day they entered Ibrox and walked up the marble staircase.

Goalkeeper Nicky Walker had worked with Jock Wallace at both Leicester City and Motherwell before hooking up again at Ibrox. Nicky recalls the day Souness was to be a Ranger: 'Firstly, I was devastated for Big Jock; he lived for Rangers, but it's a results business and the bottom line was our results weren't good enough. Souness taking over was an amazing statement of intent from David Holmes. We knew Mr Holmes was ambitious and had big plans to resurrect Rangers, but this appointment was pretty much left field!'

Despite Chris Woods being an early summer capture, Nicky Walker chose to fight for his place. Nicky did play in the 1987 Scottish League Cup success, which was determined after a thrilling penalty shoot-out, while in the following season, Walker deputised for Woods in 12 league matches, enough to secure him a league winner's medal.

Nicky is now managing director of his famous family shortbread firm, Walker's of Aberlour based in Morayshire.

After 370 appearances, Bobby Russell left Rangers in 1987

## THE SIGNIFICANCE OF SOUNESS

to hook up with his former Ibrox teammate Tommy McLean, who was then in charge of Motherwell.

Bobby recalls the influence of Graeme Souness when he came in from Sampdoria: 'I was old-school and liked tradition, where we turned up for training every day with a shirt and tie. It was unique and set Rangers apart. That changed under Graeme, and casual dress, tracksuits and toilet bags with your own shampoo and things were the order of the day. Flip-flops, too, were in. Not many of us had worn these before, but Graeme was insistent that we had to protect our feet. Diet, too, was under the microscope, as the new manager introduced things like pasta and chicken for lunch after training, but everything was designed to make us better when we took to the park for a game. My time playing with Graeme Souness was pretty brief, but I remember playing against him and thinking I had condemned myself to death when I nutmegged him in a League Cup semi-final, but he just gave me a wink and a smile. I didn't try it again, though; I had seen first-hand how he could dish it out!'

Bobby was part of the Motherwell squad that won the Scottish Cup in that epic final of 1991 against Dundee United. Bobby finished his career at Albion Rovers, where he was hugely influential in the development of their young players.

## CHAPTER 7:

# FOOTBALL REACTS

Stuart McLean spent 16 seasons with Kilmarnock and remains third on the all-time appearances list for the Rugby Park club. Stuart recalls the breaking news when Graeme Souness was confirmed as the replacement for Jock Wallace as manager of Rangers Football Club: 'Make no mistake, it was massive for Rangers, but it was equally huge for all in Scottish football! Kilmarnock were having an up-and-down time of it, constantly flirting between relegation and promotion for an extended period in the eighties, with genuine financial problems for the club all too evident. The appointment of Souness was the talking point in dressing rooms the length and breadth of the country. Everyone wanted a piece of the action! In our own dressing room, those of a blue persuasion couldn't wait to get close to the iconic Scottish internationalist, while others, who perhaps had an inkling towards the green side of Glasgow, wanted to extinguish the arrogance of Souness and see Celtic continue to dominate the domestic game. It really was such an exciting time.'

Financially, Souness raised the stakes at every club, and as stories broke of wages being paid to signings such as Chris

Woods and Terry Butcher, players elsewhere quickly re-evaluated their own position and lobbied their own managers and directors to secure wages and bonus increases to reflect the new high-profile status of the Scottish game.

McLean, who was inducted into the Kilmarnock Hall of Fame in 2016, joining such well-known ex-Killie stars as Ray Montgomerie and Rangers' Barcelona hero Tommy McLean, set his sights on a match against Rangers when it was confirmed his endeavours for Kilmarnock were to be recognised with a testimonial. The match was arranged for early January 1990. Stuart remarked: 'Graeme Souness had demonstrated a willingness to send teams to all points of the compass to promote the Rangers brand, and when it was confirmed that he would bring a strong team down for my game, I was absolutely blown away, and when Graeme himself said he would play I could hardly believe it.' Graeme was joined in the starting 11 that night by Derek Ferguson, who was such a talented boy, Neale Cooper and young Israeli international goalkeeper, Boni Ginzburg. On the night, McLean took the field wearing the number 9 Kilmarnock shirt. The reason being, it was the only number the Rugby Park stalwart had not worn in over 500 appearances for the club. For Rangers, Davie Dodds wore number 9, but it was his young Northern Irish strike partner John Morrow, who got the only goal of the game.

For the testimonial match, Stuart's sons were mascots, and even now, when you ask the boys if they were inspired to make careers for themselves in the game from that memorable night, both recall it as a very special occasion. Stuart's oldest son Steven remains one of Scotland's high-profile referees with a host of big games on his CV, including the Scottish Cup Final, and he was elevated to FIFA status in 2010, and indeed, in 2023, Steven was the first ever video assistant referee deployed at a Scottish Cup Final and was again appointed as a FIFA VAR specialist in 2025. Younger brother Brian joined Rangers as a teenager before moving on to have a very good career as a versatile defender with Motherwell, Falkirk, Dundee United and Preston North End among others, and picked up international recognition with Northern Ireland. Both Steven and Brian will tell you their dad, Stuart, was their hero, but getting close to Graeme Souness all those years ago, even pre-teenage years, was an unforgettable experience.

Stuart recalls: 'The professionalism from Graeme Souness was a delight to witness; it's no surprise he was such a success at Rangers. He had it all whether playing or managing; he had winning in his DNA.'

Gordon Smith won the domestic treble on his first season at Rangers. By the time Graeme Souness took office, Gordon was packing his bags to head off to Austria for a new footballing adventure with Admira Wacker. Gordon recalls: 'I had played against Graeme many times, and I had also played with him in the Scotland under-23s. My abiding memory of when we faced Graeme and that hugely successful Liverpool side of the day is the way the players were quick to shout at each other if they gave the ball away – they didn't hold back. Maybe that was why they were so successful: high standards and loaded with winners. When Graeme went to Rangers, yes, the appointment was a bit of a surprise, but anyone who knew him would be aware that he had the personality to straddle the demands of playing and managing.

'One story worth noting: in the summer of 1987 I was home

in the close season, and I asked Peter McCloy if I could come over to Ibrox for some training. When I walked through the front door and headed to the away dressing room, where the reserves would normally change, I met Graeme Souness and he asked where I was going. When I told him, he said, "Get yourself along to the home dressing room – you are a real Ranger." I was speechless, but delighted by such a kind gesture.'

Many years later, when Gordon was Chief Executive of the SFA, they were in the market for a new team manager: 'Graeme was my choice for the position,' said Gordon, 'but the committee had the majority and the job went to George Burley.'

Gordon Smith had the most amazing football journey and not many could equal the successes he has enjoyed as a player, a coach, pundit and agent. Apart from his time at the Scottish Football Association, Gordon also served Rangers as director of football.

David Shanks was a combative midfield player who starred for Clydebank, Motherwell and Falkirk, among others. A matter of less than a week before his 24th birthday, David remembers a massive day in the history of the original Bankies: 'We were stranded at the bottom of the league, and with games running out we had Rangers at Kilbowie. Rangers were struggling, and while Graeme Souness had been confirmed as the incoming manager, he wasn't there yet and Alex Totten was in caretaker charge. Rangers were pushing to finish in a European place, but you could see confidence was fragile when they arrived for the game. They still had real quality operators in Durrant, McCoist, McMinn and Dougie Bell, who I was asked to take care of. Surprisingly, Davie Cooper was left on the bench. We started well and were two-up inside the first half hour. Ian Durrant pulled one back for Rangers, but we saw it through to give the Bankies their first ever win against Rangers.

'Were we given added incentive to get one over Souness before he was even here? Not really. We were playing for our own futures. As it was, it didn't really matter, as league reconstruction to a top flight of 12 was on the cards, and Clydebank and Motherwell who finished second bottom were safe for next season. It was a historic day, though!'

That result at Clydebank had Graeme Souness spitting fire on the telephone to David Holmes from his Genoa base. It prompted Rangers to get Walter Smith in for the next game.

Little did Steve Cowan think that he would face such an explosive start to the season, when Souness brought his Light Blues to Leith.

'I think everyone was intrigued by the appointment. When the fixtures came out and it was confirmed we would meet them on the first game of the season at Easter Road, we couldn't wait. You want to test yourself against the best and Rangers had made some big-name signings, with a completely new spine to their team in Woods, Butcher, Souness himself and [Colin] West up front. We were desperate to get in about them.'

Steve Cowan scored the winner in that shame game in August 1986. Cowan had been at St Mirren and Aberdeen under Alex Ferguson. It was at Pittodrie he earned the nickname, 'Cup Tie', after his goal won the last ever Drybrough Cup Final for the Dons against the Saints.

From a media perspective, not many could get close to the career Archie Macpherson had behind the mic. STV, BBC, Setanta, Eurosport and Radio Clyde all had him as their main man at one time or another, while his epic commentary for the sensational Archie Gemmill solo goal in the 1978 World Cup against the Netherlands remains one of the most captivating television highlights of any broadcast sport.

Archie travelled the world to cover matches and break sports news stories. Before Souness arrived in Glasgow, Archie had already established a strong relationship with the former Liverpool captain.

'When Graeme Souness was installed as Rangers' new manager, my mind immediately went back to an interview I had with him for television in the USA, as Scotland prepared for the 1986 World Cup. Graeme was impassionate and candid as he told me: "I couldn't care less if we are defeated by Celtic four times a season – as long as we win the league!" This mindset was quite different, and it's unlikely that many Rangers fans of that time would concur with the wisdom of their new manager. I knew we were in for some special times ahead. We shouldn't forget, too, Rangers hadn't just gone for a new man in charge, they had signed an outstanding footballer. With hindsight, Graeme missing the final game of that tournament in Mexico perhaps favoured Rangers, as there is no doubt in my mind that the two previous games had taken it out of him, with the heat, humidity and the altitude taking their toll. Graeme said himself, when he came back to Rangers for pre-season, he was flying and as fit as he had ever been. He was determined to hit the ground running!'

Fittingly, Archie was the television commentator at Pittodrie on the day the league was won in that first season under Graeme Souness.

## CHAPTER 8:

# VIVA MEXICO

The sadness of the death of Jock Stein was still evident when Scotland met Australia in the play-off round to book their place in the 1986 World Cup, which was to be hosted by Mexico. In November, Scotland won the first leg with a comfortable 2–0 success at Hampden, before a goalless draw in Melbourne was enough to book their place in the finals. Davie Cooper, who got the first goal, wasn't to know his captain that night, Graeme Souness, was soon to be his manager at Rangers, while Frank McAvennie on his international debut, scored the second and was equally in the dark about how the football career of Graeme Souness would soon change.

Alex Ferguson, then manager of Aberdeen, was appointed to manage Scotland at the Mexico finals.

As Ferguson shaped his squad with the assistance of Walter Smith, who had been added to the coaching staff, there was quite a controversy when Alan Hansen was omitted from the final travelling squad. Hansen had just won the double with Liverpool! Perhaps it was confirmation that Ferguson preferred his club centre-back partnership of Willie Miller and Alex

McLeish, and was happy for them to be his first-choice central defenders in the national side, too.

An early setback to the plans was evident when Kenny Dalglish pulled out the squad citing a troublesome knee problem, despite being on the cusp of competing in his fourth finals. Many suggested the Hansen and Dalglish withdrawals were not unrelated. Steve Archibald, a striker who had formerly played under Ferguson at Aberdeen and was now with Barcelona, replaced Dalglish in the squad.

Scotland's training base was in Santa Fe, New Mexico, where acclimatisation and working at altitude were vital in preparation for the games ahead.

Souness paid particular attention to the home-based players in the squad, as they would be competition for his new-look Rangers side in the season ahead.

Of course, Graeme would soon also have teammate Davie Cooper in the squad, too – the only Rangers player to have travelled to the World Cup. Souness and Smith would also welcome the opportunity to work with Richard Gough, who was a serious transfer target, as was Graeme's old teammate from Liverpool, Stevie Nicol. Aberdeen, Dundee United and Celtic were heavily represented in the 22-man squad. It would certainly give Graeme Souness a clear indication of the quality of opposition he would look forward to facing in the season to come.

It would also give him time to talk all things Rangers with his new assistant, Walter Smith, when others weren't around; although, as captain of the team, Souness had to be careful to avoid any suggestion of conflict of interest.

The journey to Mexico got off to a difficult start when

manager Alex Ferguson let it be known that he wasn't happy that the 'suits' of the Scottish Football Association were favoured with first-class status on the first-leg flight to Los Angeles. The players were in economy.

As it was, Scotland were the last team to arrive in Mexico and set up their camp in what was an Aztec heritage site. It was described as 'spartan' by members of the squad.

Alan Rough was 34 years of age and heading to his third World Cup Finals. Roughy had been a hero in the match at Ninian Park against Wales that booked Scotland's place in the World Cup play-offs, coming off the bench at half-time to replace Jim Leighton who couldn't continue having lost a contact lens. Alan deserved his place in the travelling squad and had already amassed 52 caps for Scotland while with Partick Thistle and Hibernian. Alan was always good company and well-liked by teammates, including Souness himself.

Roughy recalls Souness and Rangers being the major topic of conversation as the squad assembled: 'We all knew it was going to happen, but equally, most of the other players couldn't believe it. Here we were, travelling the world to represent our country and everyone wanted to know what Graeme's plans were for Rangers. He wasn't for giving too much away, though, but he was always enquiring about this or that player or what way do such and such a team line-up. I'm sure he tried to avoid Rangers being a distraction as he had responsibilities as Scotland's captain. Graeme was a fantastic leader and one heck of a player. I can honestly say that for the time we were together as a group in Mexico he kept Rangers chatter to an absolute minimum. However, I remember one evening after a day off from training sitting outside our rooms, which were next door to each other, just me and him, when I tried to get him to open up about what we could expect from him as a manager. He looked at me before checking that there was nobody else about and started to unload some of his plans, and I honestly thought he was winding me up. I expected Jeremy Beadle to jump out! It just seemed so far-fetched. He told me he was going to go big-time on the fact that English clubs couldn't play in Europe because of the ban and how he would use Rangers being in Europe as a selling point. Graeme started to rhyme off the names: Terry Butcher, Chris Woods; and he also wasn't giving up on signing our Scotland teammate, Richard Gough. Another on his list was Trevor Steven, although that one took a bit longer to happen. I thought he must be having a laugh! But it was all so real a couple of weeks later when we lined up against Butcher and Woods in Graeme's new-look Rangers side for the league opener, with me in goal for home team, Hibs.'

The opening World Cup game was against Denmark, and when Alex Ferguson went with a Charlie Nicholas and Paul Sturrock partnership up top, meaning McAvennie and Archibald were on the bench, it did nothing for team harmony. In fact, it was reported that Archibald stormed out of the team meeting when given the news that he wasn't playing but would be on the bench. It was a very talented Danish side with quality throughout, including Morten Olsen, Frank Arnesen, Jesper Olsen and Michael Laudrup. On the bench was young left back Jan Bartram, who would later sign for Souness at Rangers in 1988.

Scotland lost the crucial opening game, albeit narrowly, going down to a goal from Preben Elkjaer just prior to the hour mark.

# VIVA MEXICO

Next up it was West Germany, who were fancied for the tournament by many and were loaded with star names, including Harald Schumacher in goal, Klaus Augenthaler at the heart of defence, Lothar Matthäus in midfield and Rudi Völler, their main goal threat. Genuine world-class and household name players pretty much the world over.

Stevie Archibald got his wish and started, but it was Gordon Strachan who opened the scoring in the searing heat of the Estadio Corregidora Queretaro, with a crowd of over 30,000 witnessing the unexpected start to the game. There was to be no shock on the cards, though, with Völler and strike partner Klaus Allofs on target to seal the German win.

With two defeats in two games, Scotland now needed to beat Uruguay, were they to have any chance of making the last 16 in the tournament.

For the crucial game, Alex Ferguson chose to leave his skipper on the bench, with Celtic's Paul McStay coming into midfield and the captain's responsibilities being transferred to Gordon Strachan.

The game was less than one minute old when the South Americans were reduced to ten men. José Batista was dismissed with a straight red card following a scything high challenge on Gordon Strachan, and despite that setback, it was to set the tone for the way Uruguay went about their business for the remainder of the match. The game was punctuated with fouls designed to stop Scotland finding a flow, and despite their best efforts, Alex Ferguson's side could not get the goal that would keep their World Cup hopes alive. It finished all square at 0–0 and Scotland were heading home.

The controversy wasn't over, though. Scottish FA president

# THE SIGNIFICANCE OF SOUNESS

Ernie Walker told the assembled global media that 'Scotland were on the field with cheats and cowards, who were associated with the scum of world football!'

Graeme Souness had to settle for a spectator's view of the game against the South Americans as he considered his international future. Souness had just turned 33, but with the demands of playing and managing Rangers, and the disappointment of being left out for the last match of the World Cup campaign, he was about to call time on his international career.

His game against West Germany was his last in the dark blue of Scotland.

Archie Macpherson recalls: 'It had been suggested Alex Ferguson may have left Graeme Souness out of the side to face Uruguay as a bit of a show of force that Fergie was flexing muscle as his boss, and remember, after all this was over, they would be going head to head for Scotland's top club honours in a matter of a few weeks' time. For me, though, that wasn't the way Alex Ferguson thought. Ferguson was a winner and he put out a team that he felt was best for the job, and if that meant leaving out the captain, so be it. Alex Ferguson and Graeme Souness were too very single-minded individuals, and reputations didn't mean much to either of them. Apart from this potential relationship breakdown, look at how Graeme Souness would later end the Rangers career of fans favourite Terry Butcher.'

Graeme Souness's international record spanned a period from 1974 to 1986. His first cap came against East Germany at Hampden in 1974 in a 3–0 win, with Tommy Hutchison, Kenny Burns and Kenny Dalglish the scorers. He finished with 54 appearances for Scotland and scored four goals, and remarkably for such a competitive player he was only booked four times in all those games. Souness represented Scotland at three World Cups. It was a truly memorable contribution to the national side over such an extended period, when international games were much less frequent than in the modern game. Amassing 54 caps today would be more like 100-plus.

Now, it was all about The Rangers.

On the way back from the Mexico World Cup, the Northern Ireland squad were on the same flight. Jimmy Nicholl, then with West Bromwich Albion, was part of the squad, and as he stretched his legs at the galley area he was collared by Graeme Souness. Jimmy recalls the conversation: 'Most of the Scotland guys were playing cards to put the time in. Graeme approached me and said, "You were at Rangers, weren't you? What was it like?" Well, I told him, apart from the manager John Greig resigning the day after he signed me, I loved the six months I had there, but in those days of 1983, Aberdeen and Dundee United were the dominant teams. Graeme wanted to know every detail I could offer about the club. What were the facilities like? What were the fans like? Who were the best players I played with then, and were any still there? Already his passion for his new job was shining through. He never really gave anything away about what his plans were, but he did emphasise that he was to receive exceptional support, and had to hit the ground running and to get set to chase the title. He did hint that with English clubs unable to operate in Europe, that could be helpful in enticing players north. I suppose Graeme's personality would also be a big help when it came to getting players to sign.

Little did I realise on that transatlantic flight I was actually being sounded out for a return to Ibrox!'

When the call came, Jimmy Nicholl couldn't pack his bags and head north quick enough.

# CHAPTER 9:

# NEW MANAGER, NEW SQUAD: 1986-87

As Graeme Souness was getting down to business with the Scottish national team and their World Cup adventure in Mexico, David Holmes was every bit as busy back at home, weaving his business magic to recruit the best possible players for Rangers. First to arrive was striker Colin West from Watford, a clear message of intent was then sent out when England goalkeeper Chris Woods signed, and then the big one, the capture of England captain Terry Butcher, the signing that had everyone talking on both sides of the border.

However, even now, Graeme Souness will confirm his best-ever signing was not a player, but the man he recruited as his assistant manager, Walter Smith. Souness and Smith had a good working relationship in their time together with the Scotland national team. As far back as 1978, Smith was appointed as coach to Scotland's under-18 side, and helped them win the European Youth Championships in 1982. His success with the youngsters elevated him to the same position with the under-21 team, before being brought on board with the senior team under Alex Ferguson. As a player, Walter had a journeyman-type career, with two spells at Dundee United either side of a couple of seasons with Dumbarton. But coaching was Walter Smith's forte, and as a self-confessed Rangers fan, his destiny was to be a major influence at Ibrox. Walter's coaching CV was impressive, as he operated at the side of Dundee United gaffer Jim McLean. Together they delivered United's one and only championship and took the Tannadice club to the semi-finals of the European Cup. Aged 38, five years older than his new boss, Walter Smith was ready to face the challenges ahead at Ibrox. It cost £50,000 in compensation for his services. What a bargain that proved to be.

When Graeme Souness laid out his transfer priorities to Walter an eyebrow was raised, but the look in the eyes of the new Rangers manager was one of determination and that of a man with a plan.

Colin West was first to join the revolution, with a relatively modest fee going to Watford for their number 9. He had a big physical presence, ideal for a front man, and it was clear he could complement Ally McCoist in what promised to be a fearsome front pairing. At Watford, West had scored 23 goals in 56 appearances, and had finished the 1985–86 season as their top scorer with a very creditable 16 goals. West had played alongside McCoist when they were together at Sunderland, where Colin had come through the youth ranks. Colin looks back now with fond memories: 'As soon as I heard Graeme Souness wanted me at Rangers, I couldn't get up the road quick enough. I had been brought up a Newcastle fan, played for Sunderland, but this was as big as it gets. The players coming in just added to the excitement, but I'll always be proud that I was his first signing.'

## NEW MANAGER, NEW SQUAD: 1986–87

Next up it was Chris Woods, who committed his future to Rangers. At 6ft 2in and already an English internationalist, his signing was the one that changed the dynamic of big players going south from Scotland to big players coming north from elite English clubs. Souness was reversing the trend but his philosophy was sound, in as much that if the signing didn't quite work out there would always be a re-sale market open to him back in England. Of course, there was also the thorny issue that competitors in Scotland wouldn't sell their star performers to another club operating in the same league. Souness's plans to raid the English market were made a bit easier while English clubs remained debarred from European competition following the Heysel Stadium disaster of May 1985, when violence erupted as Liverpool and Juventus fans clashed in Brussels before the European Cup Final.

Chris Woods first came to Graeme Souness's attention in the Football League Cup Final against Liverpool in March 1978, when deputising for England great Peter Shilton. Woods kept clean sheets, not just in the first game at Wembley that finished 0–0 but again in the replay at Old Trafford to ensure Nottingham Forest lifted the trophy for their incredible manager Brian Clough. Souness didn't play in either match, so had a good view as Woods produced heroics between the sticks for Forest. Woods then moved on to Queens Park Rangers in search of regular first-team football. He was only 19 years of age when he joined the London club. In March 1981, Woods was on the move again, with Norwich City his destination this time. Playing for the Canaries, he again won the League Cup as they beat Sunderland in the final, but despite their cup success, Norwich were relegated that same season. Woods's form had clearly caught the eye of England manager Bobby Robson, who took the young goalkeeper on a post-season tour to America. The following season, Norwich returned to the top league as champions and Woods was a key operator in manager Ken Brown's squad. Souness wanted a top goalkeeper who he could trust week-in week-out, and with Rangers often dominating matches it would need a special talent with exceptional concentration levels and a desire to keep clean sheets, meaning the forwards could on occasion deliver only one goal in a game but it would be enough to seal a victory.

The fact Chris Woods went from November 1986 through to 31 January 1987 without conceding a goal for Rangers was quite remarkable. It worked out that he had not lost a goal for 1,196 consecutive minutes in competitive action. The transfer fee for Chris Woods was £600,000. The fee shattered the previous British transfer record for a goalkeeper. Nobody could argue anything other than that it was money well spent; but more than that, Woods signing was another signal that Graeme Souness had no fears about spending big in the transfer market. He knew, too, that when Woods hooked up with his teammates on international duty, Rangers would be high up on the topics of conversation and Woods would be effectively selling the special history and features of the Ibrox club, on his behalf, to his English compatriots. Chris Woods remembers just how persuasive Graeme Souness was: 'It took me a matter of seconds to make my decision to join Rangers. Graeme laid out his plans and said that with Terry Butcher we were his priority targets, and reiterated that he planned to build his side around us. While Graeme was making his sales pitch he pulled no punches on what was expected of us.

## NEW MANAGER, NEW SQUAD: 1986–87

It had to be winning the Scottish Championship in that first year. Anything else would be a bonus but he laid down the challenge – deliver me the title!'

The jewel in the Ibrox crown was the capture of the English international captain Terry Butcher. He was the man Souness wanted to lead his team on the field. He was a warrior, a man with standards who drove standards in others, and was a winner in everything he did. To get Terry on board would really have all in English football sit up and take note. It wasn't going to be easy, though, as both Manchester United and Tottenham Hotspur were determined to win the race for his signature. It was going to take serious money and quite a big selling job to convince the England skipper to give up life in leafy Suffolk for the white-hot goldfish bowl that was Glasgow.

Terry Butcher had been at Ipswich Town for eight seasons and had won the UEFA Cup in 1981 when Bobby Robson was boss; they also came within a whisker in that same season of becoming champions of England. As it was, Aston Villa took the title, Ipswich were second, with Arsenal third. For context, Liverpool finished in fifth place, nine points behind Villa. At the time Rangers were in the market for experienced performers, Butcher had become available, as Ipswich had been relegated and the financial pressure was clearly on at his club, who had committed to building a new stand at their Portman Road stadium. Old Trafford appeared to be the likely destination for Butcher as Manchester United had been chasing him for three seasons. Butcher himself reportedly told close associates he was probably heading to United.

The chase for Terry Butcher's signature was pretty complex, as like Souness, he had been active at the Mexico

## THE SIGNIFICANCE OF SOUNESS

World Cup that had been won by Argentina, captained by Diego Maradona, whose 'hand of god' goal played a large part in eliminating England at the quarter-final stage. Even today, the mere mention of Maradona is enough to send Terry Butcher into a bit of a meltdown. After the finals, Butcher was off to play in an exhibition match in San Diego for the UNICEF charity, where he was at the heart of the Rest of the World team's defence as they took on an Americas select, which just happened to have Diego Maradona in their ranks. Tracking down Butcher for Messrs Souness and Holmes was proving as hard as it had been for Terry to mark Maradona in competitive action.

It was while in San Diego that Rangers made their move and put forwards their bid. Rangers met Ipswich's asking price and the terms agreed were a complete 100 per cent payment up front. Graeme Souness and David Holmes had established a budget for transfers and that included a weighty fee to get Butcher on board. Graeme Souness wasn't prepared to let this one slip through his grasp, and set up a meeting with the returning English internationalist as soon as his flight from the US touched down at Heathrow. At the time, Terry Butcher was 27 years of age and was already an established fixture in the English national side with 45 caps. Butcher was one of the best centre backs in world football at the time and Graeme Souness was committed to building his team around him. It was suggested that if Graeme got Terry, he would deliver the league title for his boss. It was a promise that David Holmes reminded him of often, and indeed, held him to on more than one occasion as the season unfolded. After a bit of a mix-up at the venue for the vital meeting in London, Graeme whisked

# NEW MANAGER, NEW SQUAD: 1986–87

Terry to Glasgow to see the impressive Ibrox stadium for himself, and after laying out his plans for the club, Butcher was fully invested in the project and a deal was established with a shake of hands. At 6ft 4in and built like a gladiator with a heart to match, Graeme Souness had his key man.

Butcher himself confirmed: 'It was quite a compliment that Graeme said he would do whatever it would take to make sure I joined up with him at Rangers. I had other options, but when Graeme Souness tells you that you are his main man, it excited me, and I just knew he was someone I could work with. I was all in from day one!'

While Terry embraced everything about Rangers, including taking on the responsibilities of captaincy, Derek Ferguson had absolutely no reservations about his new skipper: 'Maybe Graeme Souness himself didn't quite fully understand the need to win every game when you are at Rangers, but Terry Butcher got it immediately. Terry was the England captain and the dressing room gave him respect and took to him right away. We loved him, and it was obvious he had taken Rangers to his heart. He was a warrior, and yes, he was aggressive, but he could play. He was cultured in possession and could ping a ball with deadly accuracy. If you weren't producing, not just in games but in training too, he didn't hold back. Often he let you know if you had more to give or had made the smallest of mistakes. Sometimes he even did this when we won! He was the perfect man to lead us on the park.'

Season tickets, which were already selling fast, took another jump, and any concerns that Terry had about being an Englishman in Glasgow were soon history as he embraced everything about being a Ranger. Butcher was a natural for the job of skipper and he led by example, and had no hesitation in letting any teammates know if they were guilty of slack play or giving the ball away unnecessarily. Terry Butcher was a great fit for a club with serious ambitions, and that put him on the same wavelength as his new manager and his new chairman.

The final piece of the jigsaw was the signing of Northern Ireland international defender Jimmy Nicholl. Jimmy had been at Rangers before, although within 24 hours of joining on loan from Toronto Blizzard, then-manager John Greig, who brought him to the club, resigned his position. Jimmy had started at Manchester United, where he won the FA Cup in 1977, and had also played with Sunderland while both Colin West and Ally McCoist were at Roker Park. There was no transfer fee involved in this deal; it was a straight swap, with front man Bobby Williamson going to West Bromwich Albion as Jimmy came north. Jimmy was an infectious character and well respected in the dressing room, but more importantly, he was hugely physically fit and brought even more experience as the new-look defence took shape. Jimmy, who had discussed Rangers with Souness as they journeyed back from World Cup duties with their respective countries, couldn't wait to get back to Rangers. 'Ron Saunders was the West Brom manager at the time and we didn't have a great working relationship. In fact, I was training with the kids when Saunders called me in and told me, "No negotiations – no, would you consider – no – you are going to Rangers." I honestly felt I was the luckiest guy in the world! I grabbed my boots and was on my way. Little did I think that day as I swapped the Midlands for Scotland I was setting myself for the next 40 years of my life!'

# NEW MANAGER, NEW SQUAD: 1986–87

It wasn't about quantity for Graeme Souness and Walter Smith; quality was the key, and just how players would fit into their vision as they built a squad ready to mount a challenge for the league title.

# CHAPTER 10:
# EASTER ROAD: THE BIG KICK-OFF

It was quite a demanding pre-season schedule that was put in place when Graeme Souness and Walter Smith returned from their international duties in Mexico. New number one signing Terry Butcher didn't make the squad that travelled to West Germany, as he was given extended leave after his World Cup exertions. Rangers won two games, and lost and drew the other two. Rangers then came back to play Tottenham Hotspur at White Hart Lane in a testimonial match for long-serving defender Paul Miller. Again, Butcher wasn't involved. The game against Spurs ended 1–1, then next it was destination Ibrox to take on Bayern Munich in the final warm-up game for the Light Blues. Terry Butcher made his debut but Rangers still lost the game, going down 2–0 to the German giants. It wasn't the best result to head into the big league opener. There was a real sense of anticipation as Rangers travelled to Easter Road to get their league campaign up and running. Midfielder Bobby Russell sets the scene: 'We had a really busy pre-season, including games against decent lower league opposition in West Germany. Graeme limited his appearances in these fixtures but he was ready, despite the demands of the World Cup. For the game against Hibernian, I made the starting 11, and it was one of the few occasions I played alongside Graeme. New signings Chris Woods, Terry Butcher, Colin West and the manager himself were in the side, while Ally Dawson, Stuart Munro, Dave McPherson, Ally McCoist, Ian Durrant and Ted McMinn along with myself completed the line-up. Derek Ferguson and Robert Fleck were on the bench.

'The red card for the manager, despite being forewarned that perhaps one or two in the Hibs ranks were sure to go after him, gave us a mountain to climb. It was just over half an hour in, when Stuart Beedie was very late and high with a brutal challenge on Souness. You could see Graeme was furious and looking for revenge. When it came just minutes later, it was a scything challenge that warranted the early bath, but it could have been a case of mistaken identity as it was front man, George McCluskey, who copped it. I suppose with hindsight, Graeme had a policy of, "If you go over the top, I'll go higher!" It was suggested Billy Kirkwood, who would later become a Rangers coach, was the Hibs enforcer, and he was the guy Graeme had intended to give a calling card to, showing that he was nastier than the nastiest in their side if things got physical. Graeme was a sensational player. He had skill, personality, confidence and that trademark aggressive streak. On the day, perhaps the pressure to win and the need to protect his reputation took over in the heat of battle. I have no doubts whatsoever, mind you, that had Graeme stayed on the park and we had a full team of 11 we would have won the game. Of course, it all got a bit silly after McCluskey took the high boot from Graeme, and before he was carried off the

## THE SIGNIFICANCE OF SOUNESS

field and Graeme headed for the early bath, a few punches were thrown with players going toe to toe as tempers flared.'

Broadcaster and author Stewart Weir was on duty for the press agency that day: 'The look of disdain from Souness as he left the field will live with many for ever, and probably set the tone for Souness's tenure in Glasgow and launched his famous line, "no-one likes us, we don't care!"'

Weir recalls, too, the words of television commentator, Jock Brown, as he captured the Easter Road flashpoint: 'Graeme Souness maybe in severe trouble here – this game has been simmering from the start – Easter Road is going wild – and – Souness's first competitive game for Rangers has lasted only 37 minutes!' It was epic, and while many suggested referee Mike Delaney was out to make a name for himself, in reality, it was more like Souness making a name for himself back on his home patch.

Spare man in the Rangers travelling party that day was Scott Nisbet who watched the incredible scenes from the directors' box. As Souness headed down the tunnel, David Holmes turned to Scott and suggested he should head down to the dressing room to check on the manager's welfare. Nisbet made his way down to the visitors' dressing room to be met by a stern-faced Souness, who asked him, 'Front page or back page, Nizzy?' Nizzy responded, 'Both, boss, both!'

Hibernian had opened the scoring through Stuart Beedie, which was cancelled out by Ally McCoist just two minutes later from the penalty spot. Mickey Weir and Steve Cowan carved open the Rangers defence for Beedie's strike, while it was McCoist himself who was impeded by Hibs centre backs Gordon Chisholm and Mark Fulton, to win the spot kick.

## EASTER ROAD: THE BIG KICK-OFF

Super Ally gave Alan Rough no chance from 12 yards to make it 1–1. The winning strike came just short of half-time, with Cowan converting from close range after substitute Willy Irvine, who had replaced the stricken McCluskey, slipped the ball from wide left across the face of the Rangers goal.

It was an astonishing match to start the Souness era. At one point 20 players were brawling inside the centre circle. The one man missing was Hibs keeper Alan Rough.

Steve Cowan brings us his view of proceedings from a Hibernian perspective: 'We didn't want to be the sideshow, but the game had been hyped to the maximum. Everybody knew Souness was a fantastically gifted player with such a tough reputation, and I honestly think that when he lashed out at George McCluskey it was a statement of intent, in as much as, "You know of me, you know what I'm about, and I'm here to stay." Souness had previous with a similar studded challenge on Peter Nicholas in a Scotland–Wales game, and he had a leg-breaker on Siggi Jónsson in Iceland – he certainly took no prisoners. Back then, you could get away with much more than nowadays; of course there were far fewer cameras, while goodness knows what VAR might have made of the goings-on at Easter Road that day. I remember looking at George's shin, and Souness's studs had created a four-inch gash, and the wound was also about two inches deep! Then it all kicked off, with referee Mike Delaney booking nine players on the day. That figure rose when the SFA intervened and dished out another 21 yellows retrospectively.

'I was Hibs PFA representative at the time and went to Park Gardens after both clubs had been cited, to plea on behalf of my teammates. Alan Rough was innocent. Roughy never left his goal area as the melee broke out; Mark Fulton, too, did nothing wrong as he had been poleaxed by a haymaker of a right hook from Ally McCoist. Many thought it was Colin West that punched our centre half, Fulton, but it was Coisty alright. I've known Ally since we grew up together in East Kilbride and I had a ringside seat. Make no mistake though, poster-boy Ally was always quick with a quip and a smile, but he could handle himself and had a wee vicious streak when it was called for. To the game itself, it was to be our day, and I remember scoring the winner from my favourite range of about two yards! I ran off in delight to celebrate in front of the old shed packed with Hibs fans. It was a setback for Rangers, but they showed character and a real winning mentality when they got into their stride and went on to be worthy champions. It's best summed up by the old saying, "It's not how you start, it's how you finish that counts!" Under Souness, the transformation at Rangers was remarkable, and it was no surprise, especially with the signings he made, that they dominated the Scottish game for such an extended period. But that day at Easter Road, I like to think we put a wee spoke in their wheel.'

Hibernian and Scotland goalkeeper Alan Rough has a slightly different version as to why he wasn't booked, as a battle royal took place on the halfway line: 'Apart from the fact I didn't fancy running up to where it was all kicking off, I couldn't. I had already been booked, so a second yellow card and I would have been sent off along with Graeme Souness! Of course, in those days there was no substitute goalie on the bench, so I wasn't leaving my line.' Alan continues: 'My booking was harsh, and it was my tongue that got me into trouble as usual. When referee Delaney awarded the penalty as

McCoist went down in our box, I thought Ally had dived and made the most of it and I told the ref that, maybe with a wee bit of colourful language thrown in too, so I was yellow-carded. Getting involved in the mayhem later was never an option.'

On the bench at Easter Road was Ibrox starlet Derek Ferguson, and he watched the action unfold and couldn't quite believe what he was witnessing: 'The gaffer was a glorious player, and that day he was highly animated in the dressing room pre-match and determined to get off to the best possible start. I don't think he was overhyped for the match, but he used to often drum it into us how we had to protect ourselves, and also when and how to get your retaliation in first. Perhaps the fact that Stuart Beedie and Billy Kirkwood played him at his own game and lit the blue touchpaper with Beedie then coming with a very late and high challenge on Souness brought out the reaction that left George McCluskey in a heap on the Easter Road turf.'

If you look back at the highlights, you can see Graeme Souness share a point with Walter Smith in the Rangers dugout as he leaves the field, perhaps suggesting that he had eliminated the Hibs hardman, but the suggested reply from Walter according to those within earshot was Graeme had gotten the wrong guy!

As Souness made his way to the dressing room he also glanced up to the stands where his father was watching. Graeme looked embarrassed and clearly felt he had let his family down. To this day, Graeme still apologises and deeply regrets ruining his dad's day by his overly aggressive actions.

Hibernian's win was their first in the last three league visits that the Ibrox men had made to Easter Road. On their first visit to Leith in the previous season, just less than a year before this loss, Rangers had a comfortable 3–1 win, with goals from Ally McCoist, Dave McPherson and Bobby Williamson.

It wasn't a great advert, either, for the Scottish game, with such media attention from south of the border to track why Woods and Butcher had committed their future in Scotland.

As things transpired, it was probably the highlight of Hibs fans' season. Rangers would recover from the early setback and go on to win the title. Hibernian finished ninth in the 12-team league and won only nine more matches from their 44-game programme to the end of the season. When Hibs came to Ibrox in October, it finished 3–0 to Graeme Souness's side, with goals coming from Dave McPherson, Robert Fleck and Dougie Bell.

It wasn't the start Rangers wanted, and it was also an early reminder to the new management team and all the big-name signings that they weren't going to get it all their own way in the season ahead.

## CHAPTER 11:
# GRINDING OUT RESULTS

If the dreams and aspirations of David Holmes and Graeme Souness were to be delivered, Rangers would have to overcome the worst possible start to their league campaign, where they not only lost to Hibs but they lost the services of player–manager Graeme Souness to his first-half red card.

The title remained the holy grail, as it was 1978, a full nine years, since the Ibrox side had been crowned champions of Scotland.

The Scottish Premier Division in those days carried two points for a win in a 44-game campaign, meaning each team played each other twice at home and twice away. Rangers tooled up for business with striker Colin West, goalkeeper Chris Woods and centre-back colossus Terry Butcher, and of course Souness himself, all signed in the summer, and all would start for that first defeat at Hibernian. The squad would be supplemented as the season evolved, but Graeme Souness had belief in the squad that he had inherited, and was aware that some of the youngsters were showing enough in the pre-season fixtures to force themselves into his plans. The old guard, including Derek Johnstone and

Dave MacKinnon, had moved on at the end of the previous season.

After the shock of Easter Road, Rangers got back to winning ways four days later against Falkirk at Ibrox. It took a solitary penalty goal from Ally McCoist to give the Light Blues their first two points in the league. Souness had rung the changes in his starting side for this one, and another new face had also joined the squad. Jimmy Nicholl came in from West Bromwich Albion in a swap deal for Bobby Williamson. There was a recall for Derek Ferguson, who was in for the suspended Souness, and he was joined in midfield by Cammy Fraser. It was a lacklustre performance against newly promoted Falkirk, who were making their first visit to Ibrox in 13 years. Key men for Rangers, in what was described as a very dull affair, were Ian Durrant and Derek Ferguson, both orchestrating things from midfield. It may have been dull, but it was a crucial two points.

Next was another home game, one week after the Hibs defeat, with Dundee United coming to Ibrox. Rangers went down for the second time in three matches, losing 3–2, with a double from McCoist. The McCoist goals were cancelled out by two goals from Kevin Gallacher, with the winner coming only two minutes before the final whistle, and it was former Ger, Ian Redford's strike that won it for the Arabs. Souness had picked himself to start, with Derek Ferguson, despite his fine performance against Falkirk, back on the bench. What was obvious, though, was a huge uplift in the attendance. For United, 43,995 came through the gate, compared to only 27,362 who watched the Falkirk game. A trip to Douglas Park to play Hamilton was next, and Rangers won. It finished 2–1,

## GRINDING OUT RESULTS

with Cammy Fraser and Colin West on target. This new-look Rangers side were going to have to become adept at grinding out results, especially as the following fixture was the first Old Firm match of the season, and a first for Graeme Souness in a playing capacity. As it was, Souness didn't play, while Colin West missed out with a strain, and Ted McMinn was given a roving role and tasked with creating havoc in the Celtic rearguard. The gangling unorthodox front man was certainly a candidate for the Man of the Match award, but 19-year-old goalscorer Ian Durrant probably pipped McMann to the honour. The game had been moved to the last day of August, which was a Sunday, as it was to be televised live – the first Rangers–Celtic fixture ever to be a live broadcast.

Durrant and Ferguson with the creative McMinn ran the game, but it was the most magnificent pass from Davie Cooper that set up Ian Durrant to score the winner. With 16 minutes of the match remaining, Cooper dropped a shoulder and pretended to go right but went left, before playing the most visionary reverse pass into the path of Durrant, who had read the script well and timed his run to perfection. Durrant steadied himself before slipping the ball into the net beyond the diving Patrick Bonner in the Celtic nets. That goal was enough to ensure a Rangers victory, but it could have been much different had Brian McClair, who was partnering Maurice Johnston in the Celtic attack, not contrived to head over when clear and from close range. Ian Durrant remembers that goal with real affection: 'It was the perfect pass from Coop and I picked my spot. Big Paddy Bonner dived but was never getting near it. I took off in celebration looking for my brother Alan and our mates in the old enclosure, and as I did so, ran past the man who had put me through. I quickly got reprimanded from Davie not to ever blank him again. I didn't intend it. I was just caught up in the emotion of scoring my first goal against Celtic.' Durrant continues: 'It was a must-win game for us, as had we lost we would have gone five points behind Celtic.'

There was one blot on the landscape for Rangers as Terry Butcher picked up a booking from referee Kenny Hope, and that put him on the cusp of suspension before the season had even got into September. The Old Firm win gave Rangers belief, as two clean sheets and six goals scored against Motherwell and Clydebank confirmed. Another youngster made his mark in that Ibrox fixture against the Bankies, as Robert Fleck claimed a hat-trick in the 4–0 win. A trip to Dens Park on 20 September saw Rangers go down 1–0, with the only goal scored by future Rangers legend John Brown.

After losing to Dundee, Rangers went six league games in a row without being beaten. Aberdeen, St Mirren, Hibernian and Falkirk were all defeated, with draws recorded against Dundee United and Celtic, both away from home. In that run, Fleck again notched a hat-trick, this time against Falkirk. Cooper chipped in with three goals as did Ally McCoist, while Graeme Souness was on target himself in the 2–0 Ibrox win over Aberdeen, with his former Scotland boss Alex Ferguson still in charge. The good run came to an end at home to Motherwell on 8 November. In the period leading up to that, however, Souness had his first silverware in the Ibrox trophy room. In front of a crowd of 74,219 in the national stadium on 26 October, Rangers lifted the League Cup with a 2–1 win over Celtic, Durrant again on target in the Old Firm fixture with

Davie Cooper converting a stunning penalty to put red white and blue ribbons on the cup. Both goals came in the second half, while this time, McClair did score for Celtic. Terry Butcher captained his side to glory, while Maurice Johnston was red-carded by referee David Syme.

In the league, Rangers bounced back in November with wins over Clydebank and Dundee, with McCoist scoring three in the two games. As we headed to the turn of the year, Rangers put defeat at Pittodrie behind them. That match saw Ian Porterfield in the home dugout as he replaced Alex Ferguson, who had left for Manchester United a couple of weeks before. On the day, Rangers' disciplinary issues again came to the fore as Dave McPherson was sent off for a clear punch to Davie Dodds, bloodying the front man's nose.

Celtic were still top of the table and the only blemish on the Parkhead side's league record was the Old Firm defeat at the end of August. To the end of September, Celtic had 12 league wins and three draws. Rangers had work to do, and it was clear the next Old Firm fixture scheduled for Ibrox on New Year's Day, 1987, was going to be pivotal to Rangers' season. As it was, December was going to be a good month for Graeme Souness's charges. The records show Hearts (A) 3–0, St Mirren (H) 2–0, Hibs (A) 0–0, Falkirk (H) 4–0, Hamilton (A) 2–0, and Dundee United (H) 2–0. Six clean sheets in a row and 13 goals scored, with McCoist claiming three, and again Fleck was influential scoring four, with Davie Cooper contributing three. Durrant, McPherson and skipper Butcher all scored one each. Robert Fleck pretty much burst into the first team and truly shone in that first season under Graeme Souness, scoring 22 goals, including four memorable hat-tricks. Flecky's time was short at Ibrox, moving on to Norwich in December 1987, but he played a big part in that first title success.

Rangers were going into the Ne'erday fixture in terrific form, and had already racked up two wins against their biggest rivals for the season.

There really was a sense of 1987 being something special for Rangers and their fans.

On 1 January 1987, 43,206 were inside Ibrox to see the Light Blues continue their unbeaten run. It finished with Rangers winning 2–0 against Celtic and yet another shutout display from the rearguard. Ally McCoist and Robert Fleck got the goals, both strikes coming in the first half, but it was an outstanding team performance. Earlier in December, Rangers recruited Graham Roberts from Spurs, and he made a wonderful debut against Dundee United in the fixture before the Celtic game. The game was played against a backdrop of horrid weather with snow and sleet falling, but Rangers showed they were the form team and dictated the play from the first whistle. The defence looked impenetrable and Celtic didn't record a shot on target until the 33rd minute, by which time they were two down. Graeme Souness started his first Old Firm match as a player, and by full-time he could boast an unbeaten record of four wins and one draw against Celtic since he took office. Celtic's inability again to beat Rangers immediately saw the bookmakers switch their odds for title winners, and now Rangers were installed as firm favourites.

If January and the new year had gotten off to the most sensational of starts that brought joy to the Rangers faithful, they were brought back to earth with a bump on the last day of January when they were knocked out the Scottish Cup at the third-round stage by Hamilton Academical. Ibrox was silenced when Adrian Sprott slammed in the only goal of the game to give John Lambie's side the win. It was a humbling experience for Rangers and the potential for a glorious first season domestic treble under Graeme Souness was immediately off the cards. That goal ended a record 1,196 minutes since Rangers and summer recruit Chris Woods had last let in a goal.

Before that cup tie and following the win against Celtic, Rangers' undefeated run in the league had continued. The points were being stacked up as Rangers won 1–0 at Motherwell, while 5–0 and another Fleck hat-trick saw off Clydebank at Ibrox. Surprisingly, two weeks before the cup disaster against Hamilton, Rangers had a comfortable 2–0 win against the Lanarkshire side, also at Ibrox. Aberdeen then came to Ibrox and left with a point in a goalless draw. After the embarrassing cup elimination, Souness's side again got back into the winning habit and were unbeaten in the next eight games going into the Celtic match at Parkhead on 4 April. A crowd of 60,800 were in to see Celtic get their first win over Graeme Souness. For this one, it was Celtic who needed the points most, and when they went in at half-time they were two up, with both goals coming from the penalty spot. Brian McClair scored both spot kicks. Danny McGrain was back in the Celtic ranks and he was inspirational to their performance; he also ensured Davie Cooper was kept quiet for most of the game, although he did pop up with a pass for McCoist to score not long after the interval. Rangers searched for the equaliser but it was Celtic who stretched their lead when Owen Archdeacon, who had come off the bench to replace Jim McInally, took advantage of a mix-up between

# THE SIGNIFICANCE OF SOUNESS

Chris Woods and Jimmy Nicholl, and that sealed the victory for the home side. That win meant that Celtic narrowed the gap at the top of the table to only two points, but Rangers were still in the box seat.

The game wasn't without its controversial moments, as is the case most times Rangers and Celtic go head to head. From Rangers first corner Davie Cooper flighted an inswinger that Pat Bonner misjudged and the ball landed in the net. However, referee Bob Valentine chopped it off and indicated an infringement by Robert Fleck, who had taken up his position at the near post. For Celtic's second penalty, which had been awarded after Terry Butcher upended Maurice Johnston, McClair had to be patient, as a spectator ran on to the park to remonstrate with Valentine. The police intervened and the fan was hustled away.

There were five games remaining in the title race. Who would hold their nerve and be crowned champions? Rangers faced three home games and two away. Celtic conversely had three away and two at home. Ten days after the Celtic game, Rangers beat Dundee 2–0 at Ibrox, then kept the momentum going with a 3–0 success against Clydebank. Next, it was Hearts at Ibrox, and with expectations high, 43,205 were in attendance for a 3–0 Rangers win. In these last three games since defeat to Celtic, McCoist scored six goals to drive Rangers towards the title.

As it was, destiny would be decided on 2 May. Rangers faced an awkward trip to Pittodrie to take on Aberdeen. On the same day, Celtic were entertaining Falkirk. The last day fixtures were scheduled for seven days later, with Rangers due to entertain St Mirren, while Celtic were down to go to Hearts.

## GRINDING OUT RESULTS

Rangers shared the points against Aberdeen despite Graeme Souness again being red-carded, but it was a scorcher of a header from Terry Butcher for the ten men to hang on for the draw. As the drama was unfolding in Scotland's north-east corner the news came filtering through that Celtic were losing 2–1 to Falkirk at home. That's the way both games finished and Rangers were champions! Pittodrie was a sea of red, white and blue.

It also meant the last round of fixtures were academic, although the Rangers fans again sold out Ibrox to take the chance to celebrate with their heroes.

It was some campaign, and in the early part of the season Graeme Souness and his charges had to dig deep to grind out results and show the character that would see them returned to the pinnacle of the Scottish game.

## CHAPTER 12:

# A CHRISTMAS GIFT TO THE FANS

Graeme Souness had been thwarted every which way by Jim McLean every time he put a proposal to the Dundee United chief to take Richard Gough to Rangers. Graeme and Richard had played together in the national side, and the new Rangers manager was very aware of all Richard's qualities and held the belief that Richard would not just enhance the team were he to sign, but in the future would be a Rangers captain too.

Despite Rangers outbidding Tottenham, Jim McLean undersold Richard Gough to Spurs on 17 August 1986. The fee was reported as £1.5 million and it was suggested Rangers had been prepared to pay United quite a bit more than that. So, for the moment, Gough was off the radar, and as Souness had predicted, Richard's natural leadership style soon saw him rewarded with the captain's armband at the White Hart Lane club.

Since the start of the season, and in the large part while results had been good, consistency was missing, and Souness was keen to supplement his defence by finding the best possible partner for Terry Butcher. David Holmes and Graeme Souness got their heads together and remembered their trip to Spurs in pre-season that ended in a 1–1 draw. For the game in London, Rangers gave a trial to Israeli defender and former Liverpool colleague of the manager Avi Cohen, but work-permit issues meant Cohen didn't hook up at Rangers under contract until a year later. A challenge match, and in a not-so-friendly fashion, Graeme Souness had a bit of a set-to with Tottenham's imposing defender Graham Roberts. With the second half of the season closing in, another centre half was a priority. The focus switched to signing Roberts, to be that partner alongside Butcher; his physicality and commitment had stuck with Souness since that August meeting. Graham had been a bit of a late developer in footballing terms, having joined Spurs in 1980 after a couple of seasons with both Dorchester Town and Weymouth. Tottenham paid only £35,000 for him in 1980, but it was going to take a lot more money now to make him move much further north.

Roberts had been successful in his time with the north London club, winning the FA Cup in 1981 and 1982 before captaining the side to glory in the UEFA Cup Final win against Anderlecht in 1984. Graham Roberts fully fitted the profile Graeme Souness wanted of a player in his ranks. As usual, David Holmes wasted no time in getting things moving to have Roberts in place for the busy festive period fixture card. Personal terms were quickly agreed after Roberts was given the Ibrox tour, and the imposing stadium and set-up was a serious factor in influencing his decision. Graham Roberts made his debut at Ibrox against Dundee United on 27 December; at the time, Rangers were third in the table, six points behind leaders Celtic, with United themselves in second place. It was a debut to remember, with the powerhouse driving out of defence to

## THE SIGNIFICANCE OF SOUNESS

a huge roar from the home crowd, and as things opened up, McCoist was on hand to pounce and score the opening goal. The Rangers fans had a new hero. David Holmes described the signing of Graham Roberts as a Christmas gift to the fans, an acknowledgement for their commitment to supporting the team and how season ticket sales had increased.

The fee was £450k, but the figures stacked up.

Jimmy Nicholl very much welcomed Graham Roberts as a new teammate: 'Graham was a terrific signing. He was just what was needed. Hard as nails and with the winning mentality Graeme Souness wanted. He came in at the right time to keep momentum going and his experience helped everyone in the back four, but the younger guys, too, like Scott Nisbet, benefitted from Robbo's encouragement. Graham coming in when he did certainly helped kick us on to the title.'

In the first 11 home league games the previous season, 1985–86, the total attendance was 298,958, giving an average of 27,178 at each game. In the first season under Souness, the same first 11 home league games yielded a total of 362,621 in attendance with an average of 32,965 at each game. The figures showed that Roberts had been effectively paid for by fan commitment, as 63,663 more had attended Ibrox when it mattered. Rangers had the squad to mount a challenge for the league title with Roberts joining summer signings West, Woods, Butcher and Nicholl. Young goalkeeper Lindsay Hamilton also joined from Stenhousemuir in November, while one week before Roberts, Rangers raided Doncaster Rovers for Neil Woods, a young striker who was showing promise. The final signing of the inaugural season of Souness was Jimmy Phillips, a versatile defender who came in from Bolton

Wanderers, but it was Roberts who would have the biggest influence on how things would take shape.

Derek Ferguson recalls Robbo's stunning debut: 'We were a bit behind Celtic in the table and the manager wasn't happy that, in his opinion, we were losing soft goals. Robbo came in for what was a relatively modest fee and hit the ground running. On his first game against Dundee United he took out Paul Sturrock with a meaty challenge after only five minutes! He did have a reputation, of course, of not taking prisoners. But the big guy could play too, and our first goal that day was all down to him; well, nearly – McCoist provided the finish, but it was the aggressive run from Robbo going straight down the middle of the pitch leaving United players in his wake that made it. He then seemed to overrun it as Billy Thomson came out to gather the ball, but big Graham wouldn't be denied, he slid in, the ball broke to Coisty and we were one up. The punters loved it. If I remember correctly from that day, Davie Cooper was unplayable, but Robbo couldn't have asked for a better first game for his new club.'

The win that day against Dundee United pushed Rangers into second place in the table, and with a new hardman hero in their ranks the fans had the belief that it was looking like a very happy new year.

Captain Terry Butcher summed it up: 'Graham Roberts was a great signing and came in at the perfect time to set us up for the crucial second half of the season. He had the ideal temperament for the Scottish game, with a terrific winning mentality that he had cultivated while at Spurs. The fans took to him straight away too; no wonder he had a dream debut and he never looked back from his great start.'

## THE SIGNIFICANCE OF SOUNESS

Into Graham's second season at Rangers, and in the absence of Terry Butcher, Roberts captained the side to League Cup glory. Graham thrived on the added responsibility and took to the role with relish when Butcher wasn't available following his leg break. Roberts came through the October 1987 Old Firm 'Shame Game' court case trauma with a 'not proven' verdict, which is a judgement exclusive to Scotland. So, unlike Terry Butcher and Chris Woods who were involved, Roberts wasn't left with a criminal record.

Graham Roberts's Rangers career came to a dramatic and premature conclusion following a loss to Aberdeen in April 1988, when manager Souness blamed him for the goal that gave the Dons victory. Harsh words were exchanged as Roberts contested Souness's claim, an argument he couldn't possibly win. That was indeed the case, as Roberts was banished to the reserves and sent with the kids to play a game in Mallaig at the start of the following season. That ruthless streak that was a Souness trademark was in evidence as Roberts was told he wouldn't play for the club again. In the final preparations for the 1988–89 season he headed back to London, but it was Chelsea who paid £475,000 for him. At Stamford Bridge, he secured promotion with them in that first season to get Chelsea back to England's top flight. It was a sad ending to his Rangers career, as Ian Durrant confirms:

'Graham was quick to answer back to the gaffer, and that was a no-go area. If you had a grievance you could have a chat on a one-to-one with Graeme to make your point, but you daren't do it in public, and certainly not in front of the squad in the dressing room, especially with emotions running high immediately after a match. Robbo had been superb for us, but once Graeme Souness had made a decision, he wasn't the type to change it. Graham just said the wrong thing, and in the next moment he offered to lift his boots and the manager made no attempt to stop him. I got about three reprieves so I was kind of lucky.'

Roberts was a terrific signing who the fans really related to, but the lesson learned was a harsh one. When Graeme Souness made a decision it was unlikely it would be reversed, and with hindsight, Graham Roberts admitted he seriously regretted the way it all ended for him at Rangers. Even today, despite the controversy of his exit, Graham Roberts is held in high regard by the supporters who saw him play in Rangers colours. Not bad for a guy who played only 69 times for the club and scored just three goals.

# CHAPTER 13:

# PRIZE DAY AT PITTODRIE

**2 May 1987**

Rangers travelled to Pittodrie, potentially needing just one point from the penultimate game of the campaign to be crowned champions in Graeme Souness's first season in charge. Aberdeen hadn't been a happy hunting ground for Rangers, whose last win here was five years before, and their record showed only two wins in the last 13 years.

Things didn't quite go to plan when Souness was dispatched for an early bath with 12 minutes of the first half remaining following two rash tackles. Both challenges were on Brian Irvine, who was deployed in a midfield role to try and stop Rangers controlling that key area of the pitch, and both yellows were probably merited, giving referee Jim Gordon little option but to send Souness off.

It was the second successive match for Rangers to be down to ten men at Pittodrie, with Dave McPherson being given his marching orders on their last visit.

Pittodrie was packed to the rafters with a recorded crowd of 22,568, but in reality there were many more who somehow managed to find a way to get into the stadium in anticipation of

# PRIZE DAY AT PITTODRIE

Rangers lifting the title for the first time in nine years. Rangers had only been allocated around 5,000 tickets, but there were significantly more than that following the team in blue that day.

Legendary broadcaster Archie Macpherson captured the scenes at the final whistle: 'Rangers have won the league and on come their supporters. The supporters have broken ranks and there is a danger of the Rangers players being swamped. The crowd have gone berserk and it will be mayhem now, as I pity the Rangers players in there, as their supporters have taken Pittodrie over. The league championship is Rangers' for the first time in nine years in one of the most dramatic games I have seen at Pittodrie, Rangers ten men against Aberdeen's 11. The scenes are enormous, the goalposts have gone.'

Nearly 40 years later, Archie remembers that epic moment in Rangers history: 'It really was bedlam as the Rangers fans celebrated, and it was so obvious what it meant to them having been in Celtic's shadow for so long. What can you say about Graeme Souness; we saw him red-carded in the first game of the season and now here he was at it again in another crucial game; perhaps desire and the need to win again got the better of him. Despite that sending-off of their player–manager, Rangers regrouped and were fortunate to have another leader on the park in the form of their captain Terry Butcher. It was fitting that Butcher got that all-important goal late in the first half. With news coming through that Celtic were losing to Falkirk as Rangers were still tied 0–0 with Aberdeen, the anticipation was cranked up even more. It wasn't pretty at times but it was to be Rangers' day.'

It was Aberdeen skipper Willie Miller's 32nd birthday that day, but it was Rangers who maxed out the celebrations.

Rangers' goal came after 40 minutes, with Terry Butcher powering home a stunning headed goal from a precision free kick by Davie Cooper. It was a beautiful goal. The Rangers captain towered over the home defence with impeccable timing before dispatching a thundering header that flew past Jim Leighton.

It sent the Rangers fans into ecstasy, and it was quickly apparent from the celebrations that the Light Blue legions had infiltrated just about every area of the ground.

Almost on the stroke of half-time Aberdeen got back on level terms. From a Rangers perspective it was a sloppy goal to lose. Jim Bett floated in a free kick from the right and Rangers were hesitant in clearing, allowing Brian Irvine to swivel and force the ball into the net.

That sent the teams in after 45 minutes tied at 1–1.

For the second half Rangers pushed on Jimmy Phillips to tighten things up in midfield. Robert Fleck was the player who made way.

Chris Woods pulled off a few heroic saves on the day at Pittodrie as Aberdeen threw everything they had at Rangers in that second half, including a driven effort by Joe Miller that was deflected on to the post, then Alex McLeish let fly from distance, but again Woods was on point with the save. It was a day that the English international goalkeeper will never forget, as Chris himself says:

'This is what we signed up for before a ball was kicked in the season. When the manager was red-carded, we thought, *here we go again*, with minds drifting to the first league game at Easter Road, but we had fantastic camaraderie in the squad and we dug in to get the job done. When Terry scored that header, we started to appreciate that we were almost there, and then when the news filtered through that Celtic were losing at home to Falkirk, we just wanted the whistle to go and then enjoy the moment. One thing about the fans: it was crazy and took a bit of getting used to for us English guys, how they reacted to what was happening elsewhere; we always knew when our biggest rivals were up against it as our fans made sure we knew, and it always gave us a massive boost. That day at Pittodrie was no different although the volume may have been cranked up a bit, but it was certainly music to our ears!' Chris did have concerns when that final whistle blew: 'It was bedlam. The emotions and outpouring of sheer joy from the fans was really incredible. You could see exactly what it meant to them after nine years without winning the league. They appeared on the pitch from every corner of the stadium, and while it was a bit scary, the fans just wanted to celebrate and share the experience with the players. I took off towards the dressing room but got caught by a host of fans who wanted my gloves, my boots, my shirt or any other special souvenir they could get their hands on to commemorate the day. It was scintillating, if a bit frightening, but it's a memory I will never forget. When I eventually made it into the dressing room the celebrations had already started with the champagne flowing, and as you can imagine Jimmy Nicholl was leading the sing-song!'

Terry Butcher recalls his goal as if it was yesterday: 'The manager had been sent off, so we knew we would be up against it and that set pieces might be our best bet for a goal. We won a free kick out on the left; it was the perfect position for Davie Cooper to deliver one of his trademark crosses. It was in front of the Aberdeen supporters who were like sardines squeezed in behind the goal. I took up my position at the edge of the box and big Brian Irvine stepped forwards to block my run, then the jostling started. I looked over and I made eye contact with Coop, who signalled he was ready, having got his feet where he wanted them; I just gave him a nod as an acknowledgement. Next thing, the perfect ball came into the box with pace, meaning I didn't need to generate power, I just needed to make a good connection and steer it into the net. I met it sweetly having held off Irvine's challenge and the ball was in the back of the net behind Jim Leighton. I ran to the fans behind the goal forgetting for a moment that I was at the Aberdeen end, or was I? The noise from the other end was incredible but then I saw the blue and white of the Rangers fans now facing me from where they had infiltrated the Aberdeen end. What joy! It was a wonderful feeling to have scored such a crucial goal in such a big game. We were all on a high, and I was emotional, as it was probably one of the most important goals I had ever scored; it was such a buzz, but we had to get back down to earth very quickly as there was still work to be done.

'At that time, we had no idea what was happening at Celtic Park, and we hadn't even considered that we could wrap up the league that day at Pittodrie as we thought Falkirk wouldn't get a win against Celtic, meaning the title was going all the way to the last day. When the news came through that Falkirk were winning it was a bit surreal, but when the final whistle blew it was absolutely real, and we were champions. It was a unique feeling; all the hard work throughout the season had paid off. Such a special moment; the whole team and back-room staff were euphoric. My god, looking back I've got goosebumps again – it was epic! It was a concern at first that our fans had invaded the pitch as we wanted to celebrate with them, but the police were quick to intervene and efficiently restored order to allow us to go back out on the pitch and share our success with a magnificent travelling support. A day I will never forget – we had achieved what was our number-one target at the start of the season.'

Full back Jimmy Nicholl cherishes memories of that league-winning day at Pittodrie: 'I had won the FA Cup with Manchester United back in 1977. I was only 20 years of age and I naively thought this would be a regular occurrence; winning league and cup medals would be a feature of every season. It obviously wasn't, and while I also won the League Cup with Rangers on my original loan, this was the big one. This was the one that confirmed what we had worked so hard for all season. It was reward for commitment and for Graeme too, who had put together a team to secure the championship. I remember, too, it was a special journey on the bus back to Glasgow. The boys were in a party mood and rightly so.'

A footnote to that match back in Glasgow as Rangers were heading for the title. At the start of the day, Celtic were on target to finish the season on 67 points. Rangers travelled to Pittodrie on 66 points. Celtic needed to win their final two games and hope that Rangers failed to win their last two games. As it was, Celtic lost both as Rangers drew with Aberdeen and then won 1–0 against St Mirren, with an early goal from Robert Fleck sealing the points. For Celtic, they lost their last game 1–0 to Hearts at Tynecastle, but the damage was done the week before in the home game to the Bairns of Falkirk. In a quirk of fate, Falkirk, who had opened the scoring through

## THE SIGNIFICANCE OF SOUNESS

Sammy McGivern with the game only 40 seconds old, took until the 86th minute to score the winner, after a penalty goal from Brian McClair, on what was his 199th and last appearance for the Parkhead club, had pulled Celtic level. Now the twist – Jimmy Gilmour, a tricky winger, came off the bench for Ken Eadie to claim the winner with less than four minutes of the match remaining. Jimmy Gilmour was the nephew of Celtic legend Jimmy Johnstone. In another twist to the tale, Gilmour and the other youngsters of Falkirk were being coached by Rangers' Barcelona hero Willie Johnston. The win also went a long way to Falkirk retaining their top-flight status, as they finished in tenth place above Clydebank and Hamilton who were both relegated.

On the bus journey back to Glasgow the players celebrated with champagne and beers, and almost every car the bus passed tooted its horn and had scarfs and flags out of every window. It had been so long since Rangers were champions, the team and the fans were determined to make the most of the celebrations.

As the bus headed south, Graeme Souness summoned Ian Durrant to join him at the front of the coach. Ian was full of the joy: 'When I got the shout to go and speak to the gaffer, I thought he's probably going to offer me a new contract with more money. I couldn't have been more wrong! He said, "You are a great player for me, but you keep bringing me headaches by your off-the-field antics. Because of that, I am withholding your league winning bonus." It was eight grand – I needed the money! Souness continued, "You'll get your money when you prove to me that you can behave!" I was shell-shocked and couldn't find the words to reply. He then told me to go back to my seat and send Coisty down. Despite the high of winning the title and the effects of a few refreshments, I came crashing back to reality quickly. Coisty said, "What did he want, did he offer you more money? Did he want to give you a new long contract?" I just shook my head and said, "You've to go down next." Ally went forwards and sat in the vacant seat next to Graeme. The manager then repeated the words he had said to me, and qualified again that the league winning bonus would be paid when we showed more maturity and cut out the trouble that comes with youngsters on a night out. Souness then took it even further with Coisty, when he said, "In fact, you'll get your bonus when you settle down and get married!" Without any emotion, Coisty turned to the manager and replied, "Stick you f*c*en' bonus up your ar*e," before turning on his heels to come back and join me in another beer. Despite me being on the wrong side of the law again on another night out just three weeks later, and Ally still not getting hitched, we eventually got our bonuses, just in time to head to Magaluf for an epic lads' holiday! It was a bit of a lesson I suppose, and Graeme was only trying to keep us grounded.'

The title was won – mission accomplished – and the following week, Rangers brought the curtain down on their successful season with a home game against St Mirren. It was a day the players and their families were intent on enjoying and making the most of the party atmosphere. Chris Woods certainly enjoyed that last day of his first season at Ibrox: 'When Graeme sold the English guys his vision for Rangers, you only had to look into his eyes to see just how determined and committed he was to get Rangers back to the top. Now he had achieved it, and we had made Scotland our home, while the Rangers family had taken us into their hearts. Chairman David Holmes and his wife Betty had also made sure that our families all settled well into life north of the border and that nothing was ever an issue for them. For the last game, we wanted to show our own commitment to the club and to our adopted home, so we came up with the idea of special T-shirts that carried our names, with a twist: MacWoods MacButcher and MacRoberts! It was only a bit of fun, but we had taken Rangers and Scotland to our hearts, just as the fans had taken us into theirs.'

# CHAPTER 14:

# SEASON ONE, 1986-87: CUPS AND EUROPE

While the league was the priority target for David Holmes and Graeme Souness in that first season together, domestic cups and a run in Europe were still important, as both had obvious financial benefits and the early League Cup fixtures would give them an indication of the squad depth and just how ready they were for a demanding season ahead.

Before a ball was kicked in anger, Rangers tested themselves against old foes Bayern Munich in a pre-season friendly at Ibrox. The team gelled quickly and the new boys settled well into their new environment. Over 36,000 turned up to get their first look at Souness's new-look side. The game also gave outings to Cammy Fraser and Davie Cooper, who would both miss the opener at Hibernian through suspension. Bayern themselves had a galaxy of stars in their line-up, including five players from the West Germany World Cup squad who had gone all the way to the final in Mexico just a matter of weeks before. The Light Blues were wasteful in front of goal but were unlucky to lose as Bayern scored two late goals through substitutes Ludwig Kögl and Hansi Flick.

# THE SIGNIFICANCE OF SOUNESS

All things considered, Rangers were as ready for their trip to Leith as could be expected. After three league games, with only one win in the bag, the focus turned to the League Cup. The tournament saw Rangers enter at the second round in August and the final was scheduled for October, so it gave the Light Blues a real opportunity to win a trophy early, which would surely give a fantastic platform to go forwards from. There was an air of confidence in the camp ahead of the first game that paired them with Stenhousemuir away. It was a tournament that had been kind to Rangers over recent years. Stenny offered little resistance and the four goals that sealed the 4–1 victory came from four different scorers: Souness, West, Cooper and McCoist were the marksmen. In the next round, Rangers were again on their travels to take on East Fife. It was a night when not much went right for Rangers and when it finished 0–0, penalties were needed to find a winner. It took an incredible save from Chris Woods to book Rangers' place in the quarter-finals, as he high-dived full stretch to save from Hugh Hill, in what proved to be the only spot kick missed on the night. It was almost a disastrous night for cup sponsors Skol, who were relieved that Rangers and their box office power had made it through. Colin West picked up a knee injury just to add to Souness's woes.

For the last-eight tie, Rangers did manage a home draw, as they came out of the hat first with Dundee FC the opposition. But not much was proving straightforward for Rangers as Dundee took them all the way to extra-time. A last-minute equaliser from Stewart Forsyth cancelled out ex-Dees Cammy Fraser's counter, then in the added-on time, goals from Souness and McMinn saw Rangers book their place

## SEASON ONE, 1986–87: CUPS AND EUROPE

in the semi-finals, where they would face the other half of Dundee – United.

The game was scheduled for Wednesday night, 24 September, at Hampden. Rangers turned on the style for this one in a swashbuckling display that wasn't reflected in the 2–1 scoreline. Ally McCoist celebrated his 24th birthday with a goal and Ted McMinn got the second. Souness strolled through the game, with Durrant playing alongside as creator-in-chief. It was Dundee United's first defeat in 12 games, and when they did pull a goal back with five minutes remaining, through former Ranger Iain Ferguson, it was too little too late. It booked Rangers return to the national stadium for the showcase final against Celtic, who had beaten Motherwell the night before.

The final was just one month away, and it was a huge chance for Graeme Souness to lay down a marker by lifting his first trophy as Rangers' manager. It turned out to be quite a bad-tempered affair, with all three goals coming in the second half. Rangers' first came from Ian Durrant, who worked the opening with Davie Cooper. Cooper himself claimed the second with a ferociously struck penalty kick after Roy Aitken had pulled down Terry Butcher for the spot kick to be awarded. For Celtic, Brian McClair was on target to cancel out Durrant's goal. Ten players were booked in the match while Celtic's Maurice Johnston was red-carded.

Rangers had the trophy for the third time in five years. Youngster Derek Ferguson produced his best performance in a Rangers jersey and was the clear man-of-the-match recipient. They had to work hard to claim the cup as this was the genuine acid test to see if the big-money signings had the winning

## THE SIGNIFICANCE OF SOUNESS

mentality of their new boss. Celtic, of course, were reigning champions and top of the table when this final came round, despite Rangers beating them with relative ease when the teams met in August.

Souness had his trophy and he wanted more, as did the fans who felt something special was happening at their club after such a long spell of failing to hit the heights.

To Europe, and the UEFA Cup was Rangers' playground following their fifth place finish in the domestic table the season before.

First up it was a double header of Ilves of Tampere, Finland. The first leg at Ibrox was a comfortable 4–0 win with McCoist on target and a hat-trick from Robert Fleck. That made the second leg a bit of a formality although Rangers did suffer a slight scare going down 2–0. The tournament quality went up a notch or two in the second round with Rangers again given home advantage first. It finished Ranger 2 Boavista 1, with McPherson and McCoist the goalscorers. To Portugal for the return and it appeared that Rangers had learned from their errors in Finland and kept a clean sheet to win 1–0 with Derek Ferguson on target. Again the opposition got a bit tougher for round three and again Rangers were at home first with Borussia Mönchengladbach the visitors. Both matches ended in draws. 1–1 at Ibrox and 0–0 in West Germany. Borussia went through to the last eight courtesy of the away goals rule. The European dream was over before Christmas but perhaps it cleared the decks to allow Rangers to focus on bringing the league championship back to Ibrox.

The Scottish Cup proved to be the biggest disappointment of the season. What looked an easy home tie against Hamilton

## SEASON ONE, 1986-87: CUPS AND EUROPE

Accies was far from it and any hopes of a first-season domestic treble were shredded as Hamilton triumphed 1–0.

Highs and lows were regular features for Graeme Souness and Walter Smith as they assessed their first eight months in the job. Success over Celtic twice, the extreme highs, including the cup win. Being taken to extra-time by East Fife was a concern but losing to Hamilton was as low as they could surely go.

The League Cup proved to be a happy hunting ground for Graeme Souness but the Scottish Cup would be the one domestic trophy that proved elusive.

# CHAPTER 15:

# THE PLAYERS, 1986-87

| PLAYER | APPEARANCES | GOALS |
|---|---|---|
| CHRIS WOODS | 48 | |
| NICKY WALKER | 2 | |
| TERRY BUTCHER | 49 | 2 |
| HUGH BURNS | 5 | |
| ALLY DAWSON | 10 | |
| DAVE McPHERSON | 47 | 8 |
| STUART MUNRO | 48 | |
| JIMMY NICHOLL | 39 | |
| SCOTT NISBET | 1 | |
| CRAIG PATERSON | 2 | |
| JIMMY PHILLIPS | 6 | |
| GRAHAM ROBERTS | 19 | 2 |
| DOUGIE BELL | 12 | 1 |
| DAVIE COOPER | 48 | 11 |

## THE PLAYERS, 1986–87

| | | |
|---|---|---|
| IAN DURRANT | 45 | 5 |
| DEREK FERGUSON | 33 | 1 |
| ROBERT FLECK | 44 | 19 |
| CAMMY FRASER | 21 | 2 |
| DAVIE KIRKWOOD | 1 | |
| DAVE MacFARLANE | 5 | |
| TED McMINN | 19 | 3 |
| BOBBY RUSSELL | 1 | |
| GRAEME SOUNESS | 29 | 3 |
| COLIN WEST | 12 | 3 |
| NEIL WOODS | 3 | |
| ALLY McCOIST | 50 | 38 |

Rangers played 56 competitive games in the 1986–87 season.

The title was won with a total of 69 points – six more than second-placed Celtic.

Ally McCoist made the most appearances with 50, and scored 38 goals.

# CHAPTER 16:

# TIME FOR REINFORCEMENTS, 1987-88

With the Scottish Premier Division won in that first memorable season under Graeme Souness, the squad were keen to add to that success in the 1987–88 season. The Skol League Cup was also in the Ibrox trophy room while the Scottish Cup campaign was over before it ever really got started. That loss to Hamilton was a ghost that Souness wanted to exorcise in the season ahead.

For the new campaign, Graeme Souness gave a major vote of confidence to his title-winning squad by bringing only two new players in. Defender Avi Cohen finally got clearance and joined from Maccabi Tel Aviv while at the other end of the pitch Mark Falco came in from Watford to bring variety to the attack. Cohen offered versatility and experience from his time with the Israeli national squad and had been with Liverpool where he was more of a fringe player. Falco was a UEFA Cup winner while with Tottenham and scored in the penalty shoot-out final against Anderlecht, and his figures of 89 goals from 236 appearances were better than average. The season before, injury had limited the impact Colin West may

# TIME FOR REINFORCEMENTS, 1987-88

have had in the team. Mark Falco was probably more mobile than West and was of similar build. He had all the attributes to fit in well and be a success in Scotland. Both players arrived with an aggregate transfer value of under £400,000. It looked like good business, and the costs had been partly covered by the sale in January of Ted McMinn to Sevilla where he again played under Jock Wallace.

Rangers would supplement the squad as the season progressed but Cohen and Falco were the only new faces in the door by the time pre-season training came around.

On the other side of the city it was quite a different story.

Manager David Hay had been dismissed, perhaps paying the penalty for letting a nine-point league advantage evaporate to allow Rangers to be crowned champions. Celtic turned to Lisbon Lion Billy McNeill to replace him. As a player McNeill had been with Celtic for his entire career and held their record for appearances – over 18 seasons he played 822 games. His management career started at Clyde before moving on to Aberdeen. He left the north-east to answer the call to replace his mentor Jock Stein in the Parkhead hot seat. McNeill managed Celtic between 1978 and 1983 and then moved on to Manchester City and Aston Villa. McNeill won promotion for City but then the following season (1986–87) he quit to take over Villa. He holds the unenviable record of managing two teams in the season that were both relegated!

Billy McNeill was back to try and wrestle the league title from Rangers in what was Celtic's centenary year. McNeill immediately went about adding to his squad – and he had to. Celtic legend Danny McGrain had been released in May, Murdo MacLeod was sold to Borussia Dortmund in June, and in the same month Peter Latchford left for Clyde. In July the departures continued: Mo Johnston took off for Nantes in France, Alan McInally moved to Aston Villa while Brian McClair was snapped up by Alex Ferguson for Manchester United. David Provan retired with health issues and fringe players Mark Smith and Paul McGugan were also allowed to leave. In for pre-season was Mick McCarthy, a £500,000 capture from Manchester City, and actually a Davie Hay signing just days before he was fired. Free-scoring midfielder Billy Stark joined from Aberdeen, full back Chris Morris came up from Sheffield Wednesday with local boy Andy Walker bringing his goalscoring qualities from Motherwell. Like Rangers, Celtic would add to their squad when things got going. Rangers would be competing in the European Cup with Celtic representing Scotland in the UEFA Cup.

Celtic prepared for the season ahead with a trip to Scandinavia and had a testimonial match against Liverpool for long-serving Celt Tommy Burns. They also hosted Arsenal who had former Hoops favourite Charlie Nicholas in their team. Meanwhile Ibrox was the venue for the Glasgow International Tournament, which was played over two days and involved Rangers, Ajax of Amsterdam, Real Sociedad from Spain and SC Internacional from Porto Alegre, Brazil. Rangers eliminated the Spaniards, with a goal from Robert Fleck, while Internacional took care of Ajax to set up a Scotland–Brazil final. The final finished 1–1 with McCoist the Rangers scorer, meaning a penalty shoot-out would determine the winner of the tournament. Robert Fleck missed Rangers' spot kick but subsequent efforts were converted by Graham Roberts, Stuart Munro, John McGregor and manager Souness

## TIME FOR REINFORCEMENTS, 1987–88

himself. Jimmy Phillips, who had come off the bench, missed his kick, which was the 12th on the day, and handed victory to the South Americans.

That same weekend the Edmiston Club officially opened, having been financed by Rangers Pools to the tune of £400,000. Prior to the Ibrox tournament Rangers had set up their training camp in Switzerland before moving on to West Germany. In total they played six games, winning four, drawing one and losing one. It was a big loss, though, and set some alarm bells ringing with FC Zürich scoring five without any reply from Rangers.

Despite that setback, Rangers were ready for the campaign ahead.

On the first league game of the season, Rangers welcomed Dundee United to Ibrox and the league flag was unfurled prior to kick-off. By the final whistle United were heading back to Tayside with a share of the points. The match finished 1–1 with a 61st-minute penalty goal from Ally McCoist the only counter for Rangers, which cancelled out a Dave Bowman opener that came with the game only 12 minutes old. Terry Butcher and Graham Roberts were both missing, meaning a new centre-back partnership of the former Liverpool pairing of Avi Cohen and John McGregor was at the heart of the Rangers defence. The one bright spot in the afternoon was the impact of Ian Durrant when he came off the bench. Perhaps the lacklustre performance was down to some big guns missing, although it also sent the message to Rangers that as top dogs everyone wanted to get one over on them. It set the tone for a frustrating season of inconsistency.

Towards the turn of the year Rangers entertained Dundee at

## THE SIGNIFICANCE OF SOUNESS

Ibrox. John Brown looks back: 'It was Boxing Day at Ibrox, then we were scheduled to meet again ten days later at Dens. It finished 1–0 to Rangers at Ibrox, but with about half an hour to go, Graeme, unprovoked, punched me on the kidney and I couldn't move after that. I was playing in the middle of the park in direct opposition to Souness, and while I had the utmost respect for Graeme and what he has done in the game, so it was a pleasure to play against him, I hadn't expected him to stick one on me. After that I chased him about the park as best I could to try and get some retribution but I could hardly move with the pain. The game finished with Rangers taking the points.

'Ten days later we were back at it again. It was a Wednesday night and we were four down with Terry Butcher scoring a thunderous 30-yarder, and I just remembered that kidney punch from Souness at our last meeting, and I thought, *I'm going to take him out at the first opportunity*. I caught him on the halfway line and halved him in two. He went down and as I was leaning over to give him a bit, Terry Butcher grabbed me by the throat and Graham Roberts was ready to lamp one on me when I just heard Graeme saying, "Leave him – leave him, just let's get on with it". I was quickly subbed after that to probably save me from a red card. Next day we were only in briefly for a loosener and when I got home my phone went, when I answered the caller said, "John?" I said "Yes" and he said "It's Graeme here." I thought it was Graham Clark, a prominent football journalist of the day but, he confirmed no – it's Graeme Souness. He said, "Listen, I'm in agony from what you did to me last night and I'll be honest, I would rather you did that for me than against my team, so I want to sign

## TIME FOR REINFORCEMENTS, 1987–88

you – will you be keen to come to Ibrox?" I quickly confirmed I was a Rangers fan and would do whatever it takes to get there. Graeme phoned me probably three or four times a day over the next nine days until a deal could be struck.

'We agreed to meet at Ibrox and after the briefest of discussions, he handed me a three-year contract scribbled on a Tennent's Lager beer mat! This happened as I was getting my medical and they were taking my blood pressure at the time – I'm surprised it wasn't through the roof! Jan Bartram who was signed from Aarhus in Denmark the same day was getting his medical too, and Graeme said, "Are you happy with that?" I was totally over the moon and would have signed even if there had been nothing on the beer mat but that's how it was done. Graeme then told me to take it up to David Holmes the next day, which I did, but I didn't have an agent at that time. David Holmes looked at the beer mat and said, "Do you want me to rip this up and re-negotiate. Tell me what you want," but I told him no, no, I had shook hands with Graeme on those terms and I was more than happy to go forwards on those terms. He said if you are not happy with these terms you tell me what you want as we need you on that pitch, fully focused, no financial worries, no family worries and help us to win football matches. So that's how I signed.

'My home debut was the following week against Falkirk. When Graeme confirmed the team he said, "Bomber, if you are having a tough time of it out there and the fans are getting on your back [with Ibrox having a 45,000 capacity at that time it could be intimidating] keep taking and showing for the ball, even if you keep giving it away. I'll stick with you but the minute you turn your back on the ball I'll sell you!"

## THE SIGNIFICANCE OF SOUNESS

That was my home debut, so you know the expectation and what it's all about. We knew what was required and if you didn't do it for him you would be out the door. As players we looked at the number of new faces that joined the club, and some like Bartram were gone almost as quick as they had arrived. It was pressure of course but I wouldn't have changed it for the world. I was a Rangers fan, my family were Rangers fans, this was me 100 per cent living the dream.'

That first season for John Brown didn't deliver the success he was after, but in the seasons that followed Bomber became a key player for Rangers and went on to win eight League winner's medals before taking up a coaching position at Rangers.

## CHAPTER 17:

# THE SHAME GAME

**17 October 1987**

Old Firm games can be fiery and unpredictable. When Rangers entertained Celtic at Ibrox Park on Saturday 17 October 1987, it delivered unprecedented scenes and had consequences that nobody could have envisaged. The match became known as the Shame Game. It ended in a 2–2 draw but the events on the field that day led to a court case with three Rangers players and one player from Celtic charged with breach of the peace and facing a trial that would last four days.

To the game itself, Celtic, in their centenary year, arrived at Ibrox as the in-form team on a run of eight matches without defeat that stretched back to the first Old Firm meeting of the season at Celtic Park in August, which saw the home team take the points in the narrowest of wins with a goal from Billy Stark separating the sides. Meanwhile Rangers were struggling to put a run of wins together – they were four points behind Celtic going into the game and had lost at Dundee United in their last outing.

The game started in frantic fashion on a mild and sunny autumn afternoon, but the on-field heat was evident as early

## THE SIGNIFICANCE OF SOUNESS

as the 17th minute when Celtic striker Frank McAvennie, playing in his first Celtic–Rangers clash, went in on Rangers goalkeeper Chris Woods with a very late challenge. Woods had come out to gather a tame pass-back from Jimmy Phillips but McAvennie shut him down and barged into the English keeper even though Woods had the ball comfortably under control. The ball spun behind and as Chris Woods appealed to referee Jim Duncan that he had been barged and a free kick in favour of Rangers should have been awarded, the referee instead gave a corner to Celtic. Frank McAvennie, who often tried to put opposition goalkeepers under pressure early on in games with a similar physical game plan, couldn't believe he'd got the benefit of the decision and burst out laughing. Chris Woods wasn't happy with the referee but he was even more incensed by the demeanour of McAvennie.

Very quickly things got out of hand as McAvennie repeated his earlier challenge on the Rangers goalkeeper as the corner was swung in. Woods tried to protect himself with a leading elbow and in those days it was pretty much accepted that goalkeepers would take that course of action and referees tended to let it go. McAvennie stood his ground, Woods grabbed the Celtic striker round the neck and a few slaps-come-punches were thrown and that brought Rangers skipper Terry Butcher to the plot, intent on protecting his keeper. Graham Roberts also wanted a piece of the action and as they all came together McAvennie went down in a heap with suggestions that a more vicious punch from a Rangers player had landed on its target. When referee Duncan finally got in between the warring players he chose to send off both McAvennie and Woods. Terry Butcher was booked for his

# THE SHAME GAME

part in the melee. It was referee Duncan's first Rangers–Celtic match as the man in the middle and he certainly looked to be spooked by the occasion and the huge responsibility that went with it.

As the focus then turned to the actual football it was Celtic who opened the scoring through Andy Walker. Walker took a pass from Mick McCarthy, steadied himself and swept the ball into the Rangers net beyond Graham Roberts who had taken the red goalkeeping shirt to replace the departed Woods. No substitute goalkeepers were on the bench in those days so Roberts either volunteered or was press-ganged into being Rangers' last line of defence – it was probably a bit of both. Watching the drama unfold from the directors' box was Graeme Souness, who was serving a suspension at the time. Two minutes after Andy Walker's goal Celtic doubled their lead. Terry Butcher contrived to divert the ball into his own net as he tried to cut out a cross-come-shot from Walker whose movement was causing problems for the reshaped Rangers rearguard. That sent each team of ten in at half-time with Celtic two goals up and looking good for a win that would further increase their lead at the top of the table.

Into the second half and Rangers rallied and snatched a goal back on 65 minutes when Ally McCoist got on the end of a Richard Gough pass and shot home via the inside of the post. By now, and with the Light Blues reducing the deficit, the atmosphere inside Ibrox was white hot. If that was hot, the game reached boiling point just before McCoist scored when Rangers were reduced to nine men with Terry Butcher dispatched for an early bath after flattening Celtic keeper Allen McKnight as the Rangers captain desperately tried to muscle his team back into the game. Ally McCoist's goal gave Rangers a lifeline and quite bizarrely Celtic retrenched and appeared to sit back to defend their lead despite having the extra man advantage. It proved to be a poor call as Rangers equalised with the clock showing 90 minutes. Richard Gough, who had set up McCoist for Rangers' first, turned scorer himself to grab a share of the points for his team. Ian Durrant delivered a cross from the right that was misread by McKnight, allowing Gough to stretch and force the ball over the line. Ibrox erupted and how the home fans celebrated.

As the Light Blue legions lapped up the moment, where a draw felt like a victory, they were inspired by makeshift goalkeeper Graham Roberts who appeared to be conducting the Rangers choir, complete with an imaginary baton. As all of a Rangers persuasion enjoyed the late-late comeback, the players stayed on the field when the final whistle blew to take the acknowledgement of their fans while their counterparts in Celtic colours couldn't get down the Ibrox tunnel quickly enough.

There were always going to be consequences from the events on the field that day; the least of them from a Rangers perspective, at the time, was that they would be without the services of Terry Butcher and Chris Woods, as their red cards meant suspension for the League Cup Final scheduled for only eight days after the chaos and controversy of the Ibrox Old Firm clash. Graeme Souness was still under suspension for that next game too, so all things considered it wasn't the best preparation for the first domestic cup final of the season.

However, in the week of that final, both sides of the Old Firm were stunned when it was confirmed that not only the

# THE SHAME GAME

SFA but the police were to take action against players on both sides for their actions on the pitch in the match that was now being tagged 'the Shame Game'. Detectives from Govan police station requisitioned film from STV of the unsavoury incidents from the match, while officers who had been on duty at Ibrox were also quizzed on the goings-on.

By Monday 2 November the media had gotten hold of the story and press headlines that Monday morning screamed: CHARGED – OLD FIRM SHOCK AS FLARE-UP STARS FACE POLICE ACTION!

Here we had over £2m of Scotland's finest footballing talent facing criminal charges in an unprecedented case where their conduct on the pitch was deemed a breach of the peace.

First to face the music were Graham Roberts, Chris Woods and Frank McAvennie. The police would catch up with Rangers skipper Terry Butcher when he returned from a flying visit to London. The charges that made Scottish legal history were confirmed as Roberts, Woods and McAvennie were summoned to Govan police station just a quarter-mile from Ibrox where the explosive clashes had occurred. Terry Butcher was also brought to book in the same police office and all were to appear at Glasgow Sheriff Court the following month and only ten days before Christmas.

It was Glasgow's procurator fiscal Mr Sandy Jessop who instigated the probe and chose to take legal proceedings against all four players. Well-known solicitor Len Murray was recruited by Rangers to defend Butcher, Woods and Roberts, while Celtic initially offered no legal representation or support for McAvennie. With no players in attendance on the December date, Mr Murray entered a plea of not guilty on behalf of the accused Rangers players and then added Frank McAvennie to his client list at the request of Graeme Souness, who offered legal support despite McAvennie's own club showing no appetite to defend their man in court. It was even suggested that Rangers would pick up the cost for McAvennie's legal defence. The case against all four players was deferred and a new date for the hearing was set for 5 January 1988.

Again, Len Murray entered a plea of not guilty on behalf of all four players. Sheriff Craig Henry presiding committed the case to trial with again a new date set aside as 16 February. It couldn't have been easy for any of the players with this legal battle hanging over them now for more than three months.

Eventually the trial started on Tuesday 12 April, and the press quickly termed the proceedings 'the trial of Goldilocks and the three bears' after the nineteenth-century fairy tale.

There wasn't a vacant seat in Glasgow Sheriff Court as Sheriff Archie McKay brought things to order. This was a news story that captured the imagination of so many, not just football fans. It was a media circus and interest in the case was massive.

The court were advised that a goalmouth fracas between four football stars had unleashed unbridled hatred among rival fans inside Ibrox, hence the breach of the peace charges – a charge all four players denied, and all four also refused to accept that they had conducted themselves in any form of disorderly manner. When called into the witness box Strathclyde Assistant Chief Constable John Dickson stated, that in his experience, as the man on match days in charge of crowd safety and public order, incidents on the field of play had a direct relationship to incidents in the stands and terraces. Dickson continued that in his opinion fury erupted after that goalmouth incident that saw Woods and McAvennie both sent off. It appeared to be forgotten that Terry Butcher had been red-carded for a separate incident much later in the game while Graham Roberts was booked but stayed on the pitch to play out the full game. The assistant chief constable also highlighted how Celtic fans tried to climb a perimeter fence to gain access to the pitch and that after taking over in goal Graham Roberts faced a barrage of coins aimed in his direction by the visiting fans. Dickson also qualified matters with his claim that the atmosphere carried great animosity and the noise was so loud he could hardly hear himself think.

The court were then treated to a short video of rival fans squaring up to each other before moving on to the match action that had led to the court case. Dickson also added that he had never experienced such a bad atmosphere at any previous Old Firm game.

Into the second day of the trial and the focus appeared to have shifted from what the players actually did to how the fans of both clubs were intent on causing trouble with banners, chants and songs. The suggestion being that the off-field problems and disorder had influenced the actions of the players who may have reacted to the hostility of the crowd. Next up Inspector James Moir claimed that had the same fracas on the pitch happened in the street the four perpetrators would have been arrested immediately. As this was going on, the four players looked on with astonishment that they were being treated like criminals for going about their job of winning a football match – football being a sport that does carry a degree of physicality that often leads to confrontation between opponents. Surely any such on-field incidents should be dealt with by the match officials. Referee Duncan had taken action as he considered appropriate; now following the intervention by the police, football as we know it was left in a very precarious position.

Chief Superintendent William Marshall then told the court he thought Celtic front man McAvennie was trying to 'box' Rangers goalkeeper Woods' ears as they squared up, and while he couldn't confirm if any blows had actually landed, they had certainly been exchanged. The chief superintendent also reaffirmed the toxicity continued to cascade from the fans in the stands.

On day three of the trial, match referee Jim Duncan was called to the witness stand to give his version of events. Duncan quickly made his point that he was totally against the law intervening in football matches. Duncan continued that in his view if a breach of the peace charge was to apply every time a player was red-carded he would seriously consider packing it in as a referee.

On the final day of the trial Sheriff McKay summed up what he had considered to be a complex case. He stated that he was not concerned about the game of football but that his concerns were the prevention of public disorder in connection with sporting events.

Sheriff McKay said he couldn't accept the evidence against McAvennie and believed the Celtic player tried to stop himself colliding with Woods and was using his arms to brace himself.

On Graham Roberts he was unsure if he was restraining McAvennie so no guilt could be established.

It wasn't so questionable against Terry Butcher, according

# THE SHAME GAME

to the sheriff. He said Butcher was guilty of violence for which there was no excuse. For Chris Woods, McKay said his involvement was much more serious and reported that he considered that the Rangers goalkeeper, through video evidence, had clearly jabbed McAvennie sharply on the chin with his forearm.

In the final analysis, Terry Butcher and Chris Woods were convicted of breach of the peace. Graham Roberts had the charge against him not proven. Frank McAvennie was dismissed with a not-guilty verdict. Terry Butcher was fined £250. Chris Woods was hit with a £500 fine.

The sentences were slammed by Players' Union boss Tony Higgins who said that this case had opened a trapdoor and the sentences handed down had serious implications for sport in general and football in particular.

Butcher and Woods appealed the verdicts against them. A month later their appeals were dismissed with two judges, Lord Ross and Lord Allanbridge, voting that their appeals should be refused. Only Lord Murray disagreed and claimed the sheriff was not entitled to find the players guilty of breach of the peace during an on-field incident.

This prosecution was the first of its kind in the UK, where court action followed as a result of an incident in the heat of a game when the ball was still in play.

As the dust settled the media suggested that Woods, Butcher and Roberts would continue their careers back south of the border and had been totally disillusioned by the Scottish justice system and Scottish football in general.

Graeme Souness, who was no stranger himself to some on-field scraps, had also felt uneasy with his limited ability to support his players through such traumatic public humiliation. Two of his most valued players, who he had encouraged to come to Scotland to ply their trade, now carried criminal records for doing their jobs, and any fair-minded person would agree that football should police itself and that this sorry escapade did nothing whatsoever for our national game.

# CHAPTER 18:

# HIGH FIVE

**'You Got Me Singing the Blues'**
    Well I've never felt more like singing the blues, when Rangers put five past Ian Andrews,
Oh Rangers, you got me singing the blues.
    Well McAvennie he scored the first, their fans thought it was the first of many,
Oh Rangers, you got me singing the blues.
    It didn't take long to realise, when Super Ally, he equalised,
Oh Rangers, you got me singing the blues.
    Then up stepped super Ray, a 30-yarder all the way,
Oh Rangers, you got me singing the blues.
    Well I've never felt more like singing the blues when Rangers put five past Ian Andrews,
Oh Rangers, you got me singing the blues.
    Well Andrews claimed he couldn't see when Super Ally made it three,
Oh Rangers, you got me singing the blues.
    And the Ibrox fans they wanted more, so Kevin Drinkell made it four,
Oh Rangers, you got me singing the blues.

# THE SIGNIFICANCE OF SOUNESS

> Well I've never felt more like singing the blues when Rangers put five past Ian Andrews,
> Oh Rangers, you got me singing the blues.
> Old Ibrox Park came alive when the bold Mark Walters made it five,
> Oh Rangers, you got me singing the blues.
> Celtic boss Billy McNeill went home to his wife that night, and confirmed his team had got a fright,
> Oh Rangers, you got me singing the blues.

When the supporters pen a song to remember a victory over your biggest rivals it has to have been something special in the extreme.

The date was 27 August 1988; the venue Ibrox Park – it was Rangers versus Celtic and Rangers waltzed to a record-breaking Premier Division victory. It was a day when everything came together for Graeme Souness's side in a game that saw Light Blues diehard John Brown make his Old Firm debut while the manager had the luxury of leaving himself on the bench alongside Davie Cooper.

Rangers lined up Chris Woods in goal, a back four of Gary Stevens, Richard Gough, Terry Butcher and John Brown. In midfield it was Ian Ferguson, Ray Wilkins, Ian Durrant with Mark Walters on the flank. Ahead of them in a twin-pronged attack it was Ally McCoist in partnership with Kevin Drinkell.

Celtic were at full strength: Ian Andrews, Chris Morris, Roy Aitken, Mick McCarthy and Anton Rogan. Billy Stark, Peter Grant, Paul McStay and Tommy Burns. Andy Walker and Frank McAvennie were up top. Derek Whyte and Joe Miller were on the bench.

# HIGH FIVE

The 5–1 scoreline was Celtic's worst Old Firm result since August 1960.

In the build-up to the game Celtic boss Billy McNeill dismissed press speculation that star striker Frank McAvennie was set for a return to London, and in a throwaway line was reported to have said there is as much chance of Rangers beating us 5–1 tomorrow as there is of Frank McAvennie being sold. As it was, Celtic *were* beaten 5–1 and the bold Frank was soon on his way to West Ham United!

As an aside, in those days while the first teams faced off at one venue the second strings met at the home of the visiting first team. On the day of the 5–1 at Ibrox, Celtic beat Rangers 2–1 at Parkhead in front of a crowd of over 4,000. Some big hitters were in the Celtic side including Alan Rough, Mark McGhee and Paul Elliott.

But it was the game at Ibrox that stole all the headlines.

Ian Andrews was the new man in goal for Celtic, and despite a big reputation and a hefty transfer value of £300,000 he looked totally overawed by the occasion and was badly at fault, failing to stop a looping header from McCoist immediately after the interval. Andrews could do absolutely nothing about the goal of the day, if not the season, from Ray Wilkins who dispatched a volley into the net that was quite sublime. Wilkins dominated the midfield in a genuine masterclass. Ray was well supported in the engine room by both Ians Durrant and Ferguson snuffing out the creativity Celtic craved from McStay and Burns. McCoist was his usually predatory self, chipping in with a double while his strike partner caused problems for the visitors' defence all day and Kevin Drinkell duly got his reward with a headed goal from a Mark Walters cross. Walters himself

## THE SIGNIFICANCE OF SOUNESS

then capped off an excellent performance with Rangers' fifth just after the hour. Rangers even had a couple of strong penalty claims waved away by referee Kenny Hope. The Rangers fans were in dreamland and the celebrations were epic. It was arguably the best win Rangers recorded under Graeme Souness, made all the sweeter as it was against their biggest rivals with a crowd of 42,858 inside Ibrox to witness it.

Celtic midfielder Tommy Burns was a studio guest on Scotsport the day after the humiliation at Ibrox and took the opportunity to apologise to the Celtic fans for a totally unacceptable performance, especially as they had taken the lead through Frank McAvennie within five minutes of the game starting.

It was John Brown's first taste of Old Firm action as a player and he loved every minute of it, right back to Graeme Souness's pre-match team talk. Bomber said: 'We were all up for it anyway, then Graeme ran through his team. Chris Woods in goal, a back four of Gary Stevens, Richard Gough, Terry Butcher and myself. A midfield four of Durranty, Ian Ferguson, Ray Wilkins and Mark Walters. Up front it was Coisty and Kevin Drinkell. Graeme then confirmed that he would be on the bench with Davie Cooper. He then pointed to the picture of the Queen on the dressing room wall and said, "That's what this club is all about. You know who they support and what they are all about so get out there and get in about them." Ray Wilkins scored that stunning volley, and it's amazing to think we gave them the early initiative with Frank McAvennie scoring the first goal of the game. I didn't hyperventilate before this game – that came in the following match at Celtic Park – but we won that one too! With 18 minutes left to play we were cruising, and Graeme brought himself off the bench for Ian Durrant. No fears we would have got a few more goals that day but Graeme wanted to showboat while Celtic were all over the place. We have to remember too that Celtic had a very good side then, especially in midfield with Roy Aitken and Tam Burns and Paul McStay.'

Ian Durrant takes up the story: 'I couldn't believe the gaffer hooked me, I was wanting for us to really turn the screw but they went for damage limitation by bringing on Derek Whyte for Tommy Burns to shore up their defence at half-time. Goalkeeper Andrews looked totally overawed. It was 5–1 and Souness was wanting to humiliate Celtic, so the boys stopped passing the ball to him and he was raging! The steam was coming out his ears! It was a day when it all came together. The spirit in that squad was incredible. It was a unique dressing room with so many characters and personality. Ray Wilkins was a proper gentleman and he bossed the show that day. He was a proper gentleman who loved the banter. In the build-up to that game, earlier in the week, Ray came into training wearing a wig. We honestly didn't know it was him, we thought it was maybe another new signing! He didn't do it as a joke he just sat down as if it was the most normal thing in the world. He then took it off to go training, and what a trainer Ray was. His training was full pelt every day, even on the day before this crucial match against Celtic when Ray probably had his best game in a Rangers jersey.'

Kevin Drinkell has special memories of the game: 'I was still settling in at Rangers and didn't really know the history of the Old Firm fixture, nor the levels of intensity and competition it would bring. That August win was the quickest game I can ever recall playing in. The 90 minutes just flashed by. It was my first league goal for Rangers on a day that it all just clicked.'

It's a day that will live long in the memories of Rangers fans of a certain vintage, while even youngsters not born then will have learned the words to the song that commemorates this special game.

# CHAPTER 19:

# SEASON TWO, 1987-88: DETHRONED BUT DETERMINED

The Rangers faithful were still on a high from their first title success in nine years as they looked forward to the second season in the reign of Graeme Souness, who was setting the team up to defend their championship. Demand for season tickets remained unprecedented. Expectation was high. Meanwhile Celtic were hurting heading into their centenary season. Davie Hay had gone and returning hero 'Caesar' Billy McNeill was back in the manager's office.

Rangers headed off for a pre-season of games in Switzerland and West Germany. They only lost one game in six played, but it was a damaging one, going down to a 5–0 hammering from FC Zürich. Mark Falco had come in to add options to the attack, while reports suggested Robert Fleck could be looking for a move away from Ibrox for personal reasons.

The league opener yielded only one point and it took an Ally McCoist penalty to ensure the 1–1 draw with Dundee United at Ibrox in front of a 40,000 crowd who witnessed the league flag being hoisted before the game began. However, things didn't get any better with only one win in the next four in the league. That win was a 4–0 success against Falkirk at Ibrox, with McCoist claiming a hat-trick. The other games saw three defeats on the road at Hibernian, Aberdeen and biggest rivals Celtic. Rangers then went six matches unbeaten before travelling to Tannadice in October for a game that saw Richard Gough debut against his old side. It wouldn't be a happy return for Gough as former Rangers striker Iain Ferguson scored the only goal of the game.

Next up it was another Old Firm clash, this time at Ibrox. A crowd of 44,500 took in an eventful affair that boiled over with Chris Woods, Terry Butcher and Frank McAvennie all being sent off. Richard Gough popped up with a dramatic late goal to see the game end two apiece. Inconsistency was a major problem for Graeme Souness's side. Celtic were building momentum and won the New Year clash. But prior to that Rangers lost Terry Butcher to a broken leg in a defeat to Aberdeen. Ray Wilkins had made his debut too in a 3–2 win over Hearts, but the defeat to Celtic at the turn of the year saw Rangers fall seven points behind in the title race. The previous season Rangers had been five points behind their biggest rivals at one time and had turned it around. This time it wasn't to be.

The League Cup proved fruitful again albeit it took penalty kicks to win the trophy in a hard-fought match against Aberdeen. With Chris Woods suspended following the Old Firm 'Shame Game' Nicky Walker deputised in goal. Trevor Francis converted a cute spot kick with only the minimum of a two-step run-up before striking the ball. When Peter Nicholas clipped the crossbar with his effort, Ian Durrant, who had been sensational throughout the match, stepped forwards

## SEASON TWO, 1987–88: DETHRONED BUT DETERMINED

and majestically stroked the ball beyond Jim Leighton. It was Rangers' day. The chase for the other more elusive Scottish cup was ended in February by Dunfermline in a fourth-round clash at East End Park, on a day that John Brown was sent off.

Fleck got his move and was sold to Norwich. Falco too departed – he headed back to London with Queens Park Rangers. These players leaving certainly limited Rangers' goal threat and left Souness short on striking options.

Europe offered promise, particularly with a 2–0 win over Dynamo Kiev at Ibrox after going down 1–0 in the first leg to a penalty goal from a certain Alexei Mikhailichenko who would later play 134 times for Rangers, scoring 24 goals between 1991–1996. The Ibrox clash saw Graeme Souness play his trump card by instructing the ground staff to narrow the Ibrox pitch. That meant bringing in the touchlines, but Graeme was cute enough to ensure no UEFA rules were breached and it took the Russians by surprise. Rangers had struck a psychological blow before a ball was kicked. To further turn the screw, on a night that the Rangers fans really brought the noise, Souness at his arrogant best turned on the halfway line and flighted an aerial back pass over the heads of a host of Kiev forwards to keep his goalkeeper Chris Woods occupied. The fans loved it. The Soviets less so.

Next up Rangers defended their 3–1 win over Górnik Zabrze at Ibrox with a creditable 1–1 draw in the second leg in Poland. This saw Rangers then paired with Steaua Bucharest in the quarter-finals. Rangers resources were stretched to the limits with recent signings Ian Ferguson, John Brown and Mark Walters ineligible while Ally McCoist was a serious doubt because of a knee injury that required surgery.

## THE SIGNIFICANCE OF SOUNESS

With such severe limitations at the top of the pitch, having lost the first leg in Romania, back at Ibrox, Rangers won the second leg 2–1 but lost out 3–2 on aggregate. Ally McCoist was patched up and took his place in the side, but turning round a two-goal deficit against such an organised and capable team was a tall order.

In a break with tradition, but with sizeable financial benefits, Rangers agreed to face Everton in the Dubai Champions Cup. It was a meeting of the champions of England and Scotland. The game finished 2–2 and penalties came into play to determine a winner. Rangers proved to be desert champions and lifted the gold trophy scoring an enthralling eight penalties to Everton's seven.

Celtic had the title in their centenary season and Rangers were dethroned.

Graeme Souness always made the domestic championship his primary target. It was a sobering season for all at the club but it perhaps could be argued that it brought everyone back to earth with a bump, and as soon as the season was over planning was already very advanced for what would be Graeme Souness's third season in charge. There was a serious determination to increase the depth and quality of the squad to win the league flag back at the first time of asking. Finishing third in the table, 12 points adrift of Celtic and two points behind second-placed Heart of Midlothian, was not the Souness way.

Andy Walker was part of Celtic's centenary double-winning side. In fact, it was Andy's first season as a Celt having been signed from Motherwell. Andy rolls back the years:

'I had been previously tapped up by Celtic while Davie Hay

## SEASON TWO, 1987–88: DETHRONED BUT DETERMINED

was boss, and when big Billy replaced him he referred to the scouting reports and sanctioned my transfer. Billy was a family friend and my dad was his accountant. It was vital that all at Celtic reacted to the events of the previous season when Graeme Souness took Rangers to a new level. Prior to that when I was at Motherwell we faced more difficult games against Aberdeen and Dundee United than we did against Rangers. Souness very quickly turned Rangers into a very good side.

'Celtic had to become a good team to match them. We had the core of a good side with Roy Aitken, Paul McStay, Pat Bonner and Peter Grant who was probably the unsung hero of our team. We had more skilful players, for sure, but Granty was the beating heart of our side and he was a great foil for our more creative players. Billy McNeill then added to the squad with Joe Miller and Frank McAvennie coming in to form a front three with myself. These additions were great for me and we all understood the necessity to win the title back. We did, but with hindsight it perhaps only encouraged Rangers to go and raise the stakes again. They did, and after winning the title the following season they never looked back. There is no doubt in my mind that Celtic took too long to react to the new Souness signings, allowing the league flag to fly over Ibrox every year for nine in a row. It could have been quite different had Billy McNeill been supported in the transfer market after winning the League and Cup double. Billy had ambitions to sign Paul Gascoigne and Peter Beardsley. Both were serious targets and would have been sensational signings for Celtic. We can all recall what Gazza did when he did eventually move to Glasgow, while Beardsley went on to win 59 caps for England. No doubt this pair could have made a massive difference.

## THE SIGNIFICANCE OF SOUNESS

'Billy was committed to making progress and to build on our success. As it was the directors just weren't interested and the only player he managed to convince the board to sign was England under-21's goalkeeper Ian Andrews from Leicester. Later, Tommy Burns came close with some outstanding players in his team like [Paolo] Di Canio and Pierre van Hooijdonk, but despite coming close they couldn't wrestle the title back. It was only when Wim Jansen came in and fashioned a team with Craig Burley, Andreas Thom and of course Henrik Larsson that Celtic were again champions. But it was very much too late and had allowed Rangers to dominate for such an extended period even after Walter Smith had replaced Souness. Prior to that, when I returned to Celtic in 1994 we were a poor team and finished fourth or fifth without really challenging. Back in the mid-eighties – Souness changed everything.'

The question now for Rangers, going into what would be Graeme Souness's third season in charge, was how would everyone at the club react.

A youthful Graeme Souness in his Tottenham playing kit ahead of the 1972 season.

Middlesbrough FC squad line up ahead of their Division 2 campaign in July 1973. Souness is far right, middle row.

Wembley Charity Shield win August 1979 with Kenny Dalglish after Liverpool beat Arsenal 3–1.

Action shot in the national side as Scotland entertain New Zealand in February 1982. Andy Gray looks on with admiration.

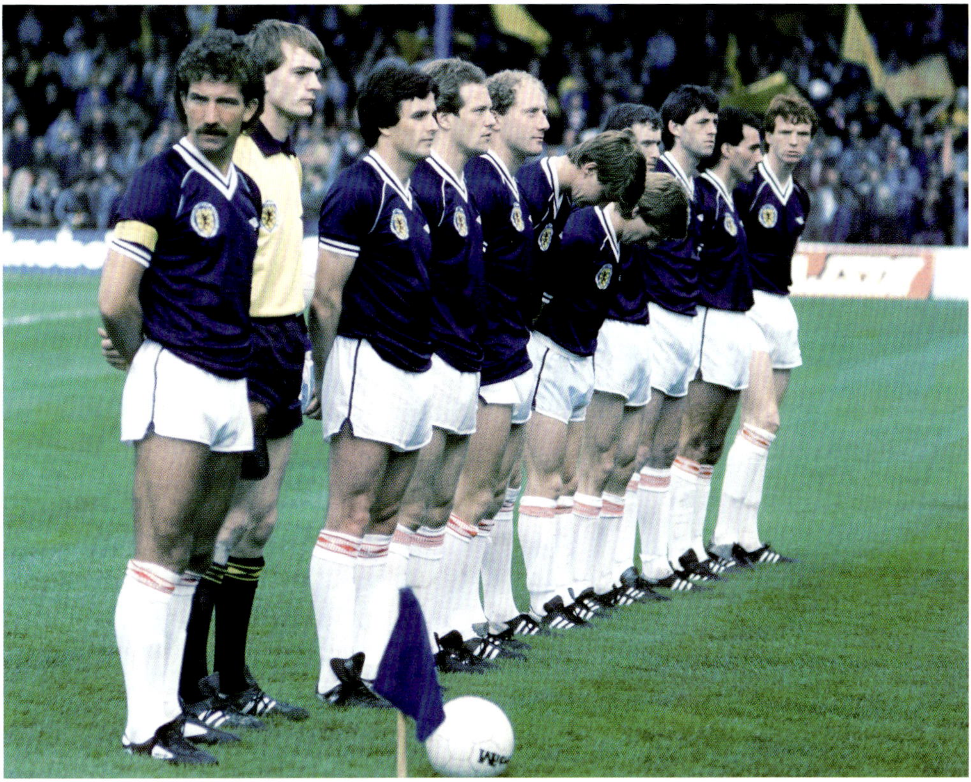

© Getty Images / SNS Group

A proud skipper. Graeme Souness lines up with his team ahead of the clash with Wales in Cardiff in May 1983.

© Alamy / PA Images

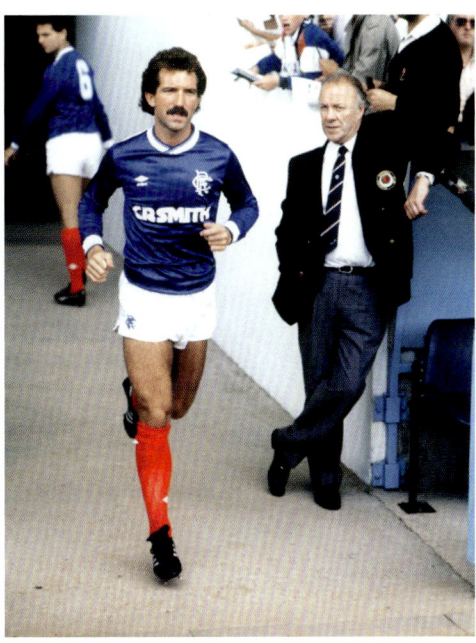

Getting familiar with his new surroundings. Graeme Souness takes the field against Spurs at Ibrox in August 1986.

© Getty Images / Mark Leech

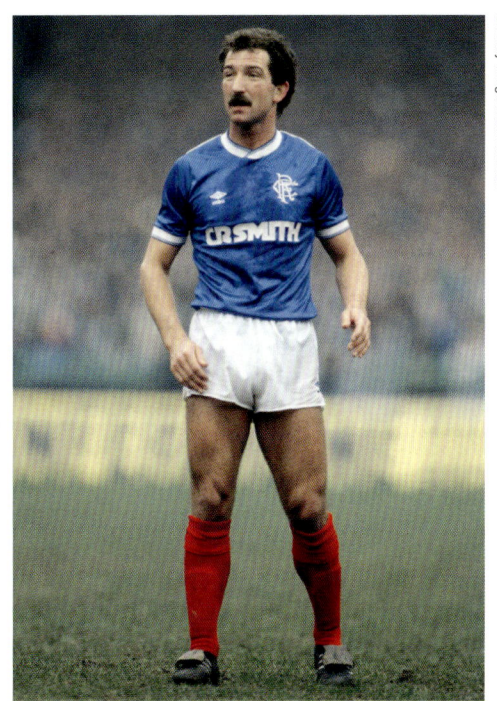

Old Firm action at Celtic Park, April 1987.

Red, White & Blue ready. The Rangers squad under Souness for the 1986/87 season. New signings West, Woods, Butcher & Nicholl are all there!

Title secured and Rangers bring the curtain down on a successful first season under Souness with a win over St. Mirren.

Chairman David Holmes and Player/Manager Souness welcome new signing Trevor Francis to Rangers in August 1987.

The contented look from Graeme Souness as he introduces new signing Maurice Johnston to the assembled media inside Ibrox in July 1989.

Early bath for Souness! Day One of the season, August 1986 and Graeme Souness gets his marching orders at Easter Road following a rash challenge on George McCluskey.

Joy all round Ibrox and from Chris Woods as Ibrox rises to acknowledge Ally McCoist's goal against Celtic in April 1990 to make him Rangers' post-war record goal scorer.

A happy camp. Manager Souness shares a joke with Mo Johnston, Mark Hateley, Richard Gough and Bonni Ginzburg as Rangers launch their new Admiral playing kit in July 1990.

Two heads are better than one. Walter Smith and Graeme Souness plot the game plan against Cologne in October 1988. Physio/Coach Phil Boersma and Doc Cruickshanks are also in the picture.

Getting his message across. Graeme Souness barks his instructions as Rangers take on Clydebank at the old Kilbowie stadium in April 1987.

The `MAC` Factor. Butcher, Woods and Roberts play up their affinity to Scotland with their Mac T-Shirts after the St. Mirren game at Ibrox in May 1987.

Brilliance from Butcher. Captain Terry Butcher celebrates the goal that effectively clinched the league title at Pittodrie in May 1987.

Suited and Booted. Graeme Souness managing Newcastle United in November 2005.

Three Amigos! Ally McCoist, Graeme Souness and Walter Smith enjoy an Ibrox reunion when Rangers took on Galatasaray in October 2000.

Graeme Souness with author Tom Miller at the launch of the authorised biography of Sandy Jardine at Ibrox in November 2016.

# CHAPTER 20:
# THE PLAYERS, 1987-88

| PLAYER | APPEARANCES | GOALS |
|---|---|---|
| CHRIS WOODS | 52 | |
| NICKY WALKER | 6 | |
| TERRY BUTCHER | 18 | 1 |
| JAN BARTRAM | 14 | 3 |
| JOHN BROWN | 12 | 2 |
| RICHARD GOUGH | 36 | 6 |
| STUART MUNRO | 22 | |
| JIMMY NICHOLL | 33 | |
| SCOTT NISBET | 29 | |
| AVI COHEN | 12 | |
| JIMMY PHILLIPS | 27 | |
| GRAHAM ROBERTS | 50 | 1 |
| IAN FERGUSON | 8 | 1 |
| DAVIE COOPER | 43 | 2 |

## THE SIGNIFICANCE OF SOUNESS

| | | |
|---|---|---|
| IAN DURRANT | 54 | 16 |
| DEREK FERGUSON | 43 | 4 |
| ROBERT FLECK | 44 | 19 |
| IAN McCALL | 12 | 1 |
| DAVIE KIRKWOOD | 7 | |
| DAVE MacFARLANE | 1 | |
| GRAEME SOUNESS | 30 | 2 |
| MARK WALTERS | 21 | 8 |
| RAY WILKINS | 29 | 1 |
| COLIN WEST | 1 | |
| MARK FALCO | 19 | 10 |
| TREVOR FRANCIS | 25 | |
| GARY McSWEGAN | 1 | |
| ALLY McCOIST | 53 | 42 |

Rangers played 58 competitive games in the 1987–88 season.

The title was won by Celtic with Rangers finishing a disappointing third. Hearts were second.

Ally McCoist made 53 appearances across all competitions. McCoist also finished top scorer with 42 goals.

## CHAPTER 21:

# NEW FACES, 1988-89

Having lost their title at the first defence, Rangers were hurting. Celtic celebrated their centenary and capped it off with Scotland's premier trophy. Rangers had bolstered the squad through the duration of the season, including long-term target Richard Gough finally becoming a member. But it came at a cost, as Spurs were demanding a serious profit on their original investment of £750,000 paid to Dundee United only one season earlier.

In November, a private jet was dispatched to Paris and returned with Ray Wilkins on board. Wilkins was the ultimate professional and had 84 England caps before he arrived at Ibrox. What a CV he had: Chelsea, Manchester United, AC Milan and now he was joining Rangers from Paris Saint-Germain. It was a masterstroke signing from Souness and a bargain at only £250,000.

John Brown, another who had his on-field battles with Souness when in the darker blue of Dundee, joined in mid-January 1988. Four weeks later St Mirren were paid £850,000 for Ian Ferguson who had won the Scottish Cup for the Paisley side in 1987. He was just 20 when he came to Ibrox. Ferguson

## THE SIGNIFICANCE OF SOUNESS

was a Rangers supporter and he didn't care who knew it. Ferguson had started his career at Clyde before moving on to St Mirren. Graeme Souness knew Ian Ferguson was someone who could have a long and successful career at Rangers but the Buddies weren't prepared to play ball and sell him to their rivals, especially after their cup win.

Fergie was hot property and very much in demand, with Liverpool and Manchester United also vying for his signature. In fact, Ian was on his way to Old Trafford to discuss terms with Alex Ferguson who was a close pal of St Mirren boss Alex Smith. On the journey to Manchester Fergie knew his heart wasn't in it. 'I was going there because Alex Smith wanted me to but I wanted to be at Rangers. We were across the border and on the M6 when I said, "Turn the car. I'm not going to Manchester, get me back up the road." I knew Graeme Souness was keen but there was nothing formal in place. St Mirren were hell-bent on making things difficult for me but I was determined to agitate for my move if I had to. I think turning back rather than going to Manchester had the Saints directors finally appreciate that it had to be Rangers for me. Like every Rangers fan I was enthused by what was going on at Ibrox under Graeme Souness and I wanted to be a part of his plans. Not only had Souness brought in the best English internationals he was also getting the best out of Scottish boys who were already there like Durranty, McCoist and Derek Ferguson. It was obvious something big was happening. Rangers came back for me with a formal bid but again the bigwigs at Saints rejected it. I was getting so frustrated and I struggled to block it out, and there is no doubt my performance levels on the park at the time dipped.

# NEW FACES, 1988–89

St Mirren were continuing to hawk me down south but when Rangers upped their offer, taking the fee to £1m with add-ons on top of the £850,000 upfront fee, Saints' resistance was worn down. Manchester United, Liverpool or Rangers? As soon as I knew Graeme Souness wanted me there was only one place I was going to be playing my football. I know it's a cliché but I couldn't wait to get started.'

One surprising new recruit was Trevor Francis who had been the first £1m-transfer between two English clubs. Nottingham Forest's iconic manager Brian Clough had sanctioned the payment to get Francis in from Birmingham City. Two European Cups later, the fee Clough paid was pretty much vindicated. Trevor Francis came to Rangers from Atalanta in Italy; he had joined the Bergamo-based club after a successful spell playing alongside Graeme Souness at Sampdoria. Francis was 33 when he became a Ranger, but he was a seasoned campaigner who had looked after himself throughout his career and of course Souness knew what he could offer.

With hindsight, maybe had the signings been made earlier Rangers would have retained their crown. As the new faces were coming in, Robert Fleck was on the move, sold to Norwich for £580,000.

So despite those earlier sizeable squad additions Souness wanted more ahead of the 1988–89 season, and he had the cheque book out again.

Avi Cohen, Jan Bartram, Graham Roberts and Jimmy Phillips were all moved on before August, as Souness showed how dispassionate he could be when it came to the playing staff. If he thought their time at Rangers was up – it was.

To the incomings, veteran front man Andy Gray finally

## THE SIGNIFICANCE OF SOUNESS

realised his boyhood dreams to play for Rangers. Gray came on board in September in the middle of a bit of an injury crisis. A couple of weeks later, versatile defender or midfielder Neale Cooper, who had been a European winner with Aberdeen, came from Aston Villa. Tom Cowan was seen as one for the future, joining from Clyde in February. In the spring, Mel Sterland came in for the run-in from Sheffield Wednesday.

The major summer recruits included powerhouse forward Kevin Drinkell, again considered a perfect partner for Ally McCoist. Drinkell had a good record of one goal every three games in an unfashionable Norwich side. Kevin was joined by another Englishman, Gary Stevens. Everton took a bit of convincing to sell their prized full back but Souness's persistence paid off. Aged 25, Stevens was to prove a very shrewd investment and would play his own part in a historic achievement for the club going forwards. Tommy Cowan proved to be one of Graeme Souness's last signings from a Scottish club, as he swooped to bring young Tom to Rangers despite serious interest and an offer already on the table from Brian Clough's Nottingham Forest. Tom recalls:

'John Clark, the Celtic Lisbon Lion, was the Clyde manager and he arranged for his son Martin and I to go to Forest with a view to signing. We flew to East Midlands Airport and were whisked straight to Brian Clough's home. It was raining very heavily, and apparently in those days if it was wet the bold Brian didn't fancy it and would give training a miss! I was wearing a big overcoat and when Mrs Clough ushered us into the front room she asked us to take a seat as her husband would join us in a few minutes. Sure enough, the door opened and the legend Brian Clough came in. Before any introductions could be made, he was giving it to me with both barrels for sitting on their couch with my wet and heavy coat on! I don't think I made the best impression.

'Forest had a double bid accepted by Clyde, and on that first meeting Martin Clark signed. I wanted longer to think about it, and that didn't please Mr Clough either, but at the time I was serving a mechanical engineering apprenticeship with British Steel and I had to consider that before making any decision. I think my lack of immediate commitment meant Forest wasn't going to happen. I was aware Coventry City were also interested but hadn't formalised an offer, and when I got back from Nottingham a scout from Tottenham Hotspur was waiting to meet me at Glasgow airport. The scout was very persuasive and he even called then Spurs manager Terry Venables on his mobile phone before passing this huge hand-held mobile brick-like telephone to me to speak to Venables myself. The Spurs boss wasted no time and was aware that Forest had made an offer and could just about recite the terms I had been offered by Brian Clough as if he had been there, including a four-year contract but for the first two years I would play in the reserves! Just as I had been told!

'Venables then said, "I want you for my first team – come down, and you will be playing top-flight football immediately." I was flattered and maybe even a bit shocked, but deep down I knew I wasn't ready for that. I thanked them for the offer but told them I wasn't ready to leave home for London. Two days later I'm at work and a colleague comes running over to tell me I had to phone my mum – it had been broadcast on Radio Clyde as an appeal for me to phone home. As an apprentice I was used to the wind-ups and dismissed it. Five minutes later and another guy came up and said the same, then another, then another. So, I plucked up the courage to phone home, not knowing why the urgency or if it was even an emergency.

'When I called, my mum was really excited to tell me that Graeme Souness had been on the phone and wanted to speak to me! It had been in the *Daily Record* for days that Rangers wanted me but I just put it down to speculation, but this was really it! I was a Rangers fan all my life – nothing else mattered now but signing for my boyhood heroes. The next night I was a guest of the club at a game at Ibrox and I signed at half-time. I couldn't wait to get started.'

Tom Cowan recalls the influence Ray Wilkins had in the dressing room: 'Ray wasn't just a sensational footballer he was an absolute gentleman. He had played with the best at the biggest clubs in the world but he was grounded. He was polite and respectful of everyone, from the laundry and kitchen staff to the directors. He had time for everybody and was always available for a chat if you needed advice. Ray used to also come along to reserve games, and while he came into the dressing room at full-time he didn't interfere with Jimmy Nicholl, who was in charge of the second team; but after Jimmy had gone through his post-match debrief Ray would take you aside and go through how you had performed. He could be critical but he always gave encouragement and finished on a positive point. He really was a special man and if I'm honest he was a bit of a hero to me. To play alongside him, even in training, was a privilege I'll always cherish.'

Rangers headed to the Tuscan hills to prime themselves to win the league title back from Celtic. The Il Ciocco complex was a facility Graeme Souness knew well as it was one Sampdoria

# NEW FACES, 1988–89

had used regularly. On returning to Scotland Rangers looked fit and well prepared, and this was evident in a comfortable 4–1 pre-season win over Ayr United.

The league campaign also delivered a comfortable opening 90 minutes with a 2–0 victory at Hamilton; Gary Stevens opened his scoring account with the first and McCoist claiming the second. Rangers looked well prepared for the challenge ahead. The first Old Firm derby was scheduled for 27 August at Ibrox. This game would give a pointer to just how ready Rangers were.

## CHAPTER 22:

# MURRAY-TIME

One other new face in and around Ibrox wasn't on the playing staff. David Murray, who was a close affiliate of Graeme Souness, effectively bought the controlling interests of Rangers Football Club in November 1988, from Lawrence Marlborough, who was still based in Nevada. It was reported to be a £6 million investment and Souness had been pivotal to the deal being struck. While Murray didn't take the reins immediately, David Holmes knew it was probably time to move on – he retained his position as chairman until the summer of 1989 when David Murray took the role on himself.

Since coming to Rangers and taking up residence in Edinburgh, Graeme Souness had become close friends with David Murray. Murray was an entrepreneur who had built up a business empire in the lucrative metals market, and had overcome serious adversity having lost both his legs in a car accident in 1976 as he returned from a rugby match. Murray was ambitious and driven and quickly diversified his business interests to include mining and property development. It's fair to say Souness and Murray were kindred spirits, and were of similar ages with David being just two years older than Graeme.

David Murray had been born in Ayr but was later educated at Broughton High School in the north of Edinburgh. In the early 1980s Murray made a bid to acquire Ayr United but the directors rejected his advances. Murray at that time had not considered the possibility that he might be able to buy Rangers. That changed when over dinner one night Graeme happened to mention that Lawrence Marlborough may have been considering selling up. Murray liked the idea of taking over not just Scotland's premier football club, but one of the biggest clubs in Britain.

By the autumn of 1988 things started to gain pace with Souness at the heart of discussions between David Murray and David Holmes and his advisors acting on behalf of Marlborough. As negotiations continued it was quite amazing that the press hadn't got wind of it. But of course, no one even speculated that Lawrence Marlborough had an inkling to sell, even with consideration to the fact he was still living in the US.

David Holmes was only partly through his business plan to reshape Rangers with Marlborough pulling the strings from afar. David Murray was a regular visitor to Ibrox but most put it down to his friendship with the manager. Then as the deal was almost finalised, out of left field came competition to own Rangers. Owner of the Mirror Group Newspapers Robert Maxwell, who happened to also own Derby County Football Club, made it known that he wanted Rangers. Maxwell was a flamboyant but controversial character who had been chairman at Oxford United, and in 1983 had tried to merge them with local rivals Reading. He wanted to form a new club as Thames Valley Royals. It was later revealed that had Maxwell got his way and bought Rangers he planned to merge them with their greatest rivals Celtic to form a super club to take on Europe. Perhaps it was just a pipe dream or he clearly hadn't done his homework. As it was, Maxwell's plans for Rangers were gazumped by David Murray.

An agreement was reached with Murray acquiring over 240,000 shares in Rangers FC PLC, at a cost of £6m. Acquiring Lawrence Marlborough's shares gave him a 69.95 per cent share of the club. To support his friend in the transaction Graeme Souness was reported to have invested £500,000 of his own money. This gave Souness the unique role of player–manager–director–investor. It was suggested the sale price was lower than it perhaps could have been, but Murray drove a hard bargain.

Murray's takeover ended a very long association for the Lawrence family at the Ibrox club. A relationship that had gone back decades to when Marlborough's grandfather John Lawrence first became a director in the 1940s and was chairman from 1963 until ill health saw him step down in 1973, the year after Rangers won the European Cup Winners' Cup in Barcelona. Murray had big plans for Rangers and had the advantage that Ibrox redevelopment had already started under David Holmes and Willie Waddell before him. The stadium was also fully paid for with no borrowings against the facility. On the field, too, the foundations were solid, with a strong pool of players, many of whom were there all the way to the amazing nine-in-a-row period. Later, under David Murray, Rangers were regularly looking for additional funding and share issues were a fairly commonplace action.

Marlborough took limited interest in Rangers after the deal was agreed, while David Holmes knew his time at the club was also coming to an end.

The methods of David Murray and David Holmes were worlds apart, and while Murray waited in the wings to take a more active role in the running of the club, David Holmes was uneasy with his presence, including his influence with the players. Murray also recruited his own non-playing staff, including Alan Montgomery coming in as chief executive, who had previously been with Scottish Television. David Murray was going to do it his way and that included influential commercial director Freddie Fletcher moving on.

Murray was a man on a mission and promised great things for Rangers, although he did qualify early on that he viewed Rangers as a football club first and a business second. Murray also claimed that he didn't see himself as Rangers' 'owner' more just a custodian. Ibrox had been redeveloped originally under former manager Willie Waddell but Murray had further ambitious plans to again increase the capacity, which involved adding a third tier to the main stand. There is no doubt Graeme Souness's and David Murray's qualities complemented each other and both were committed to take Rangers forwards without constraints. It was Murray who sanctioned the signing of Maurice Johnston after Graeme Souness floated the idea that it was Johnston's football ability that mattered – he considered it irrelevant that he had previously starred for Celtic and looked set to join them again. Souness got the deal done, and in Maurice Johnston Rangers broke the mould by signing a high-profile player who just happened to be Roman Catholic.

Under David Murray Rangers would have unsurpassed success, including winning nine league titles in a row. The success wasn't without controversy, though, and financial pressure mounted in 1999 to a level that the Bank of Scotland took a 7 per cent stake in the club, securing a charge over income and assets of Rangers to safeguard their position should Rangers default on repayments.

In August 2009, Murray stood down as chairman with the bank taking further control of the Rangers purse strings. There were also tax issues where it was a question on the legality of EBTs (Employee Benefit Trusts) where side letters indemnified players' liability. Chairman Alastair Johnstone, who had replaced Murray, was confident he and his board of directors had things in hand and could trade their way through some troubled financial waters, but everything changed when David Murray (by now Sir David Murray) sold out to Craig Whyte for a nominal £1 fee in May 2011. By February 2012, Rangers were in administration, then liquidation followed five months later.

Lawrence Marlborough did make a very rare appearance at Ibrox for the opening game of the 2011–12 season after Craig Whyte had taken control. Like everyone else, he didn't foresee what was to come next.

Graeme Souness and David Murray remain friends to this day and meet regularly at Murray's estate in Perthshire. Conversations over dinner now must be quite different to when they dined together in their favourite Edinburgh Italian restaurant and plotted to buy Rangers.

## CHAPTER 23:

# SEASON THREE, 1988-89: GET SET FOR NINE IN A ROW

Rangers had been dethroned, but there was nobody more determined than Graeme Souness to make up for the disappointment of the previous season. David Holmes made sure the manager had his backing with the summer transfer activity, and all four players who departed the club in the summer were defenders. The squad replacements were predominately more offensive operators.

The league campaign started well with an unbeaten run from day one up until a trip to Pittodrie in early October when they lost 2–1. In that run was the infamous 5–1 win over Celtic at Ibrox in late August. Earlier in August Rangers had hosted Bordeaux in a testimonial match for Davie Cooper. It was a good workout for the side to help prepare them for the season ahead. Rangers won 3–1, with Butcher, McCoist and Drinkell finding the target. In competitive action, goals were being shared about with McCoist claiming three while his new strike partner Kevin Drinkell also had three.

The defeat at Pittodrie was not the biggest concern for Rangers and the fans that day. It had started as a really bad-tempered contest, with former Dons favourite Neale Cooper, now in a Rangers shirt for his debut, smashing into tackles and looking to secure the early initiative for his new club. Animosity was in the air as both sets of fans were very vocal, and the atmosphere was bordering on toxic. The teams were scheduled to meet again in the League Cup Final later in October but it was all about vital league points that day as both teams went into the match unbeaten so far in the campaign. Rangers started brightly and Durrant was enjoying the freedom to play defence-splitting passes and getting forwards to support the front men, safe in the knowledge Neale Cooper was anchoring the midfield behind him.

Rangers won an early free kick at the edge of the Aberdeen 18-yard box after a visionary pass released McCoist who was taken out by Stewart McKimmie with a crude challenge from behind. It was a marginal decision and many thought the incident was actually inside the box. As it was, television replays later showed it to be just outside the area. Mark Walters took the set piece and his curling effort looked netbound until Theo Snelders in the Aberdeen goal rose to tip the ball over the bar.

The game was being played at a furious pace, and as Aberdeen threatened at the other end Cooper was there with a robust challenge to block Robert Connor after he first stopped John Hewitt with a timely intervention. As the ball spun clear, Ian Durrant tried to take a touch but was taken out by a horrid full-face-of-the-boot challenge by Neil Simpson. Simpson went right over the top and caught Durrant flush on the knee. The Rangers players who were close to the action were incensed by what they had just witnessed. Referee Louis Thow tried

## SEASON THREE, 1988–89: GET SET FOR NINE IN A ROW

to calm things down and booked Simpson for the shocking – and what looked deliberate – assault on the Rangers playmaker. Why it wasn't a red card, we can only speculate – perhaps the referee thought keeping 22 players on the park might allow things to be more orderly both on and off the pitch. The referee clearly didn't realise the severity or extent of Ian Durrant's injury. A very distressed Ian was eventually carried from the park piggyback-style by Phil Boersma. Many questioned the way Ian was carried off the field, but the truth of the matter remains that the only stretcher available that day at Pittodrie was outside the ground. Durrant was taken straight to the visitors' dressing room to check the injury as Stuart Munro came off the bench to replace him.

The game ended with Aberdeen winning 2–1 as Rangers suffered their first defeat of the season, but the result was academic and the 90 minutes was overshadowed by the first-half clash that saw Durrant leave the field with such a horrible injury. That evening it was reported that Ian Durrant had badly damaged knee ligaments and could be out for some time. Nobody foresaw just how long Ian would be lost to the game. Light Blues skipper Terry Butcher, who had a very close relationship with Ian Durrant, took his post-match frustration out with a kick at the referee's door – an action that would later see him fined £500 by the SFA. Graeme Souness, meanwhile, was highly critical of the referee and was quoted as saying all of Scottish football should be very concerned by that tackle and the consequences that followed. For Ian Durrant the prognosis wasn't good and he was immediately booked in for surgery the Monday after the match. It was a four-hour operation and there were no guarantees that Ian Durrant would ever be able to play football again. However, Ian was made of stern stuff and after more operations, including going under the knife with a specialist in America, he made his comeback in April 1991 – two and a half years after the sickening and shocking challenge from Simpson.

Ian doesn't dwell on the dark days but confirmed: 'I struggled to come to terms with just how bad my knee was but I was determined. I couldn't be around Ibrox much as I missed playing, I had to get away. Doc Cruickshank was magnificent but I couldn't handle being at Ibrox every day. We didn't have a big gym or the right facilities for a proper rehab. I also wanted out of Glasgow so the club arranged for me to go to Lilleshall, which was renowned for its ability to get athletes back performing, and that includes guys who were jump jockeys, many of whom had horrible injuries. It was in the middle of nowhere but that helped the focus because Glasgow could still have been full of distractions. I did three weeks on and one week off for the full period I was there. Sure I missed home but I needed to get back playing. The facility was run by ex-army men and they were demanding and just battered me physically and mentally, they were intent in making sure I only looked forward.'

Before Ian's return to the first team he was scheduled for a 60-minute run-out with the reserves against Hibernian at Ibrox. Over 30,000 fans turned out on a January afternoon to pay respects to their returning hero. Ian played the full 90 minutes and didn't want to leave the field as he defied medical opinion and took this first massive step to resurrect his career.

While Ian was in rehab his teammates were trying to put a winning run together, but a 3–1 defeat to Celtic was

## SEASON THREE, 1988–89: GET SET FOR NINE IN A ROW

damaging to their ambitions, and then back-to-back losses away at Dundee United and at home to Hearts in the run-up to Christmas also saw questions being asked about Rangers' ability to recapture the championship crown. In the rematch with Aberdeen at Hampden in the League Cup Final, Rangers lifted the trophy after winning 3–2 with two goals from Ally McCoist, including one from the penalty spot and a stunning strike from Ian Ferguson that really proved to be inspirational in his Rangers career. Author and broadcaster Stewart Weir recalls:

'Ian Ferguson had struggled for form since joining from St Mirren. The transfer fee may have been a huge weight to carry, but Fergie had also been playing out of position to help the team and he had been carrying a few niggling injuries. His cup-final goal against Aberdeen changed everything. His confidence took a huge boost and all of a sudden he felt at home at Rangers.'

The Scottish Cup was also in Rangers' sights, and they ran out 8–0 winners against Stranraer at Ibrox early in the tournament. Other than that convincing victory against lower-league opposition, Souness's side needed two wins in all the other ties against Raith Rovers, Dundee United and St Johnstone to book their place in the final against Celtic. Back on league business, momentum was building. They'd started 1989 well with a 4–1 win over Celtic and the only negative result was a 2–1 reversal at Motherwell just four days after the Celtic win. After that Rangers went 12 wins in a row before going down to Aberdeen on the last day of the season. That defeat was irrelevant, really, as the title had been secured fully three games before with a 4–0 win over Hearts

# THE SIGNIFICANCE OF SOUNESS

at Ibrox, with Kevin Drinkell and Mel Sterland both notching doubles. It would prove to be the first title of what would become nine in a row.

The Scottish Cup Final didn't go to plan, with Celtic winning 1–0 from a controversial goal that angered Graeme Souness and the Rangers support. Celtic took a quick throw-in when the award of the throw should have been given to Rangers, but referee Bob Valentine let play continue and Joe Miller raced up the park to score. The cup going to the east end of Glasgow also ended Rangers' hopes of a treble.

It had been a turbulent season but Graeme Souness had always made the championship his top priority and his team had now wrestled the title back from their biggest rivals, showing great fortitude and character after losing the services of one of the finest players this country has ever produced, by what was one of the worst tackles this country has ever witnessed. Ian Durrant played 14 games in the season and qualified for a league winner's medal.

# CHAPTER 24:
# THE PLAYERS, 1988-89

| PLAYER | APPEARANCES | GOALS |
|---|---|---|
| CHRIS WOODS | 39 | |
| NICKY WALKER | 14 | |
| TERRY BUTCHER | 51 | 4 |
| JOHN BROWN | 42 | 3 |
| RICHARD GOUGH | 51 | 4 |
| STUART MUNRO | 33 | 4 |
| JIMMY NICHOLL | 3 | |
| SCOTT NISBET | 10 | 2 |
| JOHN McGREGOR | 1 | |
| TOM COWAN | 4 | |
| GARY STEVENS | 52 | 2 |
| IAN FERGUSON | 33 | 13 |
| DAVIE COOPER | 33 | 1 |
| IAN DURRANT | 14 | 4 |

## THE SIGNIFICANCE OF SOUNESS

| | | |
|---|---|---|
| DEREK FERGUSON | 24 | 3 |
| NEALE COOPER | 17 | 1 |
| IAN McCALL | 7 | 1 |
| DAVIE KIRKWOOD | 2 | |
| KEVIN MacDONALD | 3 | |
| GRAEME SOUNESS | 10 | 2 |
| MARK WALTERS | 48 | 17 |
| RAY WILKINS | 45 | 2 |
| KEVIN DRINKELL | 47 | 19 |
| ANDY GRAY | 16 | 5 |
| MEL STERLAND | 13 | 3 |
| GARY McSWEGAN | 1 | |
| ALLY McCOIST | 33 | 18 |
| SANDY ROBERTSON | 2 | |

Rangers played a total of 53 competitive matches during the 1988–89 season.

The title was regained with Aberdeen finishing second. Kevin Drinkell was top scorer with 19 goals.

Gary Stevens, with 52, made the most appearances.

## CHAPTER 25:

# BLUE & WHITE DYNAMITE

It's fair to say Ian Durrant had a pretty unique relationship with Graeme Souness. Souness was genuinely in awe of Durranty's talent but was equally frustrated by the young midfielder's lifestyle and penchant for devilment off the park. On the park, Durrant's talent and application was never in question.

Graeme Souness had a strange pet name for his prodigy and it was simply 'Bastard', albeit it was usually said as a term of endearment.

Souness loved playing alongside Ian and probably saw a bit of himself in him, but when Durrant got together with his best pal Derek Ferguson – and with Ally McCoist usually involved, too, to make them a gang of three – away from the club they were a bit of a handful and living life to the full like most young, fit, red-blooded, financially well-heeled youngsters would. Souness himself was not averse to a night out or two, and while at Liverpool his teammates named him 'Champagne Charlie', so the new manager knew more than most about how to relax and get away from the pressures of the game. The problem was these were west of Scotland boys living and playing their football in a bit of a bubble. Perhaps his spell in Italy had changed the mindset of Graeme, as he embraced the disciplines and habits of top continental players where balancing diet, rest and avoiding the lure of nightclubs were so important, all of which were changes among many others that he was trying to instill in the Ibrox dressing room.

Ian had been brought up in Kinning Park just along from Ibrox, and even before he was seven or eight years old he used to wait until the gates opened at half-time to get into the ground to catch sight of his heroes on match days. That was if he hadn't managed to avoid the stewards by crawling under the gate in the first place. As a precocious teenager Ian fulfilled his boyhood dreams by signing for the club he loved. In April 1985, he made his first-team debut against Morton.

Everyone recognised Rangers had an enormous talent on their hands. He had pace, touch, vision and an eye for a goal. Ian was especially adept at timing his run into the danger area to get on the end of a pass or cross and he finished like a striker. Despite signing a host of international stars, Graeme Souness saw enough in the young Durrant to suggest he could build his team around him.

Souness also had Ian's close friend Derek Ferguson vying for a starting jersey in the midfield, too, and Ferguson is quick to remember just what Graeme Souness expected of his youngsters: 'When Graeme came in he wasn't just the manager – we had signed a glorious player who took Ian Durrant and myself under his wing. We were a bit in awe of him when he arrived but we learned so much. Souness would have done anything to win a game of football and that complemented what had been drummed into us from the first day we walked through the doors of Ibrox – that winning was what it was all about. Whether that was a training game or a cup final, that winning mentality was constantly promoted.'

There is a training-ground tale that suggests the competitive nature throughout the squad was always evident. It was a Friday morning before a Saturday fixture against Hearts, and the training session finished with small-sided games including a regular 'cross-border battle' of Scotland versus England. Now as the manager had played the bulk of his career on the other side of Hadrian's Wall, and despite being a Scottish international, he was given a bib to take his place in the English side. To be fair, Northern Ireland legend Jimmy Nicholl was given honorary Scottish status to even things up. The game started with the manager demanding more tempo and the ball to be moved quickly and with purpose. Ian Durrant found himself one-on-one with the manager and promptly nutmegged him to go through on goal. The trickery of Durrant was met with joy by his teammates but not so much by a certain embarrassed and livid Graeme Souness. As the game continued Ian was back in possession and as he took another touch he was felled by a thumping challenge from his boss. Souness was looking to avenge the earlier loss of face to his young dynamic midfielder. It was a sore one but Durranty wasn't going to let Souness see he had perhaps got the better of him. He jumped straight to his feet and enquired of the perpetrator: 'Was that your best shot?'

Ian's bravado was quickly dampened as Souness let loose with a right hook that struck him a glancing blow. Now to confirm how close Ian, Derek Ferguson and Ally McCoist were, his two sidekicks immediately jumped in to have a go at the manager, with Derek actually jumping on Souness's back. Others looked to get involved as it all kicked off as Jimmy

Nicholl squared up to Ray Wilkins, and Davie Cooper and Trevor Francis faced off with a few shadow-boxing moves. It was over as quickly as it had begun and the session was finished with a blast from Walter Smith's whistle.

Back in the dressing room the three amigos – Ian, Derek and Ally – waited to see what punishment they might face, although Ian was already sporting the makings of a black eye. The dressing room door flew open and the manager stormed in. Fearing the worst all heads were down focusing on the home dressing room flooring when Souness, much to everyone's surprise, said: 'Brilliant! Team spirit and all in it together – that was brilliant!' Perhaps it was a bit extreme or unorthodox but that escapade probably further cemented the bond that was so evident in the squad.

Derek Ferguson and Ian Durrant are as friendly now as they were when they both broke into the Rangers first team as teenagers. In their time together at Ibrox they were almost inseparable. That was of course until Graeme Souness sent Derek out to Dundee on loan in an effort to have him recognise that his talent alone wasn't enough and he needed to apply himself more.

Journalist Stewart Weir was another Lanarkshire lad who had good relationships with the boys and recalls: 'No doubt Souness saw a bit of himself in Derek Ferguson, and when he sent him up to Dundee it was hoped it would bring him back down to earth and realise just how far he could go in the game. You think back too to the 1989 Cup Final when Derek was left out while Souness put himself on the bench – it was another signal to Derek that he should sharpen his act. Souness was keen to develop local talent but his patience was wearing thin with Derek, and Sandy Robertson too, while he appeared to be happy to nurture Ian Durrant, as he certainly thought he was something very special. So special, in fact, I suspect Graeme Souness would have helped engineer a move to Italy where Durranty's talents would have flourished. Unfortunately, the horrid injury at Pittodrie took that potential off the table. Looking back, though, Ian Durrant was as fine a talent as Scotland has ever produced and we can only wonder how high his star would have reached had he not have had such a serious knee problem. It does say a lot about Ian Durrant – the character, mind you – that he came back to play the way he did, almost defying medical logic. So much so that when he moved on to Kilmarnock he picked up as many caps for Scotland as he did in his time at Rangers.'

Ian was just 21 when his career was almost ended by the challenge from Neil Simpson. Derek Ferguson still ponders what might have been: 'Ian was magnificent. A player ahead of his time. There was nothing he couldn't do. Aye, OK, maybe his heading wasn't the best, but he was a dream to play alongside. Ian played on instinct and didn't really have to think of his next move – that's what made him what he was and was why other fantastic creative players loved to be in the same side as Ian. When guys like Ray Wilkins tell you how sensational Ian Durrant was, you sit up and take notice – he could have played in the best teams in the world and 100 per cent made them better. I love him like a brother, that's how close we are. He's a one off and a Ranger through and through.'

A tale involving Derek and Ian in Majorca springs to mind. Graeme Souness and his first wife Danielle had a home on the Spanish holiday isle. In close season Ian and Derek had packed the 'Ambre Solaire' and headed for a couple of weeks in Magaluf, pretty much unaware that the manager was holidaying in the adjoining town of Palma Nova. After a night of clubbing and a quick stop-off for some breakfast, and before heading back to their apartment for some shut-eye, the bold Ian and Derek decided to take a stroll along the *paseo*. Within minutes a Rolls-Royce convertible pulled up with manager Souness in the passenger seat and he summoned his young midfielders to come over. Both guys drew a deep breath and hoped the excesses of the night before weren't too evident before approaching the suntanned and designer-clad Graeme. Souness took a quick glance and with a wink told the boys to keep up their early morning walks as it would stand them in good stead when they got back for pre-season training.

There were the infamous kebab-shop incidents, too, that attracted police attention, and an odd night in the Panama Jack waterside nightclub that ended up in a bit of kerfuffle, but Ian and Derek were young and up for a good time.

On another occasion Durrant and McCoist planned a trick on assistant boss Walter Smith. It was a Monday after training and Graeme Souness wasn't there – or so the bold boys thought. They were expecting it to be Walter in the shower in the manager's room, as he had taken training, but Souness had come back to Ibrox after a trip south and had chosen to freshen-up before heading home. The problem was Ian and Ally had planted a bar of trick soap in his shower room.

When both got the shout that the manager wanted a word with them they tentatively made their way into the office to discover Graeme was in the screened-off tiled shower area at the back of the office and was ready to hold contract discussions with both players while he showered. Ian looked at Ally and Ally looked at Ian: *this could be real trouble*, was their joint thoughts. Within a minute Souness popped his head round the corner as he lathered his body with the soap the guys had acquired in the famous Tam Shepherds Trick Shop in Glasgow's Queen Street. The boys looked on horrified as the coal-like coloured lathery soap suds turned their manager's face and shoulders black. At first Souness couldn't work out why Ian and Ally were stifling their laughs before he realised he was turning his body black with the joke soap. As the boys took off at pace to leave their manager distressed in his predicament, that pet name Graeme Souness had for Ian Durrant echoed round the innards of Ibrox: 'Bastard!' Although on this occasion in not quite such friendly tones.

But both McCoist and Durrant could play, and any such nonsense or high jinks was never evident when the serious part of the week came round on game day.

That horrible injury and savage tackle by Neil Simpson robbed Ian Durrant of nearly three years of his Rangers career but he fought back even after knee reconstruction and was there throughout the successful nine-in-a-row period. Graeme Souness remains one of Ian Durrant's biggest fans.

Alex Rae became a league winner with Rangers on that epic 'Helicopter Sunday' (the day Celtic lost at Motherwell and Rangers won the title) win at Easter Road while Celtic faltered at Fir Park (for the record, Terry Butcher was the Motherwell gaffer that day in 2005). Rae was another who had the utmost admiration for Durrant. Alex had started his career at Rangers but was released early in the Souness regime. Alex moved on to Falkirk before building a fantastic career south of the border, then came back to Rangers under Alex McLeish in 2004: 'Ian Durrant was the best. He could have been anything he wanted to be. A top player from the off, scoring big important goals with a knack for scoring against Celtic. He had an incredible knack of just doing the right thing at the right time and was absolutely lethal in the box. I remember my first pre-season with the squad and Ian just glided over the surface, as he covered every blade of grass when we played games, or when we were being put through the mill with some cross-country-type running and Ian was again up front making it look easy while the rest of us were blowing. He was perpetual motion and that was the way he was on a Saturday, too, full of energy and invention. Sure, Ian and his sidekick Derek Ferguson, who was another terrific player, had their run-ins with the authority of Souness, who tried to curtail their shenanigans, but it was only to make them as professional as he could.

'I think when you consider the traumas Ian suffered but had the character to come back from it speaks volumes for what type of guy he is. Add in too that when he did come back from injury, an injury that would have seen most players chuck it, he had to modify his game as he wasn't as mobile as he had been previously. He didn't just change his style to the detriment of his impact on the game, he did it and still bossed games in whichever role he chose to play. A special player and a special guy.'

Alex Rae was recruited to assist Steven Davis as interim manager after Michael Beale left the club, and was on the coaching staff under Philippe Clement. On leaving Rangers Alex was appointed assistant manager of Partick Thistle.

## CHAPTER 26:

# JULY 1989: BREAK THE MOULD, MOJO

When Maurice Johnston signed for Rangers it wasn't just groundbreaking, it was a clear signal that Rangers only wanted the best players available – race or religion was not a factor. It was a transfer that shook Scottish football to the core.

Johnston's first game for Rangers was on 29 July 1989, at the old Broomfield, home to Airdrieonians. It was a testimonial for long-serving Diamonds stars Brian McKeown and John Martin. While Rangers were without Ray Wilkins, Derek Ferguson and Ian Durrant, they did have another summer signing – Trevor Steven – in their starting line-up.

Johnston took to the field, and as you can imagine he was concerned about what kind of reception he would get. Mo was playing centre forward, and in direct opposition was ex-Ger and his former Partick Thistle teammate Dave MacKinnon. Dave recalls: 'It was the bravest most courageous decision any footballer in Scotland had taken. As we took to the field from the dressing rooms, which were down at the corner at Airdrie, Mo said, "Don't know how this is going to go today," but the travelling Rangers fans gave him a great reception, although Mo was still not a hundred per cent convinced. As the game got underway I smashed into him in a full-blooded challenge and in a moment of great hilarity the Rangers fans burst into song with a rendition of "There's Only One Dave MacKinnon!" We both laughed but I knew then my former Firhill mate had all the qualities and character to make his controversial move to Rangers' a massive success.' For the record, Rangers won 3–1 but Johnston didn't make the score sheet.

Broadcaster Stewart Weir was working with the Press Agency at the time of the controversial signing: 'On the Saturday I got a phone call from a contact in the wrestling world who tipped me off that Maurice Johnston would be signing for Rangers on the Monday. I put a call into the *Daily Record* sports desk to see if they had gotten any indication of what was going to be the most explosive story that would send shockwaves through the game. My regular contact there was in a bit of a tizzy as he confirmed the *Record* were on the case and had the exclusive news that Rangers were about to sign John Sheridan from Leeds United. Sheridan was a regular in the Republic of Ireland international side and would have been a controversial signing itself, for obvious reasons, but Sheridan was not the target, Johnston was, so I discreetly ended the call without giving anything away. If I remember correctly it was the *Sun* who were first to go to print with the news and it was some story, and of course as it broke the Celtic fans were irate!'

Johnston was a proven goal scorer, as Weir highlights: 'Look at the goals Maurice scored – big goals in big games. In his first season at Ibrox he was their top scorer in the league with 15. Graeme Souness used to say that how many goals you scored didn't really matter – you start the game with a draw, don't lose

## JULY 1989: BREAK THE MOULD, MOJO

a goal and one goal can win you the points. So, he viewed it as more about when and against whom being the important factors rather than the quantity. In fact, it also became his mantra; and when you look back, seven league games that season were won by 1–0 scorelines. In Johnston's first few months at Rangers, the man who came from Nantes for £1.5 million delivered with regularity: Aberdeen at Ibrox, 9 September, 1–0, Johnston; Hearts at Ibrox, 30 September, 1–0, Johnston; Celtic at Ibrox, 4 November, 1–0, Johnston. It was some contribution.'

The man that made the deal happen was super-agent Bill McMurdo. Nearly 40 years on, Bill looks back on that momentous transfer with great pride that his man Maurice had the fortitude to put pen to paper to become a Ranger: 'It was massive, and Maurice wasted no time in making his decision. He quite simply said, "Let's do it!" It had looked like he was Celtic-bound and the Rangers interest came about quite unexpectedly and only by a chance remark in conversation with Graeme Souness. Graeme said to me he was disappointed that I hadn't given him a shout when Maurice had made up his mind to return from France, which kind of put me on the back foot as never in a million years did I think that Rangers would have followed through to sign him. With hindsight, though, perhaps I should have been aware as it was pretty much common knowledge that Rangers had tried to sign John Collins who was of the same faith as Maurice.

'When I think back to Scotland versus France in March of that year, Maurice ran the show and scored both goals. Sitting along from me were Graeme and Walter Smith – just maybe that was the night they thought they might break the mould and bury tradition? I just had a feeling, although it took a bit

## THE SIGNIFICANCE OF SOUNESS

longer to come to fruition. Wheels were soon put in motion and a deal was structured. Now, was there a sense of devilment in it from Graeme? I think there probably was, but one thing I remember him saying was that signing Maurice Johnston made Rangers stronger and weakened Celtic. He probably laid the gauntlet down too to Maurice when he said even if Maurice doesn't play here every week we have put a spoke in Celtic's wheel and probably set them back years with the embarrassment of the media being called to herald Maurice as a Celtic player with pictures in the press and everything, yet he hadn't actually signed. Now he was joining their biggest rivals instead.

'Graeme also said some Rangers fans may not be too happy with the signing but they were in absolute meltdown on the other side of the city. It was a quiet Ibrox when Maurice and I made our way into the stadium, but it was only 5 a.m. to be fair, as we were instructed to be there early and before anyone else, while the squad had already departed for Tuscany and their pre-season training camp. When Maurice was introduced to the assembled media, I'll never forget the smile on Graeme's face, a look that said "I have actually broken the mould". For Maurice, of course he had concerns, but if he was worried he disguised it well and lapped up the attention and limelight while wearing his new club tie. This time there was no reversal – Maurice Johnston was a Ranger, and what a job he did for them.'

Another player Graeme Souness admired greatly and was also looked after by Bill McMurdo was Frank McAvennie. Bill says: 'Graeme liked Macca, as he was a terrific striker and could have played in any team. Over a coffee Graeme brought

## JULY 1989: BREAK THE MOULD, MOJO

Frank's name up but in reality that was as far as it got. I had represented Frank from day one and he was great to work with, but any suggestion that Frank could follow Maurice to Ibrox was an absolute non-starter. It was never mentioned again.'

In an Old Firm match at Celtic Park in 1987, Maurice Johnston in Celtic colours harried Graeme Souness deep inside Rangers' penalty box to win the ball. Souness held off the Celtic striker to keep possession before turning to the crowd in the old Parkhead enclosure, or 'jungle' as it was known, and in an act of defiance pulled the waistband of his shorts away from his body before pointing to the internal pocket to suggest Maurice Johnston was kept in there. Perhaps, even then, Souness was letting the Celtic fans know that he would have him where he wanted, and as things transpired a couple of years later that was at Ibrox in the blue of Rangers.

If the Maurice Johnston transfer was a move that was hugely controversial and unexpected, Bill McMurdo nearly pulled off another transfer that just failed at the final hurdle. George Best was another of Bill's clients and he came within a whisker of getting him to Rangers too. 'Maurice's transfer was the biggest ever, but if Bestie had joined Rangers it wouldn't have been far behind. Of course, it was quite different circumstances and had no religious background but George was keen to join the team he had followed since his schooldays in Belfast. He would have thrived on the Ibrox atmosphere and the fans would have adored him but it wasn't to be. It's a pity because it would have been another great step forwards for the Scottish game.

'Graeme Souness was great for Rangers and arguably left not quite fulfilled as he headed back to take on the challenge at Liverpool. Perhaps the pressures of authority in the game up here finally wore him down but we should all be thankful for his commitment and contribution to football. And when you think back to him joining Rangers as Scotland captain then, it remained the biggest transfer in history until of course Wee Maurice became a bluenose.'

Broadcaster Hugh Keevins was the leading sports reporter with the *Scotsman* at the time of the signing: 'I can remember the circumstances of the signing as if it were yesterday. I had been at Wimbledon covering the tennis for two weeks and was about to board a flight home from Heathrow when I met former Rangers and Scotland defender Iain Munro who told me Wee Mo had signed for Rangers. I had heard the rumours previously but now it looked a done deal.

'When I landed at Glasgow and went to retrieve my luggage I overheard one baggage handler say to another, "It's true, the wee b*****d has gone and done it!" The signing divided the Rangers support, in fact STV news that night reported that neither sets of supporters could accept it. By the time I had got home the call came from the *Scotsman* office to get to Ibrox to report on this hugely controversial moment impacting on Scottish football. I filed my report and still remember the opening lines: "You can't take a stick to a club while complaining that the same club had a policy of more than 100 years of not signing Catholic players, then take the same stick to the same club when they sign *that* Catholic player!" Rangers policy had been inherently wrong, but when they change that policy, clearly for the better, how can that also be wrong? It was suggested Celtic couldn't or wouldn't meet the demands of Maurice Johnston, or perhaps more accurately the demands of agent Bill McMurdo, and that

## JULY 1989: BREAK THE MOULD, MOJO

money was Mo's motivator. Don't we all work for money? Graeme Souness saw his opportunity and had the courage to make it happen. Graeme only wanted to sign the best available talent – it wasn't about a political signing. Graeme's decision was very well vindicated and when you look back at Maurice's late goal at Ibrox against Celtic to seal the win, that's [his football skills] all that mattered. Souness broke no rules when he signed Maurice Johnston and he met the demands of the player that others didn't.'

Prior to Mo Johnston crossing the Glasgow divide it was Alfie Conn who last made a similar move. Alfie Conn became the first footballer post-World War Two to play for both Celtic and Rangers.

Conn was a European Cup Winners' Cup winner in his time at Rangers before moving south to Tottenham Hotspur. Alfie had also scored in the 1973 Scottish Cup Final in a 3–2 Rangers win over Celtic. He also won a Scottish Cup medal with Celtic in 1977 after he was signed from Spurs by Jock Stein.

Alfie Conn was the trailblazer, but many years after the event, the self-confessed Rangers fan since his schooldays will look back and tell anyone interested that the move to Celtic just wasn't worth the aggravation.

Maurice Johnston won two Premier Division titles in his two years at Ibrox before leaving for Everton in 1991. That was quite a fair reward for his courage, commitment and contribution to Rangers Football Club under Graeme Souness. It was a move that paid dividends for both parties and proved a seismic shift in Rangers' previous transfer policy.

## CHAPTER 27:
# SEASON FOUR, 1989-90

With the Premier Division trophy back in the Ibrox trophy room after another successful campaign, Rangers were determined to make it three in four years. The signing of Maurice Johnston from under Celtic's noses was not just a notice of intent and confirmation of them being Scotland's number-one club, it was a move that was designed to scupper the plans of their biggest rivals. With Graeme Souness still robbed of the services of midfield maestro Ian Durrant, the manager concluded the signing of long-term transfer target Trevor Steven for £1.5m from Everton.

It was a memorable season for Rangers and one that wasn't without controversy with the Johnston signing splitting sections of the support. The league campaign didn't start well with a home defeat to St Mirren in the curtain-raiser, then losing 2–0 at Easter Road against a busy Hibs side seven days later.

Next up was the first Old Firm game of the season, hosted across the city, and Rangers got their first point on the board with a Terry Butcher-headed goal within five minutes, giving the Light Blues the early initiative, but Dariusz Dziekanowski equalised 15 minutes later. Mo Johnston got the verbals from a

## SEASON FOUR, 1989–90

home support in what was a hostile welcome back to Parkhead. They even chanted 'Who's the Catholic in the blue?' Bonni Ginzburg was in goal for Rangers and he was in inspired form. As it transpired this would be the only point Celtic would take off the champions in the four league matches of the season, and the Dziekanowski strike their only goal.

The remaining Old Firm fixtures would prove pivotal as Rangers went all out for their second successive title. Rangers started to put a terrific run together as they headed into winter and Mo Johnston became a hero of the Light Blue legions when he scored the only goal of the game against Celtic at Ibrox in early November. Johnston was then booked for celebrating the goal that came in the 88th minute. The win put Rangers back to the top of the table on a day when Rangers had cut the Celtic ticket allocation to 7,500 and their fans being housed in the Broomloan Road stand only. This game took place against a backstory of a reported Ibrox power struggle between director–manager Graeme Souness and Rangers chief executive Alan Montgomery. New owner David Murray intervened and Montgomery was redeployed within another Murray group company, Murray Media.

In between, Rangers were again active in the transfer market in November 1989 by signing Nigel Spackman from Queens Park Rangers, almost as a straight replacement for Ray Wilkins, who had left Ibrox for QPR.

Nigel was a very tidy footballer and endeared himself to the Rangers supporters by scoring the only goal of the January 1990 Old Firm Derby at Celtic Park.

Celtic were again the visitors on All Fools' Day, 1990, and again Rangers kept a clean sheet in a comfortable 3–0 win. The goals were shared between Walters, McCoist and Johnston, who again made his mark. This was the first game shown live by BskyB. Summer signing Trevor Steven was a clear man of the match as he constantly dictated the Rangers play. It was a great way to bounce back as Celtic had knocked Rangers out of the Scottish Cup at the end of February.

The title was all but won and it was finally wrapped up at Tannadice on 21 April with a 1–0 win. It was Rangers' 40th league crown. In the European Cup Rangers were eliminated at the first attempt by old foes Bayern Munich. On League Cup business, Rangers knocked out Arbroath, Morton, Hamilton and Dunfermline on their way to the October final but lost to Aberdeen in extra-time. Across all competitions Mo Johnston scored 17 goals, proving that the only gamble Graeme Souness took on signing the former Celtic star was on how the fans would react. His goal return, and Rangers again being Premier Division winners, was really all that mattered, and for Mo's contribution the fans were grateful.

## CHAPTER 28:

# TERRY'S ALL GOLD

Graeme Souness's skipper Terry Butcher talks teammates.

### Chris Woods

Simply the best! Fantastic guy – fantastic goalkeeper. He was my room-mate but unfortunately he had a shocking taste in music. He listened to Jason Donovan and Kylie! Please! He also offered to be my interpreter for Durranty, but he really couldn't understand a word he said either!

### Jimmy Nicholl

What a raconteur. Jimmy had a story for every event. A great character and terrific in the dressing room. Got about the park like a gazelle. A great teammate who was always there for you.

### Graham Roberts

We also played together with England. Quite the perfect partner. Graham was a warrior who loved the heat of the battle. He also loved Rangers and he was shattered when he had to leave the club.

# THE SIGNIFICANCE OF SOUNESS

## Stuart Munro

The quiet man. A lovely guy. He always had your back. He was Mr Dependable and consistently delivered real stability. He just did everything right. Graeme tried to replace him with a host of other left backs but Stuart just fought them off and had a terrific career at the club.

## Dave McPherson

Big Slim – what a guy. A thoroughbred the way he glided over the pitch. Another quiet unassuming guy until he got out to play the match when his whole demeanour changed and he tackled like a lion. He hit hard. Great versatility, too, that was such an asset to the squad.

## Graeme Souness

The gaffer! He had such a presence. He gave us all confidence and when he was in the side we felt unbeatable. Was as hard as nails in every which way. A wonderful motivator, and Rangers proved to be the perfect fit for his first steps in management. What a player – a Rolls-Royce. One of the finest these shores have produced.

## Robert Fleck

Partnered McCoist to great effect. Always a willing front man who would take it in even when he knew he was going to get clattered. He had the knack of making great runs in behind defences, and when I got the 'Winchester' out to deliver a 60- or 70-yard pass you just knew Robert would get on the end of it.

## Ally McCoist

Where do you start? He could score with any part of his body and he frequently did! A natural finisher. The poster boy and the housewives' choice. Off the park a master blaster, and when he and his sidekick Durrant were about anything could happen – on and off the pitch! Great company, and probably he and Durranty aged Graeme by years in his time trying to manage that pair.

## Ian Durrant

Tweedledum and Tweedledee – double trouble with Coisty. Nobody escaped Ian's banter, and if you come in any day with some dodgy clobber you can guarantee he was first to let you know. He called me Lofty as a term of affection (I think?). A genius of a player and one of the best young players I have ever seen. What character, too, to come back from the most horrific of injuries. Another whose company I love, but even after all these years I still have no idea what he's on about half the time!

## Davie Cooper

We called him Albert Tatlock after the old *Coronation Street* character who loved a moan. Coop soon let you know if you didn't pass it to him. He could have played in any side in the world and excelled. Davie loved the game and the game loved him. If you took up a position when Coop was on corners or free kicks you could guarantee he would find you with the perfect delivery. A superb entertainer who did so much to win us games. Strikers thrived on his service. Sadly, taken too soon. It was a genuine honour to have played with him.

## Colin West

Graeme's first signing, and he blazed the trail north for the rest of us. He was nicknamed Oscar but nobody knew why. If you wanted defenders roughed up a bit Colin was an expert in that side of the game. A big honest front man that didn't quite hit the heights at Rangers because of injury and the form of Fleck and McCoist.

## Derek Ferguson

The biggest compliment I can pay Fergie is that I signed him when I was manager at Sunderland. I loved him as a player. A player ahead of his time. So mature for a young guy. He was the straight man to Durranty and they were almost inseparable off the pitch – on a Monday morning in the dressing room it was like the *Tales of the Unexpected* as the boys told us what they had got up to over the weekend. He was quietly bonkers. I honestly think Graeme Souness saw a lot of himself in Derek and that maybe restricted the number of games he played at the time, but a quality operator.

## John Brown

I would have rather played alongside Bomber than play against him, that's for sure. I had never seen a player hyperventilate before a game before, but prior to just about every Old Firm game Bomber would be up to high doh and blowing into the brown paper bag to try and find some kind of calm. A leader and a standard setter. What a bargain signing he was for the club that he loves so much. John could be mad, measured and an animal but with fantastic technique, all evident within a three-minute spell. Fantastic to see him back at Rangers in an ambassadorial role. Not many are better equipped to represent the club in that way.

## Richard Gough

A true leader who was a nine or even ten out of ten just about every game. Graeme knew exactly what Goughie could do, hence he made such a determined effort to get him on board. Richard also demanded a hundred per cent from his teammates, not just in a match environment but every day in training too. Strong as an ox but he could play too. What a legend of Ibrox – 11 years at the club and a winner in everything he embraced.

## Scott Nisbet

Nizzy just wanted to do so well but often found himself on the wrong side of a tongue-lashing from Graeme. Maybe a victim of his own versatility as he would play anywhere he was asked to: up front, full back or centre back. A top guy with that strange Edinburgh sense of humour. Full of energy and could hold his own in the banter stakes.

## Ian Ferguson

Ian matured very quickly at Rangers. When he joined the club he was a non-drinker – we soon knocked that out of him. Another Rangers fan who lived the dream, and how! Had it all: tackle, shoot, score and he was one of many players of that time that was an absolute machine. Like Durrant I had no idea what he said when he spoke, I just nodded and gave him a knowing wink. To go on and be a nine-in-a-row hero means the world to Fergie, nobody deserves it more.

## Ray Wilkins

An absolute gent on and off the pitch. Ray was a really class operator who could turn a game on its head with a pass. What a signing he was for Rangers. Ray would sit quietly in the dressing room with his broadsheet newspaper sipping an espresso. Quality. He loved the banter and buzz, and while he didn't contribute much to it he sat back and soaked it all up. I miss Ray enormously – I loved playing with him just as much as I loved his company. Not many will have the career that Ray had, and despite Chelsea, Manchester United, PSG and AC Milan on his playing record he really cherished his time at Rangers.

He will never be forgotten.

## Mark Walters

What a brave guy. Came to Rangers and took all the flack but he had the courage and conviction to overcome it. Mark had a strong mentality and he was so focused for the team. He was rapid and sharp in everything he did. He also had very quick feet and could shuffle the ball from one to the other then leave defenders trailing in his wake. He created so many goals for others, he would be a phenomenon in the modern game. In his time at Rangers all the boys went out of their way to protect Mark from verbal and physical abuse he so often faced – he was one of us. Loved his cars, too, and if a new Porsche appeared in the car park you couldn't get a bet on that it was Mark's car.

## Trevor Francis

Came to Rangers late in his career but I knew Trevor from way back. We were international teammates, too, but I was in direct opposition to him on his debut for Nottingham Forest after his £1m move – the first seven-figure transfer in British football. As I took to the field in my Ipswich kit I wished Trevor all the best and then advised him that if he went past me I'd break his legs. I didn't really mean it, but Trevor didn't take the chance just in case! He will be forever remembered by Rangers fans for the coolest penalty in the 1987 League Cup Final shoot-out. Typical Trevor, never flustered and an absolute perfectionist.

## Gary Stevens

This man had three lungs! What an athlete. Could run for fun and if there had been no gates at Ibrox he would have run right out the stadium. At pre-season Gary set the pace and we were all expected to follow it, or try to match it, but Gary was miles ahead, so far ahead in fact that it was practically impossible to get near him. It was in the days prior to computer tracking of player runs, but he would have blown the system up. In a match he had incredible speed of recovery, too, if a team counter-attacked us. Another quiet guy but he was a top teammate.

## Ally Dawson

Special mention for a special fellow. Ally did so much to educate me on all things Rangers. We struck it off together immediately. A gentleman and a very capable player, who if I am correct was Rangers' youngest-ever captain. Ally was my centre-back partner in the 1986 League Cup Final. Special memories, as it was our first trophy under Graeme Souness. Ally is another that is no longer with us and he's a huge loss to his own and the Rangers family.

# THE SIGNIFICANCE OF SOUNESS

*Not many soft centres in this box of goodies but there are a few nutty ones in there as well.*

*It was a joy to play alongside all these guys and working with them every day has left me with memories that will last a lifetime.*

Terry Butcher
6 August 2025

# CHAPTER 29:
# THE PLAYERS, 1989-90

| PLAYER | APPEARANCES | GOALS |
|---|---|---|
| CHRIS WOODS | 37 | |
| BONNI GINZBURG | 8 | |
| TERRY BUTCHER | 43 | |
| JOHN BROWN | 30 | 2 |
| RICHARD GOUGH | 31 | 0 |
| STUART MUNRO | 45 | 1 |
| CHRIS VINNICOMBE | 9 | |
| SCOTT NISBET | 9 | |
| NEALE COOPER | 3 | |
| TOM COWAN | 4 | |
| GARY STEVENS | 44 | 1 |
| IAN FERGUSON | 32 | 2 |
| TREVOR STEVEN | 43 | 3 |
| DEREK FERGUSON | 8 | |

| | | |
|---|---|---|
| SANDY ROBERTSON | 1 | |
| GRAEME SOUNESS | 1 | |
| NIGEL SPACKMAN | 23 | 1 |
| IAN McCALL | 5 | |
| RAY WILKINS | 22 | |
| MARK WALTERS | 36 | 12 |
| KEVIN DRINKELL | 7 | |
| MAURICE JOHNSTON | 45 | 17 |
| DAVIE DODDS | 15 | 4 |
| ALLY McCOIST | 40 | 18 |

Rangers played a total of 48 competitive matches during the 1989–90 season.

The title was won; Aberdeen were runners-up.

Chris Woods and Gary Stevens both finished with 48 appearances – the most in the squad.

Ally McCoist was top scorer with 18 goals.

# CHAPTER 30:
# SQUAD CHANGES, 1990-91

Despite the signing of Maurice Johnston in July 1989, a year later Graeme Souness was still not completely satisfied by the goal threat and striking options in his squad, even after being crowned champions for consecutive seasons. Leaving aside the war years and a run of six Southern League titles in six seasons, Rangers were going for their first major three-in-a-row since 1935.

Andy Gray and Kevin Drinkell had been moved on to clear the way to sign long-term target Mark Hateley from AS Monaco. Hateley was the number-one target, but with Davie Cooper away, Rangers went Dutch to sign winger Pieter Huistra from FC Twente. Souness himself decided it was time to hang up his boots and saw the signing of Terry Hurlock from Millwall as a potential midfield enforcer in his own image. It took £1m to secure Mark Hateley, while Huistra and Hurlock both cost £300,000 each.

Mark Hateley had an impressive CV, with rich European experience from his time in French football and in Italy with AC Milan. His development at Coventry and then Portsmouth saw a rapid rise to fame confirmed by his first cap for England in 1984 aged 22. In his second appearance for his country just days after his debut, he scored in the Maracanã Stadium in a memorable 2–0 win for England against Brazil. He was signed by Arsène Wenger for Monaco – in fact Mark was his first signing for the club.

Pieter Huistra missed the 1990 World Cup with the Netherlands because of injury but he hit the ground running at Ibrox with his direct style and ability to stretch defences from a wide left position. Hurlock was no youngster when he joined Rangers and his signing was quite a surprise, as before the Light Blues he had been with Brentford and Reading before joining Millwall in 1987. Rangers would be quite a step up for the long-haired Londoner but he wasn't short on character, personality or confidence.

A real eye-opener was the signing of Oleg Kuznetsov, but while the deal was finalised in the summer the USSR World Cup star couldn't join up at Ibrox until the end of the Soviet season in November. Rangers fans did get a look at the flame-haired all-action central defender before that, though, as Rangers hosted Dynamo Kiev at Ibrox in a pre-season challenge match. Kuznetsov ran the show and comfortably won the match 3–1, with John Brown scoring Rangers' consolation goal. There was one other significant signing as they headed into early 1991: Brian Reid, another defender, was snapped up from Morton. The significance? Reid turned out to be Graeme Souness's last signing for Rangers. There was one other significant signing that year, Nigel Spackman for Queens Park Rangers.

On the field Rangers also hosted Manchester United in preparation of their title defence but again it was a loss. United triumphed 1–0 at a rain-drenched Ibrox. To be fair to

# SQUAD CHANGES, 1990–91

United their own pre-season programme was well advanced with their win against Rangers meaning they were unbeaten in seven games. In the summer Derek Ferguson had joined Hearts for a fee of £750,000, and before the turn of the year Terry Butcher would also depart the club in controversial circumstances.

Graeme Souness wasn't one to let reputations or relationships stand in his way as every decision was about making Rangers better.

When the real stuff started, we got a glimpse of what Mark Hateley had to offer, as he scored Rangers' first goal of the league campaign with the opener in a 3–1 home win over Dunfermline Athletic. Mark had such terrific experiences with Milan and Monaco but the persistence from Graeme Souness finally paid off after a chase of nearly three years when he persuaded Mark to join him at Ibrox. Mark says:

'I knew Graeme well and I could see what he was doing at Rangers. We were still pals but the family were settled in Monaco. I had a chat to Arsène Wenger and he wanted me to stay but I felt perhaps with a new start and putting injuries behind me I might get back to really enjoying my football. I knew I was facing a massive reduction in income, and paying tax, but I missed the British dressing-room culture. The banter and mentality. The pace of the game in Britain was also faster than on the continent and for strikers you would get so many more chances compared to France or Italy where genuine scoring chances were pretty much limited. After a chat with the family, I instructed my agent Dennis Roach to get the deal done. Rangers had good players coming in and he [Souness] set standards that he expected to be met – if they weren't

## THE SIGNIFICANCE OF SOUNESS

you wouldn't be there. It was interesting times at Rangers with Graeme's a reflection of his own personality. We had a fantastic dressing room with big personalities too. I was often asked about the team that drinks together winning together. Sure, our boys liked a night out but it was done when the time was right then it would be parked and time to reset. Graeme just said, "Stay off the front pages!"'

Mark probably never considered that by the end of the season Graeme Souness would leave for Liverpool.

## CHAPTER 31:

# SEASON FIVE, 1990-91

The big signings kept coming, with no geographical barriers to the sourcing of the latest recruits. Players from French football, the Netherlands, Russia and closer to home and again south of the border added to the cosmopolitan nature of the squad. The biggest change was Graeme Souness himself hanging up his boots to concentrate purely on managing. With this in consideration, it was quite a surprise when Souness accepted a bid from Hearts for Derek Ferguson who could easily have been Graeme's midfield successor. The Tynecastle club paid £750,000 for Derek and perhaps it was perceived as an offer the club couldn't refuse for a young player they had developed since he joined Rangers straight from school.

Terry Butcher also moved on to become player–manager at Coventry City. Rangers had lost 2–1 away at Dundee United in September and Graeme Souness was openly critical of Butcher and blamed him for both United goals. Four days later Terry Butcher was left out of the squad to play Aberdeen in the League Cup semi-final at Hampden. It was a bold decision by Souness and one that signalled the end for Terry Butcher at Rangers. Butcher had been a sensational signing for Souness

## THE SIGNIFICANCE OF SOUNESS

but the Rangers manager was again showing how ruthless he could be in his quest for trophies. He didn't look back, only forwards, and was always intent on improving his squad. Some may say Terry hadn't been the same player since coming back from a leg break, but Souness showed no compassion. It was the end of an era.

As it was, Rangers progressed to the League Cup Final with Trevor Steven scoring the only goal of the game. This set up a return to Hampden to take on Celtic in the final. It took extra-time to determine a winner with Rangers prevailing through goals from Richard Gough and Mark Walters. Celtic got revenge in the Scottish Cup with a 2–0 victory and the hoodoo continued for Graeme Souness in Scotland's foremost cup tournament. In the European Cup, a 10–0 aggregate score saw off Valletta of Malta; but in the next round Red Star Belgrade were too strong for Rangers, winning 3–0 at home and leaving Ibrox with a 1–1 draw in the return leg. Red Star were a top side and went on to become European Cup winners that year, beating Marseille in the final.

To the Premier Division, and Rangers were again slow starters with wins against Dunfermline and Hearts but had to settle for draws against Hibernian and Celtic. As autumn turned into winter Rangers hit their stride and put a winning run together. In the New Year Old Firm fixture, Celtic were first foots to Ibrox but it was Rangers who were celebrating with a comfortable 2–0 win – Walters and Hateley were the scorers.

Life was good for the Rangers faithful but little did they think that 1991 would see Graeme Souness leave the club, especially with the most bizarre sense of timing, as their third league title

# SEASON FIVE, 1990–91

in a row was very much a potential reality with Aberdeen their biggest rivals for the trophy.

Souness left for Liverpool with four games left in the league campaign. Speculation was rife as to who would replace him but the players were adamant that there really was only one man for the job and that was Walter Smith. A number of senior players approached chairman David Murray and made their thoughts known. David Murray agreed and Walter Smith was installed as Rangers' new manager. Walter brought in his good friend Archie Knox from Manchester United as his assistant, but in his first game Rangers lost 3–0 away at Motherwell. This set up a winner-takes-all last-day shoot-out at Ibrox against title favourites Aberdeen. Step forwards Mark Hateley whose two goals on the day confirmed Rangers as champions.

Graeme Souness may have gone but he had masterminded a huge part of the league success, even though it was Walter Smith who got it over the line.

# CHAPTER 32:

# DEPARTURE AND LAST-DAY DRAMA

### 16 April 1991

While Graeme Souness had arrived at Rangers quite unexpectedly, his departure five years later was equally a bolt from the blue when he confirmed he wanted to return to Liverpool to replace his good friend and former teammate Kenny Dalglish.

The timing was odd to say the least. Rangers were still in contention for the league title and had only four games left to play. Another championship would have put Rangers on a run of three in a row.

Kenny Dalglish had resigned as Liverpool manager in February despite having won three league titles and two FA Cups in his previous five seasons in charge. Liverpool too were in contention for both these trophies again when he resigned. Souness had been tipped as favourite to replace Dalglish but he constantly played it down when asked if that's where his future lay. Ronnie Moran had been given temporary charge of Liverpool while the board looked for Kenny's successor.

By this time Graeme Souness was not just Rangers' manager but a director too, and had been the main influence in David Murray acquiring the club. Souness himself had

## DEPARTURE AND LAST-DAY DRAMA

committed £500,000 to support the buy-out from Lawrence Marlborough. Playing was no longer part of Graeme's role at Ibrox, having hung up his boots after Rangers' last home game of the previous season against Dunfermline. Rangers had a comfortable 2–0 win against the Pars that night but the players had hatched a plan not to pass the ball to the gaffer when he came off the bench with 20 minutes remaining in what would be his swansong. It was all done in a jocular manner but the longer it went on the more frustrated Souness was that he wasn't getting a look in. When the penny dropped, he took it in good part and found the funny side of it too. Now a year on he wasn't just giving up playing for Rangers he was leaving to take on another challenge.

When Graeme told David Murray that he would like to leave at the end of the season to take up the position at Anfield, Murray showed he had a ruthless streak the equal of his outgoing manager when he refused Graeme's request and invited him to leave the club immediately, although a press conference was hastily arranged to let Souness explain his decision for himself. Rangers had a title to win and David Murray was intent on ensuring that would happen, with or without Graeme Souness.

The lure of Liverpool appeared too strong for Souness to resist but the timing could not have been worse. Only a matter of days before the shock news, Rangers had beaten St Johnstone 3–0 at Ibrox to maintain their title challenge. Midfielder Ian Ferguson remembers how the Ibrox dressing room and the fans reacted to Souness moving on:

'We were all stunned and the fans were shocked too. Here we were on the brink of another title and Graeme was heading out the door and could possibly destabilise everything. The chairman was decisive too in as much that if Graeme didn't want to be here he knew a man that did, and that was Walter. It wasn't a gimme, though, that Walter was getting the gig. We were at him immediately for the inside track but he would give nothing away. There was next to nothing in it between ourselves and Aberdeen but we were weighed down by a huge injury list going into those last few games. We were all sorry to see Graeme go, he had been wonderful for the club and I will always be grateful for him making me a Ranger and making me a better player. But players are resilient, they just want to play, and we all had our eyes on another prize. We did, however, hope that the job would go to Walter Smith. The dressing room was unanimous on that shout.'

Tommy Cowan was signed by Graeme Souness for Rangers, and the former Clyde full back was taken aback that he was losing his mentor: 'Graeme Souness moving on was a shock to the system. He signed me, he made me a better player, although occasionally he would test you and throw you in at the weirdest times, like Bayern Munich away, when he played me on the left wing. No inclination, no warning – just named the team and I was in it. Walter was the right call to replace him – it was pretty seamless.'

With hindsight perhaps there was more to Souness leaving than just his attachment to Liverpool. Graeme's run-ins with the football authorities in Scotland were getting more regular and his conflict with officialdom often led to confrontation. Some post-match interview content didn't sit well with the Scottish Football Association and their counterparts at the Scottish League. These breaches of rules in his guise as

## DEPARTURE AND LAST-DAY DRAMA

a manager, as the authorities classed them, led to touchline bans that Souness failed to respect by naming himself as a substitute to circumvent the rules and still give him access to the dugout in his playing kit. That didn't go down well with the rulers of the Scottish game. In May 1990, Souness was hit with an SFA fine to the value of £5,000 for being in the Ibrox tunnel while banned, but to frustrate him even more, it was only television evidence that the SFA used to convict him.

Frustration also got the better of Souness in 1991 when he had a confrontation with St Johnstone's tea lady Aggie Moffat. Aggie wasn't happy that the Rangers players had left mud in the McDiarmid Park dressing room, and on the next visit when some china had been broken Aggie went hunting for Souness to voice her displeasure. Graeme didn't take kindly to her confrontation. A storm in a teacup, perhaps; but it may have been the final straw for Graeme Souness.

Mark Hateley wasn't overly surprised when Graeme accepted the Liverpool opportunity: 'It had been mentioned for weeks and speculation was rife that Graeme wanted to be the man to replace Kenny. Nothing ever surprises me in football, even when Graeme left with four games left to play. The chairman David Murray was decisive; and after counselling the senior players, Walter was the only man for the job. On the park, we got the job done but you wonder what might have happened had we lost to Aberdeen on that last day and lost the league. Walter may not have had the Rangers managerial career that he did.'

On Graeme departing, Rangers chairman David Murray publicly claimed Graeme Souness was making the greatest mistake of his life.

# THE SIGNIFICANCE OF SOUNESS

Rangers would move on, and David Murray wasted no time in installing Walter Smith as his new manager. Walter's appointment was fully endorsed by Graeme Souness who knew better than anyone just how ready Walter was for the step up.

Walter got straight down to business and raided Old Trafford to have Archie Knox swap his position as assistant manager at Manchester United for the same role at Ibrox. It really was a remarkable period. Liverpool were in a bit of disarray when they handed Graeme Souness a five-year contract, and by the time he took office their trophy hopes for the season were all but drifting away. At Ibrox it was a baptism of fire for Walter Smith and his new assistant Archie Knox – they had four games to become champions. Spare a thought, too, for Alex Ferguson at Manchester United – in the week that Archie Knox joined up at Rangers, Manchester United were playing Barcelona in Rotterdam in the European Cup Winners' Cup Final. As it was, United still took the honours with a 2–1 win, and former Barca man Mark Hughes scored both goals.

For Archie Knox there was no immediate success, and a bit of a scare, as Rangers lost 3–0 away at Motherwell, meaning the title would be decided on the last day of the season against Aberdeen who were now favourites to become champions. We can only wonder what was going through Graeme Souness's mind as this drama was unfolding.

Aberdeen now only needed one point from their visit to Ibrox to take the crown.

A favourite in the Dons ranks was local lad, David Robertson. Robertson epitomised the changing role of full backs in modern football. Pace was a crucial part of his game and the Aberdeen youngster had it in droves. Robertson was a very capable defender and when going forwards was very creative, almost like an old-fashioned winger. It was no surprise that Graeme Souness reportedly had him in his sights to make him a Ranger. In fact Rangers had been tracking his progress since his early days with Deeside Boys Club.

Robertson was given his Dons debut under Alex Ferguson as a 17-year-old, so he was a player Archie Knox also knew very well, and despite his lack of experience he performed with a level of consistency and maturity that belied his tender years. Even when Ferguson moved on in 1986, to take on the job of transforming the sleeping giant that was Manchester United, his successor Ian Porterfield, who had been appointed in the November of that year, recognised he had a prized talent on his hands. Robertson won both the Scottish Cup and the League Cup with the Pittodrie club but this trophy haul would be hugely eclipsed by his success when he eventually joined Rangers. The twist in the tail is that David wasn't signed by Graeme Souness but was taken to Ibrox by Walter Smith – a fee of £970k saw the move go through in 1991. Now this is the interesting fact . . . Robertson and his representatives had struck a bargain with Graeme Souness and Walter Smith before Graeme left for Liverpool. In fact, it was a real hush-hush cloak-and-dagger move by all parties, as Aberdeen were on target to win the league with Rangers in their wake going into the final rounds of fixtures in the Scottish Premier Division.

On the way to training with his Aberdeen teammates on 16 April 1991, the team minibus radio burst into life with breaking news. The news was that Graeme Souness had left

## THE SIGNIFICANCE OF SOUNESS

his role at Rangers to take up the vacant manager's position at Liverpool. The Aberdeen players were overjoyed with the news with one exception. Guys like Alex McLeish (who would later manage Rangers to terrific success), Brian Irvine and Stewart McKimmie were hammering on the roof of the minibus and chanting in delight, buoyant and full of belief that they would now be champions with Rangers facing this Souness setback, especially as the teams were scheduled to meet at Ibrox a few weeks later. The one man who kept his own counsel and didn't react to what was going on around him was David Robertson. Why? Well, Robertson, whose representatives had been in regular communication with Souness and his assistant Walter Smith, had agreed a package to move to Rangers in the summer. David could only imagine his dream move would now be a non-starter with Souness moving on.

As it was, Walter Smith honoured the unwritten agreement to sign David for Rangers at the start of his first full season in charge. It left Robertson very relieved, although he had been denied a league winner's medal on his last appearance for Aberdeen. As things transpired, the Dons arrived at Ibrox on the last day of the campaign needing only one point to lift the title. However, Mark Hateley, in particular, had other ideas. Rangers were struggling with a serious injury list with captain Richard Gough missing, while John Brown was taking injections to negate a troublesome Achilles injury. Despite being nowhere near fit Ally McCoist and Ian Durrant took their places on the bench just to make up the numbers.

Aberdeen had a full squad to pick from, with the exception of experienced defender Brian Irvine.

Rangers midfielder Ian Ferguson remembers the day with

great fondness: 'I knew we would win. From the minute I woke up and to taking to the field for our warm-up, I knew we would win. We wanted to do it for Walter and I suppose for Graeme, too, who had signed so many of the team that played that day. Aberdeen were nervous favourites – we got to them, the crowd got to them and we got a comfortable win despite the injuries, which got worse throughout the game with Mark Walters struggling with a hamstring and Tommy Cowan playing to the 20-minute mark despite, miraculously, what proved to be a broken bone in his leg (which occurred in a clash with Hans Gillhaus only ten minutes into the game). We were champions – the first for Walter – but I will always be grateful to Graeme Souness for his determination to sign me and give me the chance to play for my boyhood team.'

It was an emotional day, too, for Tommy Cowan, who started the match but lasted just over 20 minutes: 'I got caught by Hans Gillhaus and it was later confirmed I had fractured my shin. I wanted to play on but it was impossible. As I was being stretchered back to the dressing room, TV commentator Jock Brown said it was a "tactical change" from Walter Smith. I was in agony but I managed a laugh when I was told that one. The drive and determination in that squad was unbelievable, epitomised by John "Bomber" Brown – he would have run through brick walls for the club and he pretty much made sure everyone else would have too. Despite the injury, I got a pair of crutches and got on the pitch at full-time – there was no way I was missing the celebrations!'

The game finished 2–0 to Rangers with Hateley scoring both, and Walter Smith had captured his first title of what would go on to be nine in a row.

## THE SIGNIFICANCE OF SOUNESS

Of course Souness had played his part but it was Walter Smith who got it over the line. It was as dramatic a finish to a league season as anyone could have imagined.

It was a bittersweet day for David Robertson, playing the full 90 minutes for Aberdeen as they came so close, but his sadness was tempered by the fact he knew he would be a big part of Walter Smith's plans for the following season.

As it was, David Robertson – who thought his Rangers dream was over before it began – went on and won the league with Rangers for six successive seasons after signing, before moving south to join Leeds United.

David will always be grateful to Walter Smith for his opportunity to be a Ranger but it's fair to say he was more than anxious when Graeme Souness left before his move could be finalised.

# CHAPTER 33:
# THE PLAYERS, 1990-91

| PLAYER | APPEARANCES | GOALS |
|---|---|---|
| CHRIS WOODS | 48 | |
| BRIAN REID | 3 | |
| TERRY BUTCHER | 9 | 1 |
| OLEG KUZNETSOV | 2 | |
| JOHN BROWN | 36 | 1 |
| RICHARD GOUGH | 37 | 1 |
| STUART MUNRO | 21 | |
| CHRIS VINNICOMBE | 11 | |
| SCOTT NISBET | 19 | 1 |
| TERRY HURLOCK | 35 | 2 |
| TOM COWAN | 7 | |
| GARY STEVENS | 48 | 4 |
| IAN FERGUSON | 15 | 1 |
| PETER HUISTRA | 36 | 5 |

## THE SIGNIFICANCE OF SOUNESS

| IAN DURRANT | 4 | 1 |
| SANDY ROBERTSON | 18 | 1 |
| GARY McSWEGAN | 3 | |
| NIGEL SPACKMAN | 45 | 1 |
| TREVOR STEVEN | 31 | 5 |
| JOHN SPENCER | 6 | 2 |
| MARK WALTERS | 39 | 15 |
| MARK HATELEY | 42 | 15 |
| MAURICE JOHNSTON | 39 | 19 |
| DAVIE DODDS | 6 | 1 |
| ALLY McCOIST | 36 | 18 |

Rangers played a total of 48 competitive matches in the 1990–91 season.

Rangers won the title; Aberdeen were runners-up.

Chris Woods and Gary Stevens both finished with 48 appearances – the most in the squad.

Maurice Johnston was top scorer with 19 goals.

# CHAPTER 34:

# THE REVOLVING DOOR – THE TRANSFERS

Graeme Souness was never fully satisfied with the squad at his disposal. He was always striving to be better, stronger, more competitive – and he always wanted to have winners around him. He had some quite terrific backing from the board, too, firstly with David Holmes and latterly with David Murray. Not every transfer worked out but his strategy was decisive, and if a player wasn't delivering to expectation he was soon shipped out.

The fact of the transfer market from a Rangers perspective was that they had to get as many right first time as possible, as mistakes would prove costly and it would also be evident when trying to move players on that Scotland was a very shallow market. And as players were made available for transfer, England would be the likely destination for most who found themselves surplus to requirements under Graeme Souness.

Two extreme examples of how Souness operated in the transfer market could be the Rangers careers of Mark Falco and Ian Ferguson. Both were highly gifted and technical operators. Falco arrived in 1987 from Watford and scored 10 goals in

19 competitive appearances. By December of the same year he was on his way to Queens Park Rangers and the Light Blues banked a £70,000 profit along the way. Ian Ferguson joined after scoring the only goal of the 1987 Cup Final for St Mirren against Dundee United. It was a bit of a protracted transfer for Fergie, who was a true Rangers fan, but his Paisley bosses weren't keen to let him join their rivals.

Souness was determined, though, and parted with £850,000 for his signature – a fee that remains a record for a St Mirren transfer.

Ian Ferguson became an Ibrox icon, winning every title in the nine-in-a-row era, with Richard Gough and Ally McCoist the only other players to achieve this, and he was rewarded with a testimonial against Sunderland in 1999 before moving on to Dunfermline after 12 years at Ibrox and nearly 350 appearances.

From Graeme Souness taking office in April 1986, to leaving for Liverpool in 1991, only four players were still at the club from before his arrival: Ally McCoist, Ian Durrant, Scott Nisbet and Stuart Munro. All overcame adversities to prolong their Rangers careers. It was suggested Nisbet had the *Rothmans Book of Football* launched at him on more than one occasion by his manager and told to go and pick himself a new club. Durrant had that horrible knee injury to overcome. The position of left back was one Souness signed a number of players to displace Stuart Munro, but the former Alloa man saw them all off. McCoist, the top scorer in the history of Rangers Football Club, had been given the nickname 'the Judge' by his teammates as he spent so much time on the bench while Souness was in charge. He had the character to overcome it. In fact, all the boys above did.

# THE REVOLVING DOOR – THE TRANSFERS

Here is a list of player movements, in and out as signed or sold by Souness. There are one or two who may have thought it was a bit of a revolving door at the entrance to Ibrox.

When you analyse the names and numbers of players who arrived at Ibrox while Graeme Souness was boss, it's remarkable that he and his assistant Walter Smith had time to prepare players for matches and then deliver results with such consistency. Factor in the time both Graeme and Walter will have spent travelling the length and breadth of Britain and beyond to scout potential signings, and the hundreds of games they will have taken in over the years, their commitment to the job was much greater than any regular nine-to-five employment. It was a hundred per cent full on, a hundred per cent of the time. The trophy rewards over the years are testimony to the hours and commitment the Rangers management team gave to the club. Every signing was about improving the team on the park. Some they got right, some didn't meet expectations, but no matter what any squad achieved in any season, standing still and resting on previous laurels certainly didn't happen, not on Graeme Souness's watch.

## Transfers In

MAY, 1986
Colin West: signed from Watford (£200,000), 16 May

JULY, 1986
Chris Woods: signed from Norwich City (£600,000), 1 July

AUGUST, 1986
Terry Butcher: signed from Ipswich Town (£725,000),

# THE SIGNIFICANCE OF SOUNESS

1 August
Jimmy Nicholl: signed from West Bromwich Albion (part-exchange), 8 August

NOVEMBER, 1986
Lindsay Hamilton: signed from Stenhousemuir (£25,000), 14 November

DECEMBER, 1986
Neil Woods: signed from Doncaster Rovers (£120,000), 22 December
Graham Roberts: signed from Tottenham Hotspur (£450,000), 23 December

MARCH, 1987
Davie Kirkwood: signed from East Fife (£50,000), 19 March
Jimmy Phillips: signed from Bolton Wanderers (£95,000), 27 March

MAY, 1987
Avi Cohen: signed from Maccabi Tel Aviv (£100,000), 17 May
John McGregor: signed from Liverpool (free), 24 May

JULY, 1987
Mark Falco: signed from Watford (£400,000), 14 July

AUGUST, 1987
Trevor Francis: signed from Atalanta (£75,000), 6 August
Ian McCall: signed from Dunfermline Athletic (£200,000), 28 August

# THE REVOLVING DOOR – THE TRANSFERS

OCTOBER, 1987
Richard Gough: signed from Tottenham Hotspur (£1,500,000), 2 October

NOVEMBER, 1987
Ray Wilkins: signed from Paris Saint-Germain (£250,000), 28 November

DECEMBER, 1987
Mark Walters: signed from Aston Villa (£500,000), 31 December

JANUARY, 1988
John Brown: signed from Dundee (£350,000), 14 January
Jan Bartram: signed from Silkeborg IF (£180,000), 15 January

FEBRUARY, 1988
Ian Ferguson: signed from St Mirren (£850,000), 15 February

JUNE, 1988
Kevin Drinkell: signed from Norwich City (£500,000), 30 June

JULY, 1988
Gary Stevens: signed from Everton (£1,000,000), 19 July

SEPTEMBER, 1988
Andy Gray: signed from West Bromwich Albion (Free), 17 September

# THE SIGNIFICANCE OF SOUNESS

OCTOBER, 1988
Neale Cooper: signed from Aston Villa (£250,000), 3 October

NOVEMBER, 1988
Kevin MacDonald: on loan from Liverpool, 25 November

FEBRUARY, 1989
Tom Cowan: signed from Clyde (£100,000), 6 February

MARCH, 1989
Mel Sterland: signed from Sheffield Wednesday (£750,000), 4 March

JULY, 1989
Trevor Steven: signed from Everton (£1,525,000), 1 July
Maurice Johnston: signed from FC Nantes (£1,500,000), 10 July

AUGUST, 1989
Boni Ginzburg: signed from Maccabi Haifa (£200,000), 15 August
Davie Dodds: signed from Aberdeen (£100,000), 30 August

NOVEMBER, 1989
Chris Vinnicombe: signed from Exeter City (£150,000), 3 November
Nigel Spackman: signed from Queens Park Rangers (£500,000), 30 November

JUNE, 1990
Mark Hateley: signed from AS Monaco (£1,000,000), 21 June

AUGUST, 1990
Pieter Huistra: signed from FC Twente (£300,000), 2 August
Terry Hurlock: signed from Millwall (£300,000), 23 August

OCTOBER, 1990
Oleg Kuznetsov: signed from Dynamo Kiev (£1,400,000), 9 October

MARCH, 1991
Brian Reid: signed from Morton (£300,000), 25 March

## Transfers Out
MAY, 1986
Derek Johnstone: free transfer (joined Partick Thistle), 9 May
Dave MacKinnon: free transfer (joined Airdrieonians), 9 May
Eric Ferguson: free transfer (joined Dunfermline Athletic), 9 May
Billy Davies: free transfer (joined Jönköpings Södra IF), 9 May
Andy Bruce: free transfer (joined Heart of Midlothian), 9 May

AUGUST, 1986
Bobby Williamson: transferred to West Bromwich Albion (part-exchange), 9 August
Iain Ferguson: transferred to Dundee United (£150,000), 22 August

NOVEMBER, 1986
Colin Miller: free transfer to Doncaster Rovers
Stuart Beattie: free transfer to Doncaster Rovers
John MacDonald: free transfer to Barnsley, 29 November (debut for Barnsley)

DECEMBER, 1986
Dougie Bell: transferred to Hibernian, 3 January (debut for Hibernian)
Craig Paterson: transferred to Motherwell, 1 January (debut for Motherwell)

JANUARY, 1987
Ted McMinn: transferred to Sevilla FC (£225,000), 19 January

MAY, 1987
Cammy Fraser: retired (eventually came out of retirement)
Ronnie Yule: free transfer (joined Hamilton Academical)

JULY, 1987
Dave McPherson: transferred to Heart of Midlothian (£325,000), 8 July
Hugh Burns: transferred to Heart of Midlothian (£75,000), 8 July
Bobby Russell: free transfer (joined Motherwell), 8 July
Neil Woods: transferred to Ipswich Town (£120,000), 27 July

AUGUST, 1987
Ally Dawson: transferred to Blackburn Rovers (£50,000), 11 August

# THE REVOLVING DOOR – THE TRANSFERS

**SEPTEMBER, 1987**
Colin West: transferred to Sheffield Wednesday (£150,000),
3 September

**DECEMBER, 1987**
Mark Falco: transferred to Queens Park Rangers (£375,000),
4 December
Robert Fleck: transferred to Norwich City (£580,000),
16 December

**MARCH, 1988**
Trevor Francis: free transfer (joined Queens Park Rangers),
23 March

**MAY, 1988**
Avi Cohen: free transfer (joined Maccabi Tel Aviv), 31 May

**JULY, 1988**
Jan Bartram: transferred to Brøndby IF (£300,000), 1 July

**AUGUST, 1988**
Graham Roberts: transferred to Chelsea (£475,000), 26 August
Jimmy Phillips: transferred to Oxford United (£100,000),
26 August

**OCTOBER, 1988**
Dave MacFarlane: transferred to Kilmarnock

## THE SIGNIFICANCE OF SOUNESS

DECEMBER, 1988
Kevin MacDonald: loan return to Liverpool, 22 December

MAY, 1989
Andy Gray: free transfer (joined Cheltenham Town), 26 May

JULY, 1989
Mel Sterland: transferred to Leeds United (£600,000), 5 July
Jimmy Nicholl: transferred to Dunfermline Athletic (£50,000), 26 July
Davie Kirkwood: transferred to Heart of Midlothian (£100,000), 29 July

AUGUST, 1989
Davie Cooper: transferred to Motherwell (£50,000), 11 August
Nicky Walker: transferred to Heart of Midlothian (£125,000), 22 August

OCTOBER, 1989
Kevin Drinkell: transferred to Coventry City (£800,000), 2 October

NOVEMBER, 1989
Ray Wilkins: free transfer (joined Queens Park Rangers), 28 November

JANUARY, 1990
Ian McCall: transferred to Bradford City (£200,000), 10 January

THE REVOLVING DOOR – THE TRANSFERS

JUNE, 1990
Lindsay Hamilton: transferred to St Johnstone

JULY, 1990
Derek Ferguson: transferred to Heart of Midlothian (£750,000), 4 July

NOVEMBER, 1990
Terry Butcher: transferred to Coventry City (£500,000), 15 November

## Debuts
**9 August 1986:** Hibernian 2 Rangers 1 – Chris Woods, Graeme Souness, Terry Butcher, Colin West
**13 August 1986:** Rangers 1 Falkirk 0 – Jimmy Nicholl (first game of second spell)
**27 December 1986:** Rangers 2 Dundee United 0 – Graham Roberts
**17 January 1987:** Rangers 2 Hamilton Academical 0 – Neil Woods
**4 April 1987:** Celtic 3 Rangers 1 – Jimmy Phillips
**9 May 1987:** Rangers 1 St Mirren 0 – Davie Kirkwood
**8 August 1987:** Rangers 1 Dundee United 1 – John McGregor, Avi Cohen, Mark Falco
**29 August 1987:** Celtic 1 Rangers 0 – Ian McCall
**12 September 1987:** Rangers 4 Dunfermline Athletic 0 – Trevor Francis
**10 October 1987:** Dundee United 1 Rangers 0 – Richard Gough
**28 November 1987:** Rangers 3 Heart of Midlothian 2 – Ray Wilkins

**2 January 1988:** Celtic 2 Rangers 0 – Mark Walters
**16 January 1988:** Heart of Midlothian 1 Rangers 1 – John Brown
**23 January 1988:** Rangers 3 Falkirk 1 – Jan Bartram
**27 February 1988:** Dundee United 1 Rangers 1 – Ian Ferguson
**16 April 1988:** Rangers 1 Hibernian 1 – Gary McSwegan
**13 August 1988:** Hamilton Academical 0 Rangers 2 – Gary Stevens, Kevin Drinkell
**21 September 1988:** Rangers 3 Heart of Midlothian 0 – Andy Gray
**8 October 1988:** Aberdeen 2 Rangers 1 – Neale Cooper
**26 November 1988:** Rangers 1 Aberdeen 0 – Kevin MacDonald
**11 March 1989:** Rangers 3 Hamilton Academical 0 – Tom Cowan, Mel Sterland
**6 May 1989:** Dundee 1 Rangers 2 – Sandy Robertson
**12 August 1989:** Rangers 0 St Mirren 1 – Trevor Steven, Maurice Johnston
**15 August 1989:** Rangers 4 Arbroath 0 – Boni Ginzburg
**30 September 1989:** Rangers 1 Heart of Midlothian 0 – Davie Dodds
**2 December 1989:** Heart of Midlothian 1 Rangers 2 – Nigel Spackman
**9 December 1989:** Rangers 3 Motherwell 0 – Chris Vinnicombe
**21 August 1990:** Rangers 5 East Stirlingshire 0 – Mark Hateley, Pieter Huistra
**28 August 1990:** Rangers 1 Kilmarnock 0 – Terry Hurlock
**2 October 1990:** Rangers 6 Valletta 0 – John Spencer
**13 October 1990:** Rangers 5 St Mirren 0 – Oleg Kuznetsov
**30 March 1991:** Dunfermline Athletic 0 Rangers 1 – Brian Reid

# THE REVOLVING DOOR – THE TRANSFERS

It was a huge turnover of players and John Brown was very aware of expectation: 'We knew exactly what was required and we knew if we didn't deliver we would be out the door. In my second season Graeme signed Oleg Kuznetsov. I was performing better than any other defender at the club and he called me in one Friday and said, "I'm going with Oleg tomorrow. I know you've been outstanding, Bomber, but I've signed this player who will play against St Mirren and you will be at Love Street with the reserves." John McGregor took the second team at that time – he was sympathetic to my situation and I assured him I would do my best, as I deep down wanted to show that I should still be playing in the first team. As it was, Oleg did his cruciate on his first game and I was straight back in. Had the big Ukrainian performed well and not got seriously injured it might have signalled the end for me. Graeme was ruthless that way and his track record in moving players on was there for all to see.'

Despite all these regular personnel changes the harmony in the squad was exceptional and they regularly got together for a midweek dinner and drinks together. Graeme Souness would be part of it too. John Brown again: 'The camaraderie was unique. We had so many characters and top players. At times the players took over training and Graeme was happy to go along with it. If we had a Wednesday off, we would head out to an Italian restaurant in Great Western Road after training on Tuesday. Sometimes we would take the place over and we could be there from lunchtime to closing time. Graeme would be part of it but he usually left before we got a bit boisterous and headed into the town to keep the party going.'

Ian Durrant chipped in: 'Derek [Ferguson] and I met the

gaffer in Palma [Majorca] one day, and he insisted we join him for a drink. It was just about the end of our holiday and we were kind of skint. He took us into a champagne bar that was right top-end, and beer was not their normal. Derek and I were scratching about our pockets to try and pull together enough of the old pesetas to buy a round. He could be good company but he knew when to draw the line between players and manager. We had been on it all day and were looking a bit of a mess while Souness was looking a million dollars. We had our beer and after the initial small talk he reminded us that next season was going to be a big year for us both and we had to pull our finger out. He managed to get us relaxed but he knew just how to get his message across, even in Spain in the close season!'

John Brown goes back to pre-season: 'We were in Il Ciocco and my daughter Lauren had just been born, and he [Graeme] picked up the tab for the champagne to toast the new baby. After the best part of a week working flat-out and being at altitude the bubbles went straight to our heads after just two glasses. I started spraying the drink around the room and a few more bottles were ordered before Graeme stepped in to send us all to our beds. He didn't mind a bit of leeway but you weren't allowed to ever take it too far.'

Maybe one exception was a trip to St Andrews. Bomber remembers one visit that was pretty epic: 'Normally you have to pay for any extras charged to your room and you were expected to settle up as you checked out. As we left the hotel Walter was standing with the bills. It was a classic sketch: Butcher and Wilkins, £600; Gough and Gary Stevens, £500; Brown and Ferguson, £250; Durrant and McCoist, £42.50!

## THE REVOLVING DOOR – THE TRANSFERS

What!? Next it was the bill for kitman George 'Doddy' Souter: £12,500! The bold lads – Coisty and Durranty – had been on the Bollinger and progressed to the Dom Pérignon then the Cristal, and had perfected Doddy's signature! Souness had already gone home to Edinburgh, so fortunately he wasn't around, but the boys made sure they settled the bill and the kitman wasn't out of pocket! Yes, as a squad we knew how to enjoy ourselves when the time was right and it was effective in the team bonding and helped integrate the regular new boys into the group. Happy days!'

## CHAPTER 35:

# THE LURE OF LIVERPOOL

All the way back to the days of Bill Shankly, Liverpool had a policy of promoting from within when a manager needed to be replaced. Bob Paisley, Joe Fagan and Kenny Dalglish were testimony to how that succession planning had benefitted the club.

Graeme Souness taking on the manager's position after Dalglish was quite a departure from Liverpool's previous recruitment process, but Souness had a stellar career at Anfield as a player and despite the passing of the years he was still revered by the Liverpool fans.

Before Graeme Souness accepted the invitation to replace Kenny Dalglish, he had advances from a third party operating on behalf of Liverpool to gauge whether he had any interest in swapping Ibrox for Anfield, where he had enjoyed incredible success on the park and had a very good relationship with the fans. Souness also enjoyed living in the city, where two of his children had indeed been born, but things at Ibrox were going well, even though outside influences, like the SFA extending his touchline ban and the intrusion into his private life by the press, were serious frustrations. The idea appealed to a degree, but with his financial investment in Rangers and a wonderful relationship with his chairman David Murray, the notion was dismissed and his focus remained on taking Rangers forwards.

As the end of the season got closer, and after the Aggie episode at St Johnstone, Graeme Souness began to believe that going back to Liverpool was probably the thing to do. Graeme wanted his Rangers back-room team of Walter Smith and Phil Boersma to join him in the challenge of reviving Liverpool, who had an aging squad and had been without a full-time manager for more than two months. However, when Dalglish left, Liverpool were still very much in contention for honours, including the league title and the FA Cup. Walter Smith debated the potential of joining Graeme at Liverpool but had concerns about displacing the existing Anfield back-room staff of Ronnie Moran and Roy Evans, both of whom were Liverpool to the core. Phil Boersma meanwhile was fully behind the idea and was keen to get back to the club he had served as a player from 1968 to 1975 when he left for Middlesbrough. Boersma was excited by the prospect while Walter decided it wasn't for him, in the hope that David Murray would position him as Graeme's successor. Before that could happen, David Murray had to be informed that he was losing Graeme. It was late March when Graeme sat down with Murray and told him of his plans. Murray immediately pulled out all the stops to keep his friend at Ibrox and even offered an improved long-term contract. It was a huge decision for Graeme Souness to leave Rangers, especially as they were on target for another league title.

On 16 April 1991, Graeme Souness was confirmed as

# THE SIGNIFICANCE OF SOUNESS

Liverpool's new manager on a lucrative five-year contract. Phil Boersma, who combined coaching with his physiotherapy skills and had an extraordinary working relationship with Souness, also left Rangers to continue to work with his friend. It felt like they were going home. With five league games remaining, Graeme Souness had a fine chance of retaining Liverpool's title, but Arsenal remained favourites, under another Scot, George Graham.

Three straight wins in April had kept the Reds in contention, before successive defeats to Chelsea and Nottingham Forest ended any hopes Graeme Souness had of a glory title-winning return to Liverpool. The season finished with a 2–0 home win over Tottenham Hotspur, and it was enough to see Liverpool finish second in the table to champions Arsenal. It was the tenth consecutive season where they had delivered a top-two finish. Now it was to be a summer of change.

The Liverpool directors had warned Graeme that the squad needed to be refreshed and in their opinion the dressing room lacked leaders. Team spirit was also much diluted compared to Souness's time as a player at the club. Under director Peter Robinson, Graeme was offered the responsibility for negotiating player contracts, and while it would prove to be useful as he went into the transfer market to bring his own players in, it also created problems, too, particularly with the existing team. Rejecting requests from senior players for more money, for instance, then trying to motivate them come a Saturday match day, led to some awkward confrontations.

Traditionally, Liverpool had the luxury of buying players and integrating them into the first team over time, often playing reserve-team football to ensure they fully understood the Anfield way – but this was different. Graeme Souness had to make some big decisions on who he brought to the club, and they had to be ready and capable of being launched straight into the first team and delivering results. There were some very talented youngsters in the squad Souness inherited but it's debatable if they were primed for the step up and could deliver the level of consistency the team needed. Graeme Souness had a fantastic record at Rangers for signing players who did just that, and now he was going to have to replicate it to have Liverpool challenging from the start of the new season. Club captain Alan Hansen, who had missed almost a year with injury, retired not long after Dalglish had resigned, while other senior players like Peter Beardsley and Gary Gillespie were facing a questionable future.

Souness's first foray into the summer transfer market saw him recruit his marquee signings: Mark Wright arrived with teammate Dean Saunders from Derby County. Saunders was Liverpool's record signing, with a transfer fee just short of £3m going to Derby for his services. Souness went back to raid Ibrox for Mark Walters despite his middle name being Everton! Before the season started in earnest, Gillespie joined Celtic, now managed by Liam Brady, who had replaced Billy McNeill in June. Peter Beardsley joined city rivals Everton, while Steve Staunton was shipped out to Aston Villa. David Speedie, who only joined the previous January and was Kenny Dalglish's last signing for Liverpool, was sold to Blackburn Rovers. Scottish international Speedie had enjoyed a dream start to his Anfield career, scoring on his debut at Old Trafford then claiming a double in his next game in the Merseyside derby. It wasn't enough to keep him a Red, though.

## THE SIGNIFICANCE OF SOUNESS

It was suggested other established Liverpool players were concerned that the new boys were being paid salaries in advance of the dressing room average and even more than guys like Ian Rush, who was a Liverpool legend; although lucrative testimonials were in the pipeline for Rush and others including Ronnie Whelan and Bruce Grobbelaar.

It was going to be quite an uphill task to pacify the senior players and then find the mechanism to get the best out of them on the pitch. Graeme's first full season in charge also combined with the club's centenary celebrations.

It was clear on the park that they were a team in transition. It was a mixed bag of results for his first month in charge, the highlight being a 3–1 win over Merseyside rivals Everton. John Barnes was lost to injury for a few months and that gave an opportunity to teenage winger Steve McManaman, who had progressed through the club youth system. Another youngster, Jamie Redknapp, was also knocking on the first-team door, and another new face joined the club in October. Rob Jones was recruited from Crewe Alexandra and proved to be money well spent at £300,000.

Into 1992, and Liverpool's form saw them move up to third in the table by the end of January. Manchester United were top, with Leeds United in second place. If January was good then February was a disaster, when a poor run of results effectively ended any hopes they had of becoming champions. March saw them eliminated from Europe with a 4–1 aggregate defeat to Genoa. Michael Thomas was now on board from Arsenal and he kept hopes of FA Cup glory alive with the only goal of the game in the quarter-final tie against Aston Villa. The semi-final paired Liverpool with Second-Division Portsmouth, and it took

# THE LURE OF LIVERPOOL

a late equalising goal by Ronnie Whelan to see the match finish 1–1, meaning a replay would be required to determine who would go on to the showcase final.

However, there was more drama to follow, and it wasn't on the park. A matter of hours after the Portsmouth clash Graeme Souness was taken ill and rushed to hospital for an emergency triple-heart bypass operation. Liverpool turned to Ronnie Moran to take temporary charge again and tasked him with booking them a place at Wembley.

The semi-final replay played at Villa Park went all the way to a penalty shoot-out. Souness wasn't there to see Barnes, Rush and Saunders convert their spot kicks, while three players missed for Pompey. Liverpool would now meet Sunderland in the final. The FA Cup became the major focus for Liverpool and Graeme Souness was determined to be back and fit enough to lead his team out at the final, which was scheduled for 9 May.

The league title was now a straight shoot-out between Manchester United and Leeds. After going five games without a win, Liverpool beat Manchester United 2–0 at Anfield and that effectively handed the title – the last ever old First Division championship – to the Elland Road club. After the match against the Old Trafford side, reserve-team coach Phil Thompson, who had stepped up to assist Moran, became very critical of Souness and he didn't care who knew it. Graeme did not hear it for himself, of course, as he was still recuperating in hospital. When word did reach him, through a very unlikely but reliable media source, and alerted him to the unsavoury nature of Thompson's comments, Souness immediately made up his mind that Thompson had no future at Anfield. Here was

## THE SIGNIFICANCE OF SOUNESS

a Liverpool club official going public with his opinion that the manager wasn't capable. This was a situation Graeme Souness did not need after his major health scare and with a Cup Final on the horizon.

Phil Thompson and Tommy Smith were two individuals who Graeme considered friends from his playing days, and yet here was Thompson undermining him. Tommy Smith, who was involved in the local press, used his column to attack his old teammate, with particular emphasis on changes that Graeme had made at the club that in his eyes weren't for the better. Smith also questioned the calibre of his signings, claiming they were not of Liverpool class. Phil Thompson's actions were probably not the biggest surprise – back in their playing days he had been stripped of the captaincy, with Bob Paisley giving the job to Souness. Perhaps the change of policy of not promoting the manager from existing coaching staff members had not gone down well with Thompson.

Souness approached the board, and the directors supported his decision to sack Thompson – but they would wait until after the FA Cup Final and until Graeme was fit and healthy enough to do the deed himself. Thompson sued the club for unfair dismissal, and reached a settlement out of court. Thompson later returned to Anfield as assistant manager to Gérard Houllier. Tommy Smith had enjoyed many privileges around Anfield on match days that were not afforded to other journalists covering the game, including access to the inner sanctum – like the boot room – and sharing after-match beers and thoughts with the coaching staff and visiting manager – this was ended swiftly after the departure of Thompson.

The FA Cup Final went to plan with a 2–0 victory over Sunderland. Graeme Souness led his team out and on to the Wembley turf but he certainly did not look well.

There were other issues for Souness to deal with, including his obvious relationship with the *Sun* newspaper, which didn't sit well with the Liverpool public. The *Sun* under editor Kelvin MacKenzie generally lacked any sensitivity and had gone to print with questionable reporting following the Hillsborough disaster.

Graeme Souness made a mistake. A mistake that he deeply regrets and he has said so in public many times. As Souness was recovering from his heart surgery he gave an interview to the *Sun* after the semi-final win over Portsmouth, and while that wasn't well received the timing of the publication could not have been more insensitive. The *Sun* carried it on the front page with a picture of him embracing his girlfriend Karen Levy while he was still wearing his pyjamas. It was a *Sun* exclusive and there were suggestions Souness had been paid for the article. The newspaper hit the streets on Wednesday 15 April 1992. The issue date coincided with the third anniversary of the Hillsborough tragedy and on the same day Anfield was hosting a memorial service. Any payment Souness received from the exclusive was reported to have gone to Alder Hey Children's Hospital. It may have been a serious error of judgement by Souness and it was one that probably signalled the beginning of the end of his time at Anfield.

The following season a fully fit Souness was at the helm, but again Liverpool failed to hit the heights. New signings goalkeeper David James and Hungarian midfielder István Kozma joined, as did Danish defender Torben Piechnik

## THE SIGNIFICANCE OF SOUNESS

with the versatile Paul Stewart coming in from Spurs. Barry Venison moved on as did Dean Saunders, who had finished as Liverpool's top scorer the season before. Souness almost recovered the full transfer value he had paid for the Welsh international as he joined Villa to team up with other former Reds, Steve Staunton and Ray Houghton. The season ended with Liverpool sixth in the new-look Premier League, while their defence of the FA Cup had been halted in the third round by Bolton Wanderers.

For the 1993–94 season, again expectations were high, with Nigel Clough and Neil Ruddock joining the squad before Julian Dicks arrived only a month into the season. One major positive was the debut of teenage striker Robbie Fowler. Fowler quickly became the poster boy of the supporters, scoring five goals in one of his early games against Fulham.

January 1994, started quite well for Liverpool. A win on their travels to Ipswich was followed up with a 3–3 draw with Manchester United. Next up Oldham were defeated, as were Manchester City as the month progressed. The FA Cup saw them come out of the hat with Bristol City. The first leg finished 1–1, and then in the return at Anfield over 36,000 supporters saw the unthinkable happen – a goal from Brian Tinnion put the Robins through. Three days later Graeme Souness resigned; Roy Evans would replace him.

Graeme Souness was committed to the job and had the belief that he could deliver success, but ultimately he failed to restore the glory days. He had been in the position for 33 months and had two-and-a-half-years remaining on his contract. David Murray had suggested taking the job was a mistake, and so it proved.

The FA Cup win in the 1991–92 season was his only trophy, and for a club like Liverpool, who had dominated at home and abroad not that many years before, that was just not acceptable.

# CHAPTER 36:

# THE MADNESS OF MANAGEMENT

After leaving Liverpool it was the first time in 23 years that Graeme Souness found himself on the outside of football looking in – all the way back to when as a teenager he left his Edinburgh home to join Tottenham Hotspur. The heart operation and the loss of his father in the final weeks of his Liverpool reign had taken their toll and a bit of a sabbatical was required to charge the batteries. Travel was therapeutic, and on a trip to Las Vegas he married his girlfriend, Karen. Graeme also enjoyed gardening as a way of divorcing himself from the game. It was a self-imposed exile, and although his former club Middlesbrough were suggested as a possible return to management it was Bryan Robson who got the nod.

Then, quite out of the blue, a call came from a representative of Galatasaray requesting a meeting. Apparently the Turkish side had targeted former Sheffield Wednesday and Leeds boss Howard Wilkinson but he in turn proposed Souness as his recommendation for the post. It was 18 months since Graeme left Anfield but here was the chance to join another big club, based in the football-crazy city of Istanbul – the passion of the fans was in parallel with his experiences in Glasgow and Liverpool.

A one-year contract was agreed with the understanding that if the elected board were voted in again for a longer period, Graeme's contract would be extended accordingly.

Local rivals Fenerbahçe were the team to beat, and in an attempt to mount a challenge Souness went for the tried-and-tested players that he had worked with previously, and all ex-Liverpool: Barry Venison, Dean Saunders and Mike Marsh. American goalkeeper Brad Friedel, who would later play for Liverpool, also joined from Brøndby in Denmark. The star man in the Galatasaray ranks was Tugay Kerimoğlu. Tugay was a wonderful talent but a bit of a maverick. In January 2000, he joined Rangers but found game-time restricted under Dick Advocaat, as he considered him to be a bit of a circus act. Souness rated Tugay so highly that he later signed him for Blackburn Rovers where he became a cult hero and served the Ewood Park club for eight seasons. Tugay had been Galatasaray's youngest-ever captain and he would enjoy a fine period playing under Graeme Souness in the Turkish capital.

Another foreigner joined the ranks as Souness looked to shore up his defence. Ulrich van Gobbel came in from Feyenoord and he impressed Souness so much that when he later moved to Southampton he made the big Dutchman a priority signing.

It wasn't the best of starts for Souness at Galatasaray and the press appeared to be having a go at every opportunity, and not just about results but the fact that he was playing expensive imports ahead of local talent. As the league challenge slipped away, the Turkish Cup became the key target for the season, so very much like Liverpool in 1992. Beşiktaş were beaten in the quarter-finals to set up a double-header semi-final against Samsunspor, and two goals from

# THE SIGNIFICANCE OF SOUNESS

Dean Saunders eased Gala to a 3–1 win in the first leg at home. In the return match Galatasaray lost 1–0 but they were through with an aggregate scoreline of 3–1. They were now set to face Fenerbahçe in the final.

The Ali Sami Yen stadium in Istanbul would host the first leg of the 1996 Turkish Cup Final on 11 April. Galatasaray would then travel to Fenerbahçe's home, the Şükrü Saracoğlu Stadium, 13 days later for the second leg. This was a date that would go down in Galatasaray folklore, and with Graeme Souness involved it would be an event not without drama or controversy.

The first game was a tight affair but an early goal from Dean Saunders gave Souness's side the advantage for the second game. Aykut Kocaman gave Fenerbahçe the lead after 35 minutes and that's the way the 90 minutes ended, meaning extra-time would be played. With barely four minutes remaining of the added-on 30, the ball fell kindly for Dean Saunders and he smashed it into the net from the edge of the box. Galatasaray were cup winners! The celebrations from the Gala fans were extreme, and as the heroes in red and yellow went across to enjoy the moment with their supporters a huge Galatasaray flag was handed across to the players to bring extra theatre to the party. Each player took it in turn to raise the standard high and relish the special moments that winning trophies provides as the adrenaline takes over. Eventually the huge flag made its way to manager Souness. Graeme Souness couldn't resist the opportunity to leave his mark on proceedings and made for the halfway line before planting the flag deep into the turf of their biggest rivals Fenerbahçe.

Now there may have been a secondary agenda at work here,

## THE MADNESS OF MANAGEMENT

as before the final an official of Fenerbahçe had been critical of Souness and questioned the wisdom of Galatasaray employing a 'cripple' as their manager, this being a far-from-accurate and offensive term for Souness in reference to his previous open-heart surgery. Perhaps this gesture by Graeme was his way of saying he was fit and the planting of the flag was an act of defiance. But the home fans who were still in the stadium were incensed and baying for blood. The drama with the flag didn't end there. It all kicked off in the tunnel and punches were thrown, but it didn't detract from a fantastic day for all those of a Galatasaray persuasion.

The next day, pictures of Graeme's flag-planting effort were everywhere and fans had T-shirts printed with the same image to further embarrass their city rivals. The board of directors that brought Graeme to Galatasaray didn't win the election, meaning Graeme's time in Turkey was over. But that cup win and the subsequent celebrations are still held in the memories of the Gala fans as one of the best days in their history. Only Graeme Souness could have come up with such a ploy. He will tell you it wasn't premeditated, but he always did have the ability to come up with something spectacular.

Next up, it was back to England, with Southampton becoming his fourth managerial appointment. There is no doubt, even with consideration to the Galatasaray ending, Graeme had mellowed and matured and had a less confrontational style than he had perhaps employed at both Rangers and Liverpool.

On 2 July 1996, Graeme Souness was confirmed as successor to Dave Merrington, who had kept Southampton in the top flight the previous season by finishing 17th –

## THE SIGNIFICANCE OF SOUNESS

just one point above the drop zone. Southampton had plans to build a new stadium as The Dell was very short on capacity for Premiership football. Austerity measures meant that Souness was going to be at his wheeler-dealer best.

Graeme cast his net far and wide to find the quality he wanted within the narrow budget he had to work to. Norwegian defender Claus Lundekvam was signed from Brann, then Graeme went back to Galatasaray for Van Gobbel and Graham Potter came in from Stoke City. Wayne Bridge, who was destined for a huge future in the game, also proved to be a really shrewd capture, and as the season unfolded Eyal Berkovic arrived in October on loan from Maccabi Haifa. In the same month an SOS went out to Graeme's old Rangers keeper Chris Woods who was now with Colorado Rapids. Players taking their leave from the south-coast club included players so very well known to Souness: Mark Walters and Bruce Grobbelaar were allowed to leave on free transfers, but Richard Hill, the former Scunthorpe defender, was sold to West Ham United for a huge fee of £1.4m, delivering a profit of £1.2m for the five years he was at The Dell. Boardroom changes also weren't helpful as Graeme set about trying to improve Southampton.

Survival was the name of the game. The highlight of Graeme's time at the club was an impressive 6–3 win over Manchester United in a match that had a bizarre post-match quip from United boss Alex Ferguson, who claimed his players couldn't see each other because of their bland grey shirts that was then United's away kit. The Saints were three up at half-time. An appeal was made to the referee and Manchester United took the field for the second half in a blue-and-white strip.

# THE MADNESS OF MANAGEMENT

It didn't make a slightest bit of difference, as Southampton scored another three after the turnaround.

If that was the highlight then the lowlight would be the game-time given to Ali Dia, who claimed to be a Senegalese international. Southampton brought him in on trial on the strength of a reported tip-off from former World Player of the Year George Weah. At the time Southampton had the worst injury list probably in their history, and with a small squad to start with Dia was invited to show his qualities. First impressions were that Ali was not suitable for Saints and no contract would be offered. However, in the week he was there more players were sidelined by injury, and with a match scheduled for the weekend against Leeds United, Southampton were struggling to make the numbers up for a starting 11, never mind a bench. Matt Le Tissier was the only fit front player at that time and was patched up and asked to lead the line, but 20 minutes into the game he aggravated his injury and had to come off. Ali Dia was thrown on to maintain the numbers but it was clear he was nowhere near the standard he claimed to be, or as Southampton required. He was quickly hauled off and was never seen again. Were Southampton duped? It is maybe best summed up by Matt Le Tissier, who made the comment that he thought Ali had won a competition to spend a day with the team.

The season ended with Southampton positioned 16th in the Premier League, and Graeme Souness left the club. In reality, the way the club was run proved to be a very different proposition than the one he had been sold on by Lawrie McMenemy. So much so, McMenemy himself left the club he served as manager for just short of 12 years before switching roles and returning in the summer of 1992 as director of football.

It was the first time as a manager that Souness had failed to deliver a trophy for his club.

Graeme's next chosen position can only be described as a bit of a disaster. The concept and potential were favourable: Torino were languishing in Italy's Serie B, but Souness's reputation from his time in Sampdoria had kept his stock high. The target was clear – win promotion and restore once-great Torino to former glories. The problem was the squad had already been assembled by the time Souness arrived in Turin and there were no funds available to expand it. Graeme did coax the directors to sign Tony Dorigo from Leeds but no fee was involved.

It was a long time ago that Torino had Joe Baker and Denis Law as the jewels in their crown, and it was neighbours Juventus who were the dominant force. The football environment in Italy had changed since Souness played with Sampdoria in Serie A, and it was also suggested the language barrier was a problem as Souness tried to force his personality style of management on the squad. Early results were not good. Six games in, Torino had won two, lost two and drawn two, leaving the club 14th in the league. It was apparent to all parties that it just wasn't working, and after a 4–0 defeat to Verona it was all over – Souness was sacked after just 98 days in charge. Graeme Souness himself commented that he had pretty much taken the first offer he had received after leaving Southampton and had not done enough research before committing himself to Torino.

*

# THE MADNESS OF MANAGEMENT

Have passport, will travel, and it wasn't long until Graeme Souness was back in management, but again he had to head overseas to try and rebuild his reputation.

On 2 November 1997, Graeme Souness replaced Manuel José as boss of Benfica. The recurring theme here was another club turning to Souness in their attempt to restore former glories. It was how it all started for him at Rangers and he had been successful in doing so, but he'd found that success much more difficult to replicate in his time at Torino. Would Benfica be different?

Again, Souness looked to England for signings. Scott Minto was signed from Chelsea in the summer before Souness came in but he did engineer the transfer of Brian Deane from Sheffield United within a month of arriving in Portugal. Benfica were sitting seventh in the table when Souness took over but the gap wasn't huge and a challenge was considered possible.

In need of pace, Souness agreed with his president that Karel Poborský at Manchester United would fit the bill. Poborský had enjoyed a very good Euro 96, and that prompted Alex Ferguson to sign him, but the emergence of David Beckham had relegated Karel to being a squad player at Old Trafford. Nothing was simple at Benfica, though, and payment for Poborský had not been made. It was an embarrassing situation for Souness, especially as he thought signing the Czech international was the first of many new faces to join. Remember, too, that at foreign clubs the president and directors are voted into position, so politics posturing and promises being made are common place.

Brian Deane was a prime example of the transfer goings-on at Benfica. Souness agreed a fee of £1.5m with Sheffield United, although the Blades also had to wait to receive the transfer funds, but the following season Souness sold him on to Middlesbrough for £3m. Graeme's record of returning a positive balance in his transfer dealings was better than excellent. That first season in Portugal was a success, with Benfica finishing second to champions Porto, and qualification for the Champions League was the reward.

Expectations were high that Benfica under Souness, in his second season in charge, could go all the way. More UK players were brought into the squad, including the ever-reliable (in the eyes of Graeme Souness) Dean Saunders, while another Welshman and ex-Liverpool star Michael Thomas also put pen to paper to commit himself to the club who played their home games at the impressive Estádio da Luz.

Inconsistency was to be Benfica's downfall, along with a revolving door that saw players come and go, often without the manager being consulted. At the turn of the year Benfica had never been out of the top three places in the Primeira Liga, but failure to make the knock-out stages in Europe clearly frustrated the hierarchy, and Souness had seen the signs before. The pressure was on. In April, defeat to Boavista meant their tilt for the title was over and Porto were on track again to be champions. On 3 May Souness was relieved of his duties. It was time to come home. Graeme and Karen were keen to put down more permanent roots, especially with a new baby on the way.

## CHAPTER 37:

# BOUNCE BACK AT BLACKBURN

On Tuesday 14 March 2000, Blackburn Rovers confirmed Graeme Souness was their new manager, and his trusted sidekick Phil Boersma had his bags packed and was ready to join him. It had been pretty much an open secret that Souness was the man Blackburn wanted to replace Brian Kidd who had left the club in November. (Iconic Blackburn former centre half, Colin Hendry, who was a league winner in his time at the club and was also a serial winner at Rangers under Dick Advocaat, was an outsider for the job.) The local newspaper carried the headline SOU-YES. On the day before Graeme's appointment Bruce Rioch had resigned as boss of Norwich City, and speculation mounted as he had been mentioned in dispatches for the Blackburn job, but Souness was the man Jack Walker wanted to take his club forwards. Rioch's move was just coincidental.

Graeme Souness had been out the game since the summer when he'd left Benfica. During his time in Portugal he'd got his mojo back for management and was fully enthused by the task in hand of restoring the good times to Blackburn Rovers. It was the type of challenge Graeme responded to, especially

## THE SIGNIFICANCE OF SOUNESS

when it was confirmed that funds were available to improve the squad. Jack Walker had already poured millions from his vast fortune into the club over the years. There was still time left ahead of the pending transfer deadline, so it was important that Souness got to work immediately, refreshing the squad and moving players on that weren't in his plans. Graeme Souness also had the expertise of Tony Parkes to call on, who had been in temporary charge since Kidd's departure. It was a role that he was familiar with as Parkes had previously taken the reins on three previous occasions before his most recent experience after Brian Kidd, including when Kenny Dalglish left. Graeme Souness recognised what Parkes had to offer and installed him as his assistant manager. Tony Parkes first joined Blackburn as a player in 1970 and he was the epitome of a one-club man, staying with Rovers until he retired from playing in 1982 when he then joined the coaching staff. Tony knew the club inside out.

Graeme Souness was given the stability of a three-year contract, which would take him through to the summer of 2003. This effectively gave him breathing space to have a genuine tilt at promotion the following season. Blackburn Rovers remained an ambitious club, albeit they had lost their way since winning the Premier League in the 1994–95 season. After that title success, Kenny Dalglish moved upstairs to become director of football and his assistant Ray Harford became manager. A season later Harford left, as Rovers failed to offer any obvious defence of their title. Sven-Göran Eriksson was a contender to replace him but it was Roy Hodgson who came in from Inter Milan to be next in the hot seat. It wasn't a move that proved productive, and Hodgson was sacked in December. Brian Kidd replaced him but he couldn't stop Blackburn being relegated. The job in hand for Graeme Souness was quite simply to secure promotion and secure it as quick as possible.

Graeme would soon be on Blackburn's Brockhall training ground and working with some familiar faces. Steve Harkness worked with Souness at both Liverpool and Benfica, and also in the Blackburn squad was Egil Østenstad who Souness had signed for Southampton from Viking Stavanger. Souness was quick to make his mark, and results improved immediately as they took ten points from a possible 12 in his first four league games in charge. But the real game plan was about putting down the right foundations to pitch for promotion the following season. The season ended with Blackburn finishing 11th in the First Division.

For the following season Souness was again busy in the transfer market to bring quality to the squad, and, more importantly, to bring in players he could trust and who would blend well with the younger players. Striker Matt Jansen, who had joined the year Rovers were relegated, had a terrific season, scoring 23 Division One goals. The defence had also been shored up by the return of Henning Berg, three years after he had been sold to Manchester United.

As the season unfolded, Graeme recruited Brad Friedel on a free transfer from Liverpool, Eyal Berkovic came in on loan from Celtic and the hugely experienced Mark Hughes signed on after his release from Everton – three big personalities and players who understood the standards Souness expected. Others arrived too: Marcus Bent and Alan Mahon joined in time to bring impetus to the promotion bid.

By the spring, Rovers were on target for that dream return to the top league. In April a 5–0 win over local rivals Burnley was a particular highlight. By the penultimate game of the season, Souness needed a win at Preston North End to seal promotion. The points were secured with Matt Jansen scoring the only goal of the game. It was a short journey from Preston to Blackburn but the celebrations started on the coach, as they were most certainly going up. Rovers finished second with 91 points. They were ten points behind champions Fulham but four better off than Bolton Wanderers, who were also promoted but through the play-offs.

Sadly, Blackburn's benefactor and chairman Jack Walker died in August 2000, and didn't get to experience the promotion success. Jack Walker was 71 years old when he succumbed to cancer. Captain Garry Flitcroft went to the visiting fans after the win at Deepdale wearing a T-shirt with a simple message: WE DID IT FOR JACK!

There is no doubt that Walker's choice of Graeme Souness as the man to get Blackburn back up was the right one. The Ewood Park Club could now look forward to life with the big boys after a two-year absence.

Rovers made a solid start to life back in the top flight, losing just three games from the first 14 played. The club were also making good progress in the Worthington or League Cup.

At the end of December, Souness coaxed Andy Cole to join his squad. Cole was a real talismanic striker but had been edged out of things at Manchester United by big-name signings Juan Verón and Ruud van Nistelrooy. Cole was expensive, and it took an offer of £8m before Alex Ferguson agreed to sell him. It may have appeared to be a big transfer fee but he delivered crucial goals, including the winning strike at Cardiff's

Millennium Stadium in February as Blackburn beat Tottenham Hotspur in the League Cup Final. It was Blackburn Rovers' first major cup since 1928. Cole scored 13 goals in 20 appearances for Blackburn in the second half of that first season back in England's top division. League results through the winter months had delivered a mixed bag; however, inspired by the cup triumph, Rovers started to find some form and won six of their last 12 games of the league campaign, which pushed them up to a tenth-place finish. They had also qualified for Europe with the Worthington Cup success.

Former Galatasaray technician Tugay was pulling the strings in midfield for Blackburn after Souness finally got his man in the summer of 2001. Previous attempts to get Tugay on board were unsuccessful and had been held up by international work permit red tape. Now he was here, having left Rangers at the end of the previous season as a league and cup double-winner. The Ewood Park faithful had a new hero and took to him immediately, while Tugay seemed to be very much at home in his new surroundings. Goalkeeper Brad Friedel was also having an excellent season and made the PFA Team of the Season as Blackburn ended the campaign in a very commendable sixth place in the table. Their attempt at defending their League Cup trophy was ended by Manchester United at the semi-final stage while their lack of European experience was evident as they were knocked out of the UEFA Cup by Martin O'Neill's Celtic. It was the season Celtic went all the way to the final in Seville, but lost out to Porto. Overall, the report card would clearly have said progress was being made, and Graeme Souness was getting the best out of his players and enjoying every moment of it.

## THE SIGNIFICANCE OF SOUNESS

The following season, 2003–04, was not so positive for Blackburn and they were flirting with the relegation zone for most of the time. Barry Ferguson had come in from Rangers as Souness once more rang the changes in his playing squad.

Ferguson was almost forced out of Rangers by the financial pressures at the club and the need for austerity on costs. Barry had been captain and a sensational treble winner at Rangers while also being a regular for the Scottish national team. Barry was in demand and before signing for Blackburn, Rangers rejected a £6m bid from Everton, who at that time were managed by another Scot, David Moyes. When Blackburn made their approach and agreed a £7.5m fee, Barry was attracted by the proposition of playing under Graeme Souness. Barry recalls, 'It was one of the hardest decisions I ever had to face. Rangers were my club but while I did fancy a crack at the English Premier League, my heart was still at Ibrox. When I was informed that Rangers had accepted a bid from Blackburn, my first thought was, "I want to play for Graeme Souness." When Graeme came to Rangers in 1986, I was only eight years of age and was just really getting into football. Of course my big brother Derek was in Souness's side back then, and now I was getting the chance to play for a guy of Graeme's "obvious" calibre, as he was one of the greatest midfielders these shores have ever produced.

'Graeme had a presence and when he spoke you sat up and took notice. I liked his honesty and the way he conducted himself, I still do even now when I hear him on radio or TV. He was a demanding manager, Derek had tipped me off on that, but I knew what to expect I was 25 and ready for the new challenge. There was a mini Ibrox at Blackburn back then, Souness, Big Amoruso and the incredibly gifted Turkish midfielder Tugay. After a game we would all be wanting to know how Rangers had got on and when we got back into training on a Monday that would again be the topic of conversation in the dressing room.

'Graeme Souness was a hard taskmaster and he soon let you know if you didn't do what was asked of you. He could give you it with both barrels if he felt you deserved it and that was the same for young players coming through the ranks to the most senior pros. I learned a lot in my time with Graeme at Blackburn and I really enjoyed working with him. One thing remains sure though: he was and still is, all these years later, a massive Blue Nose!'

The next season for Blackburn was a difficult one. The team were again quickly out of Europe at the first round and their FA Cup hopes were ended in a 4–3 home defeat to Liverpool. A run of good results towards the end of the season were enough to stave off any fears of facing the drop and Rovers finished in 15th place. After the highs of the previous season, this was considered pretty disappointing and a section of the fans started to lose their faith in Souness.

The following season Barry Ferguson was appointed captain, while Dwight Yorke and Andy Cole moved on after confrontations with Souness in the later stages of the previous season. Another former Rangers captain, Lorenzo Amoruso, had joined the ranks but his season was all but over by October when he suffered a serious knee injury. Barry Ferguson's influence on the side was also lacking, as he too had a horrible knee fracture that would see him sidelined for 15 months.

Not a lot was going right for Souness. Against the odds,

## THE SIGNIFICANCE OF SOUNESS

Blackburn retained their Premier League status but it was Mark Hughes who steered them through the bulk of the season, as Graeme Souness had jumped ship for Newcastle United in mid-September. It was a bizarre decision by Newcastle to sack Sir Bobby Robson when they did, with the season only a few games old. When Graeme Souness was offered the chance to replace Robson, he didn't hesitate. Graeme had enjoyed life at Rovers but there were no comparisons on the size of the club or the scale of support between Blackburn and Newcastle. The Toon Army were also one of the most passionate group of fans in English football. It's quite clear that Graeme Souness enjoyed his time at Benfica and then at Blackburn, enough to give him the belief that he was ready to take on another big job – and they didn't get much bigger than bossing Newcastle United.

## CHAPTER 38:

# NORTH TO NEWCASTLE

The opportunity to prove his qualities again with a massive club meant Graeme Souness swapped Blackburn for St James' Park. Leaving Blackburn Rovers was a wrench but he had achieved what Jack Walker had charged him with, and that was getting the Ewood Park side back to England's top flight. Winning a cup along the way was a major bonus too. Trophies were the holy grail, and in Graeme's mind he was confident he could deliver silverware to the hugely passionate Newcastle fans who had been starved of success for too long.

At 51 years of age, it appeared to be the perfect fit for Souness, who had matured from his early days in management at Rangers. However, there had been reports of training ground bust-ups between Souness and Trinidad and Tobago striker Dwight Yorke while at Blackburn. Souness had played it down, confirming that passions can run high, but it was also well documented that Souness wasn't comfortable with his striker's 'busy' social life. That episode was history, but not before Souness had shipped Yorke out to Birmingham. Now it was Newcastle and some big personality players to deal with. United chairman Freddy Shepherd was confident

## THE SIGNIFICANCE OF SOUNESS

he had the right man to succeed north-east legend Sir Bobby Robson. To secure the post Souness had to fight off serious competition from Terry Venables and Steve Bruce (Bruce would later manage Newcastle between 2019 and 2021), while David O'Leary and Gordon Strachan were also touted for the job. But it was Souness who was given the mandate to revitalise the fortunes of the Magpies.

Souness had to be patient to get started in his new managerial position, as in the week he struck an agreement with the Newcastle board his Blackburn side were due to travel to St James' Park to face Newcastle that weekend. The Blackburn directors took the early decision to have Graeme leave the club right away to allow Tony Parkes to take temporary charge again while Graeme faced a few days 'garden leave'. But the temptation to take the game in from a seat in the stands was too great for Graeme Souness and he enjoyed the moment as his new club ran out 3–0 winners, with goals from Alan Shearer and Andy O'Brien to add to the own-goal opener from Garry Flitcroft. It was Newcastle's first win of the season and Souness had quite a platform to go forwards from. For Blackburn they banked a hefty compensation payment from Newcastle to allow Souness to officially take up his new role from Monday 13 September.

John Carver had taken temporary charge pending Souness coming in officially. Also set to join the coaching staff was Terry McDermott, who was an old teammate of Graeme's from Liverpool and had originally been appointed as first-team coach at Newcastle by Kevin Keegan in 1992. McDermott had left to hook-up with John Barnes at Celtic in 1999 but Souness brought him back early in 2005. Another former teammate,

# NORTH TO NEWCASTLE

Alan Murray, who had been part of Graeme's back-room team at Southampton came in immediately as assistant manager, and, as ever, Mr Reliable Phil Boersma was there too. Dean Saunders also left Blackburn to continue to work with his close friend, originally with the responsibility of coaching the strikers but this soon changed to a wider role as first-team coach. Another former Newcastle defender, Steve Clarke, was in the position of chief scout, and would later manage West Bromwich, Reading and Kilmarnock before taking on the daunting task of managing the Scottish international side in May 2019.

While Graeme Souness confirmed he was ready to face the challenge, the Newcastle fans were not convinced. His appointment divided opinion. In the season before his appointment Newcastle finished fifth in the Premier League, while in the two seasons prior to that they had qualified for the Champions League. Souness inherited a capable squad mixing seasoned professionals and a host of talented youngsters ready to step up. Some big-name international players were in the dressing room, including Shay Given, Nicky Butt, Craig Bellamy, Laurent Robert, Patrick Kluivert and, of course, local hero Alan Shearer. The youngsters that were exciting the fans included James Milner and Charles N'Zogbia. Graeme Souness had serious talent at his disposal and he was confident he could mould them into a team that could challenge for honours.

Despite a flying start things weren't quite right, and Souness supplemented the squad with more internationals like Ronny Johnsen, Celestine Babayaro and Amdy Faye (later Faye would have a brief spell at Rangers under Walter Smith), and then went back to Rangers to recruit Jean-Alain Boumsong in January of 2005 for a fee of £8m. Including Boumsong the total outlay on squad additions came to more than £13m. In the same January window Graeme Souness moved on Olivier Bernard and Craig Bellamy, two players who were regulars under Bobby Robson. The following summer the overhaul continued and the Robson squad was dismantled with Lauren Robert and James Milner going out on loan with permanent exits for Andy O'Brien, Jermaine Jenas and Hugo Viana. The summer spending was in the region of £40m with record signing Michael Owen accounting for a big percentage of the outgoing cash.

Towards the end of his first season in charge Souness had to deal with another major fall-out that saw teammates Lee Bowyer and Kieron Dyer exchange punches. Newcastle were three down to Aston Villa when it all started, and both players were sent off. It could be argued that Bowyer and Dyer were similar – both wanted to get forwards and offer a goal threat from midfield, but that is no excuse for the moment of madness that left their team down to nine men when they were already chasing the game. Graeme Souness chose to put both Bowyer and Dyer up for post-match media duties. Arguably this only added to the negativity, and as you can imagine Graeme Souness was livid with his players, especially with an FA Cup semi-final against Manchester United coming up. The cup tie didn't go Newcastle's way, losing 4–1 to Manchester United at the Millennium Stadium.

In Europe things didn't offer any positivity either in the week leading up to the Manchester United meeting – they beat Sporting Lisbon at home but were comprehensively outplayed in the away match, and Europe was over at the first hurdle. Injuries may well have been a factor in the run of poor results, and Graeme Souness criticised the club's training ground and claimed it was the main reason for the extensive injury list. Graeme also stated publicly that the playing squad lacked depth, and the combination of these comments set the manager on a collision course with chairman Shepherd.

The season ended with Newcastle finishing in a disappointing 14th place. Two points better off than his old club Blackburn who finished 15th and just avoided a genuine relegation battle.

For the 2005–06 season Souness was back wheeling and dealing in the transfer market. Former Ranger and Australia defender Craig Moore joined from Borussia Mönchengladbach, Dutch keeper Tim Krul came in from Den Haag with 'locals' Scott Parker and Lee Clark supporting the marquee signing of Michael Owen. Before the transfer window closed Nolberto Solano left Villa to rejoin the new-look Newcastle, and James Milner went off in the opposite direction on loan as part of that deal. Souness had been backed with a huge transfer war chest and expectations were high for the new season. In the season just past Newcastle averaged home crowds of more than 51,000. The Toon Army wanted success.

Sadly, Souness was not the man to deliver it. On 2 February 2006, Graeme Souness was sacked after a 3–0 defeat away at Manchester City. It reflected a run of six league games without a win. In contrast Glenn Roeder came in and went on a run of five league games without defeat.

To be fair to Souness, his plan to partner Alan Shearer with Michael Owen looked to be a sure-fire winner and indications were clear that they were building a lethal understanding together, but that ended when Owen broke a metatarsal in a match against Tottenham Hotspur which kept him out for the rest of the season. It was a devastating blow to Souness and with Owen out injured the team's form dipped. A case of what might have been . . .

The Newcastle–Souness relationship was always less than harmonious with suggestions that Graeme had his favourite players, which impacted on dressing room morale, while the fans who weren't convinced from day one had their worst fears confirmed. A team who had contended Champions League football regularly prior to Souness coming in had lost its way.

Former Fleet Street reporter John 'Gibby' Gibson, a football legend in the north-east, which has been his beat since 1966, looks back on where it went wrong for Graeme at St James' Park: 'It was almost impossible to follow Sir Bobby Robson at Newcastle. Bobby was the complete Geordie and the Geordies loved him. Bobby had pulled us up by our bootlaces from the lowest of positions imaginable to get us up to third in the title race. Bobby Robson was our Bill Shankly.

'Graeme Souness was a magnificent player but as our manager it didn't work out. He wasn't alone in that one – we had Ossie Ardiles, Ruud Gullit and Kenny Dalglish as well. In typical Geordie black-humour style, the fans say it's a pity we didn't have them as players as they were all pretty crap as managers! Graeme's signings weren't good. Take Michael Owen for instance – he was a record signing, meaning we paid more for him than we had for Alan Shearer! That just wasn't right. By the time Owen came from Real Madrid he had lost that electrifying pace and he lacked commitment, refusing to relocate to the north and choosing to commute every day to training and games by helicopter! That didn't endear him to the fans. But Graeme could also be very confrontational and arguably his style was dated – he was perhaps one of the last tough-guy managers.

'I still have a good relationship with Graeme, and many years ago he actually wanted to be at Newcastle before he finally did get to St James' Park as manager. Graeme was playing with Middlesbrough but wanted a bigger stage for his skills. Graeme was enjoying life at Boro, but wanted more. He was such a talented boy, with George Clooney looks and a liking for the champagne lifestyle – he knew he was more than capable of playing with any of the top clubs in the country.

'He called me, aware that I had contacts with the top decision makers at United and he asked me to sound them out to determine if Newcastle would be interested in signing him. I made the call and it got a very favourable response, and for a while it looked like Graeme was on his way to Newcastle. However, perhaps it was a bit of penny-pinching or lack of full agreement between all the directors, but as Newcastle prevaricated Liverpool nipped in and took him to Anfield. It's such a shame he couldn't make it work when he did join Newcastle all those years later.'

Glenn Roeder, who succeeded Souness, won the 2006 Intertoto Cup, delivering Newcastle's first trophy since 1969. By May 2007, Roeder himself was another casualty of the Newcastle poisoned-chalice managerial hot-seat.

Fast forward to the 2024–25 season when Newcastle next won a cup. Under Eddie Howe the Football League/EFL Cup was secured in March 2025, with a thrilling Wembley win over Liverpool – their first domestic trophy in 70 years.

# THE SIGNIFICANCE OF SOUNESS

What next for Graeme Souness? Well after the disappointment of Newcastle a career in the media looked the most obvious option and he wasn't short of offers to bring his unique insight to both radio and television.

In 2007 the City of London Police opened an enquiry looking at the transfer goings-on at Newcastle, with particular interest in the movement of two Souness signings: Jean-Alain Boumsong and Amdy Faye. The enquiry involved Newcastle, Rangers and Portsmouth. The Quest report published their findings in June 2007, and emphasised that it was clear that no evidence of irregular payments was found in the transfers. Willie McKay was the agent involved, and, like Graeme Souness, he cooperated fully with the investigators. Souness issued his own statement: 'I cannot understand why my name features in this report. I volunteered full information to Quest as a witness and heard nothing further from them.'

It was all part of the Stevens Inquiry into football corruption.

Following this unfortunate and unnecessary experience, you can understand why Graeme Souness perhaps decided his days in football management were pretty much over.

However, that hankering for the day-to-day involvement at a football club wasn't quite extinguished and he did come close to taking over at Bolton and Crystal Palace. There was also a suggestion that he could return to Blackburn; and while in his role as chief executive of the Scottish Football Association, Gordon Smith wanted Graeme to take on the job of national team manager. Gordon's proposal to appoint Graeme was overruled by the SFA committee at the time.

None of the later managerial potential actually did

materialise, and it was the numerous and varied media options that appealed to Graeme, and he was soon in high demand for his no-nonsense and forthright opinions.

It may have been a major loss to the dugout but Graeme Souness proved to be a major gain for broadcasting. Graeme was fearsome on the park as a player, and he was and still is equally so in the TV or radio studio.

# CHAPTER 39:

# MEDIA, HEALTH & CHARITY

### Media

Ian Crocker has spent more than 30 years in the football broadcast business and has enjoyed working with Graeme Souness on numerous occasions. Ian recognises the insight Graeme offers when on radio or television: 'Graeme Souness has an aura; indeed he has an incredible presence. He's a fascinating guy. When you are in his company, whether he's on air or just in conversation, it's an education. He knows what he's talking about – big time. Audiences and studio colleagues hang on his every word. He was a top-level player and manager and now he's a top-level pundit.

'No matter wherever or whenever I meet him over the years when covering games, his first question to me is always, "What's happening at Rangers?" His affinity to the Ibrox club doesn't diminish – he clearly holds Rangers deep in his heart. However, that doesn't impact on his view of the game, and it's always an honest and informative analysis and insight that he offers. When he first came on Sky he was a revelation and he clearly set the tone for others to follow. He doesn't suffer fools gladly and is forthright, straight-talking and fearless in offering criticism if he thought it was due. He was equally authoritative when it came to praising players or managers when he felt it was justified. Graeme set the bar high, as did Martin O'Neill, and I have no doubt guys like Roy Keane took on board the way Graeme went about his job as inspiration – albeit Roy would clearly put his own spin on things too. I've been lucky to spend time in the company of these legends of the game, including Martin and in Graeme Souness and Walter Smith, with whom I had terrific working relations. Arguably the best of them all, but that might be a bit harsh on Craig Brown who was another special man to deal with.'

Mark Donaldson covers many sports for ESPN in the US, but his major passion remains football. Like Souness, Mark was born in Edinburgh and remains a Hearts fanatic despite his home now being on the other side of the Atlantic: 'I've always really enjoyed watching and listening to Graeme Souness on television and radio. Working with Graeme's former teammate Stevie Nicol at ESPN, I've heard loads of stories about Graeme the player, most of them involving pranks at Stevie's expense! But Souness the pundit is always no-nonsense and sprays honest opinions around without caring who is in the firing line, who takes offence or who gets upset. Also, if Graeme is at the match as a pundit, then you just know it's a big game. His presence elevates the importance of the television broadcast for the viewer. Very few pundits have his gravitas on the small screen. For those who say his views are old-school and football has moved on since he was involved as a player and manager, I'd say that's nonsense – there should always be a place for someone like Graeme Souness as a football analyst because he tells it straight.

He's forgotten more about football than some of the current crop even know.'

Graeme Souness has been prominent on our television screens while working with Sky Sports, ESPN, RTÉ and Al Jazeera Sports. Graeme also has had newspaper columns and remains a regular on talkSPORT radio.

Another man who is regularly in demand across many media platforms is former top referee Jeff Winter. Jeff was the man in the middle at the 2004 FA Cup Final between Manchester United and Millwall. Jeff's love of football was cultivated watching both Middlesbrough and Rangers. Jeff confirms it was Jim Baxter who sparked his interest in the Ibrox club and recalls many enjoyable hours watching Graeme Souness after he transferred from Spurs to his home town team on Teesside. Jeff confirms: 'You could see from day one that Graeme was a special talent and it's no surprise that he had such a successful career. I never had the opportunity to officiate a game he played in or managed, and perhaps I was lucky? I had a few run-ins with Sir Alex, and while they were daunting I don't think I would have liked to bump into Graeme Souness in a dark alleyway. However, I do love his punditry. Now Graeme may not be very PC but he calls it as it is and can hold his own in any company debating anything football, and those talkSPORT pundits can be very vociferous. Graeme treats his media work the way he treated his job on the park as a player – he gives a hundred per cent, he's honest and straightforward. He's respectful when it's called for but most importantly when Graeme speaks you do really have to sit up and listen. He's got such an authoritative aura about him. I loved watching him as a player and all these years later I love listening to him when he is broadcasting.'

John Gibson has reported on football in the north-east since 1966 and established a fantastic relationship with Graeme Souness while he was a player at Middlesbrough: 'I got to know Graeme really well, and he truly was a sensational footballer. When he called time on his managerial career and moved on to a number of different roles in the media he was a revelation. Graeme has absolutely no peers when you look at his punditry. His knowledge and ability to offer deep-dive analysis is unmatched. Graeme found his niche again in the TV studio in particular and when he spoke it was an education.'

Former Rangers player, coach and interim manager Jimmy Nicholl is a huge fan of Graeme Souness when he is on TV: 'Graeme says things in a way we can all understand. He doesn't use terms like "low-block" and "high-press" – he keeps it simple and I suppose it's the phrasing that's different as he cuts through all the jargon. Graeme has done it all as a player and manager, so when he speaks, you listen, as he does so from experience and is better placed than most to make his point with his authority and passionate but almost relaxed style.'

## Health

At the age of 38 and during his tenure as Liverpool manager, Graeme Souness was diagnosed with coronary heart disease and underwent a triple bypass. The operation was a clear success and he continued to live his life.

The only clues he had to his condition, at that time, was a feeling of extreme tiredness on a regular basis and he had been diagnosed with alarmingly high blood pressure.

In November 2015, he was rushed to hospital after experiencing a heart attack while at home. Quick action and the fitting of a new stent quickly had him fighting fit and back on our TV screens in next to no time.

In September 2024, Graeme faced emergency surgery after experiencing chest pains as he made a cup of tea while watching an England v Finland match on television at his home. No time was wasted and a couple of stents were again required. His local cardiologist in Bournemouth, Suneel Talwar, was praised by Souness for his skills and the way he had handled him as a patient over the last 15 years.

Graeme is now a committed advocate for health awareness and has shared his own experiences to encourage others to be more proactive in checking their blood pressure, as it could be a lifesaver.

## Charity

Graeme Souness is vice president of DEBRA UK. He remains a committed fundraiser to support those who suffer from the skin disease epidermolysis bullosa (EB), which is also often referred to as 'butterfly skin'. Graeme has previously described the condition as 'the cruellest disease out there'. Graeme got involved with the charity after meeting teenager Isla Grist from Inverness who endures severe blistering and has a life of constant pain because of EB. Isla has suffered from the condition since birth and has to be swathed head to toe in bandages which are changed three times a week, and it's a terribly painful process. On a TV interview, a very emotional Graeme described young Isla as 'the most unique person' he has ever met.

DEBRA UK provides community support to assist and improve the quality of life for those who suffer from EB, while

# MEDIA, HEALTH & CHARITY

assisting too with funding for research into potential drug treatments that may ease the pain.

In November 2024, Graeme Souness was awarded a CBE for his services to football and charity. Graeme was presented with the honour from William, Prince of Wales at Windsor Castle. Prince William, a committed Aston Villa fan, no doubt took a moment to chat football with Graeme, especially as his team had just recently been beaten by Graeme's old team Liverpool. Prior to his investiture Graeme was part of a relay team who swam the English Channel in 2023 and raised £1.5m for further research into the EB condition. The swim was again completed in 2025 when the team went non-stop from England to France and back, achieving this inside 22 hours.

Next, it was an 85-mile cycle challenge. Despite recovering from shoulder surgery required to address an injury picked up on the previous swimming challenge, Graeme committed to the project, which saw the relay team travel from Dover to London. Another £1m was secured for the EB cause, with the target to stop the pain.

Graeme also supported the Sky Bet 'Every Minute Matters' campaign that ended at Wembley after a gruelling 28 days and 4,000km on the road of almost non-stop walking, running and cycling. The event set out to unite football fans and deliver them skills to perform lifesaving CPR. Over 24,000 fans took the opportunity to support their communities to learn how to perform this vital skill. Graeme was joined on this campaign by former England international team managers Sam Allardyce and Glenn Hoddle.

Graeme Souness remains committed to supporting good causes and sees it as his way of giving something back.

# CHAPTER 40:

# PHIL B – MR RELIABLE

When Graeme Souness took his first steps in football management it was vital he had the correct network of support with him. Walter Smith was the obvious one to get on board for his huge level of awareness of the Scottish game and his work with the international squads, and with Dundee United regularly competing in Europe he was invaluable. Walter was also a Rangers fan and players could relate to that. Of course Walter went on to have a wonderful career in his own right and managed Rangers on two separate occasions, and also had a spell managing the Scottish International side. Graeme Souness says that Walter was his best-ever signing. Quite a compliment. While Walter was a well-known and respected figure in the Scottish game, Graeme's choice for another back-room role at Rangers was a bit more of a surprise.

Phil Boersma first got to know Souness when they were teammates at Middlesbrough. When Graeme came to Glasgow Phil Boersma was there with him, pretty much always in the background but totally loyal, trustworthy and hard-working. After his playing career was over Phil trained in physiotherapy

## PHIL B – MR RELIABLE

and that made him a very unique and useful addition to any coaching staff.

When Graeme Souness joined Middlesbrough from Tottenham he shared digs with Phil who had arrived from Liverpool. They hit it off immediately – two young lads away from home but with ambitions to make it big in the game. Phil Boersma was at Anfield from 1969 to 1975, and in that period he made 120 appearances and scored 30 goals. Some of the goals were important, with four claimed in the successful UEFA Cup run of 1972–73. In the same season he scored seven times in the league as the Reds won the title. For a front player at Liverpool in those days, things were difficult, with Kevin Keegan and John Toshack the regular front pairing under Bill Shankly, and Steve Heighway another terrific front man also in the squad. At that time, too, David Fairclough was an emerging talent who was termed 'Super Sub'. Boersma was growing more and more frustrated by the lack of first-team football opportunities.

When Liverpool started to show an interest in his friend Souness, it was Phil Boersma who encouraged Graeme to take the opportunity to reverse the transfer journey he himself had completed when swapping Anfield for Ayresome Park. Phil still had contacts back on Merseyside and they kept him up to date on just how determined Bob Paisley and his staff were to bring Souness to Liverpool. When the deal finally went through and Souness signed for Liverpool, Phil Boersma was soon on the move himself, leaving Middlesbrough and joining Luton Town. His former Reds teammate John Toshack was boss at Swansea City and he then swooped to take him to the Vetch Field. It was while with Swansea that Boersma suffered a serious ankle injury in a game against Swindon Town. It pretty much ended his playing career prematurely.

It was at this point he focused on coaching and his physio career. In 1983 he left Swansea to become assistant manager at Lincoln City and then moved to a first-team coaching role with Doncaster Rovers. Boersma was at Doncaster when Souness invited him to join him at Rangers where he could combine coaching with physiotherapy duties. Phil accepted the proposal immediately and was soon heading north to hook up with his old Middlesbrough pal.

It's fair to say they have been pretty much joined at the hip ever since, with Phil joining Graeme on his coaching journey from Glasgow to Liverpool and on to Istanbul and Benfica before working together again at Southampton. Circumstances precluded Phil from joining Graeme in Turin. Phil was not on the payroll as any kind of old-pals act – Boersma was an acute judge of player and was Graeme's sounding board and confidant. Phil's personal fitness levels were up there with the best in squad players over the years and he was capable of doing any drill the players were at every club he was at. Graeme Souness called him 'Peter Pan' for his youthful looks and natural zest for the job in hand. Phil was not a 'yes man' and had his own ideas and was happy to express them, even when they didn't always agree with Graeme's view of things. It was a healthy, honest and rewarding relationship for both. They were on the same wavelength and it remains important that Phil is recognised for his contribution to the success Graeme delivered and the magnificent trophy haul they achieved together at Rangers.

# CHAPTER 41:
# MEMORIES, LEGACY AND THE SIGNIFICANCE OF SOUNESS

'If you asked me about Graeme Souness's legacy from his time at Rangers you would have to start with the way he took professionalism in the Scottish game to new levels. Other clubs really had to follow suit. He increased standards by example.'

**David MacKinnon: Rangers, Airdrie and Kilmarnock**

'Graeme Souness didn't just sell Rangers to the main players in the English international side at the time, he sold them Scotland as a wonderful place to live and to embrace the culture. The Butchers, the Woods and Wilkins all did, and even now nearly 40 years on Mark Hateley still lives up here.'

**Iain Ferguson: Rangers, Dundee United and Motherwell**

'Souness signed big-name players who were almost mercenaries, as Rangers were paying top dollar to get them to come north. By the time the bulk of these players left they were Rangers fans for life. When most come to Ibrox, nearly 40 years later they are still loved by the fans.'

**Alex MacDonald: Barcelona Bear**

'Rangers blazed the trail with the imaginative appointment of Graeme Souness. It raised the profile of the Scottish game beyond belief.'

**Gordon Smith: Rangers treble winner**

'Souness raised the bar and then some. Other clubs had to assess their own position and decide which way to go.'

**Archie Macpherson: legendary broadcaster**

'Graeme Souness coming in was definitely to Rangers' benefit. Was it best for Scottish football? I'm not convinced. Some clubs spent more than they probably should have to try and keep up with what was happening at Ibrox.'

**Alex Totten: former assistant manager, Rangers**

'Graeme Souness came to Rangers an icon of Scottish football and left a hero in the eyes of the Rangers fans. If I am being honest, I think he should have stayed and kept that upwards trajectory going and eventually left with a status similar to that of Bill Struth himself. I suppose though Walter took the job on, and what a job he did! His legacy remains obvious, he re-awakened a sleeping giant.'

**Bill McMurdo: football agent**

## MEMORIES, LEGACY AND THE SIGNIFICANCE OF SOUNESS

'Ticket sales went through the roof. It was then we started the Premiere Club in the Govan stand rear, and it sold out in days. We then extended the option to season ticket holders in the Govan front and again it sold out in days. The impact of Graeme Souness saw an unsurpassed demand for tickets, it was phenomenal. Our numbers shot up to 32,000 in next to no time and it was all down to the new manager and the exciting new players he was bringing in.'

**Jim Hannah: Rangers ticket office manager, 1986**

'Winning the league in that first season will live with me forever. Souness demanded success and he was so focused. Seeing the joy on the faces of the fans when we were crowned champions was magnificent. It had been a long time since Rangers last won the title but that first one for me was so special. I played over 30 games that first season and while we had our ups and downs Graeme Souness certainly made me a better player.'

**Derek Ferguson: Rangers, 1982–1990**

'I loved working with Graeme Souness. Scottish football still owes him a big debt. He totally transformed the Scottish game and other clubs had to sit up and take note, then change or be left behind.'

**Colin West: Graeme Souness's first signing for Rangers**

# THE SIGNIFICANCE OF SOUNESS

'When Aberdeen lifted the Cup Winners' Cup in 1983 it made people south of the border think that maybe Scottish football isn't so bad. They took more of an interest, but when Graeme Souness took over at Rangers – wow! – that was a totally different proposition. People sat up and took note. Souness laid foundations for a whole new era for the game north of the border, including reversing the transfer trends by bringing in huge personality players from England.'

**Ian Crocker: Sky Sports football commentator**

'I hold Graeme Souness in the highest possible regard. He was my captain when I made my Scotland debut in 1983. He had such a big personality and commanded the dressing room. When he signed me for Rangers, he had already proven that he was an equally capable manager as he had been a player. He changed everything at Rangers and it was clearly for the better. One area that Graeme was quite open about was that he was sometimes less than willing to give youth a chance, as he often said "young players won't keep me in a job!" When he then gave me the opportunity to coach the reserves I did my very best to develop players that could prove him wrong, but he was a very single-minded guy. I then progressed to coach the first team, and when Walter replaced Graeme he had a terrific foundation to take the team forwards and a few young players did break through. Graeme was brilliant for me – I'll always value the fact he signed me and that I went on to spend eight years at the club and tried to put some of Graeme's characteristics into my coaching methods.'

**Davie Dodds: former Rangers player and coach**

'Rangers bringing in Graeme Souness was probably the biggest appointment since Bill Struth, and even with consideration to Scot Symon, Dick Advocaat and Steven Gerrard we have not made such a big appointment since. It was a revolution. Graeme was strong-minded and refused to be bound by rules. Jock Wallace left when Willie Waddell refused to break the established wage cap, whereas Graeme ripped up the wage structure and committed to pay what was required to sign the best. With Graeme Souness there would have been no Walter Smith, and while Walter was an outstanding coach and tactician I think it was working with Graeme that sharpened his instincts for winning. Souness reversed the trend of the best Scottish talent being drained to England by raiding the English market for the cream of their international side. The closest Rangers came previously to Chris Woods and Terry Butcher was the signing of Herbert Lock from Southampton in 1907 – that was a big deal then as he became a mainstay of the title-winning side over the next few years. Graeme didn't operate by the book in the transfer market as he lifted the bar with his signings, many of whom took the view that if it's good enough for Graeme Souness, Rangers is good enough for me. He went beyond our own shores to get the quality he wanted and it's a strategy that was taken too by Walter Smith when he succeeded him.'

> **David Mason: Rangers' official historian, who took the job six weeks after Graeme Souness had been appointed and was still in his post in 2025**

'Taking on a role as player–manager is a daunting task, as I know first-hand from my own first steps in management at Motherwell while continuing to play. It's challenging and all-consuming. I only managed to play a handful of games as the pressures to succeed in both were huge. That's also when you need your backroom staff to be so switched on. For Graeme Souness to come in and make it look so easy with a title win in his first season was incredible. Although looking back to the red cards he picked up it shows you how he also felt the pressure. Again, he was fortunate he had Walter Smith as his number two. It wasn't a bad partnership, was it?'

> **Alex McLeish: Rangers' treble-winning manager**

'I had many ups and downs with Graeme Souness. On one occasion I was leaving Ibrox after a game and was stopped by Peter the long-service steward on Rangers' reception. He asked me to wait a moment while he made a phone call. The phone was then handed to me to be told by Graeme Souness on the other end of the line that I was now barred from Ibrox. Apparently, my crime was I had reported that one of his players could be out for an

# MEMORIES, LEGACY AND THE SIGNIFICANCE OF SOUNESS

extended period as I had witnessed him leave the stadium on crutches. Graeme told me I had abused the privilege of position and overstepped the mark. I offered to come upstairs to talk about it and the call was terminated with a "No you f****n' won't!" The ban didn't last and quickly Graeme was back to his usual engaging self. But that incident summed up how tight a ship he ran. He was such a strong character and personality. In the west of Scotland people have sectarianism almost as a lifestyle. Graeme signing Maurice Johnston and Mark Walters, albeit in different circumstances, broke down barriers. I am myself in a mixed marriage that this year in 2025 will see us celebrate 54 years together. Having spent all my life in Glasgow, I know better than many what strengths of character it took from both Maurice and Graeme to make it work at Rangers.

'Graeme Souness remains the most charismatic man I have ever met in football. A singular human being with an incredible aura. He had something about him that set him apart. I was heading to Fir Park one day not that many years ago and had my huge Radio Clyde umbrella up to protect me from the elements when a head popped under the brolly and enquired, "Are you still causing trouble on that radio?" It was Graeme Souness with a huge smile on his face. Graeme taking the Rangers job and bringing Walter Smith with him was pivotal for them both, but more importantly it changed Rangers for the better on and indeed off the park.'

**Hugh Keevins: broadcaster and writer**

'Graeme Souness changed the whole landscape of the Scottish game. I know a lot of players at other clubs up here benefitted by having their wages increased because of the money Rangers players were earning. I remember one broadsheet published a table of the difference in player earnings between Rangers and Celtic. It was accurate down to the penny and I know because my income had been listed. My dad, being an accountant, saw this report as a real breach of confidentiality. Celtic fans saw it differently and saw it as Celtic keeping a close tie on the purse strings, as did some Celtic players who wanted parity. Apart from the finance, Souness changed everything; and despite everything he had gone through as a player at Liverpool, in Italy and with Scotland he still got caught up in the unique and extraordinary Old Firm experience and was red-carded as we won 1–0 at Celtic Park. He lost it completely that day and with hindsight would probably admit he underestimated the intensity of the fixture. Believe me that game gets to you. Graeme Souness made Rangers the team to beat.'

**Andy Walker: 198 Celtic appearances and 69 goals**

'I'll always be grateful to Graeme for giving me the opportunity to play for the club I loved. It was quite a contrast in management styles from Craig Brown and Alex Smith who I had worked under previously. Both Craig and Alex went on and had fantastic managerial careers but Graeme was different. He wasn't big on tactics but was big on motivation. He used to say, "Turn

## MEMORIES, LEGACY AND THE SIGNIFICANCE OF SOUNESS

your opponents – earn the right to play by winning the battles," but more importantly he also said you need to earn the right to pull on this blue strip. Graeme believed you were a good enough player to be here and didn't need coaching, and he was always quick to remind us that nobody likes us and to use that to help us win the game. When I look back, Graeme converted me to a more defensive-holding midfielder from the young adventurous more offensive guy he signed. In my own coaching career I have tried to take a few wee bits I learned over the years from Craig, Alex and then Graeme, and before it was Walter and Dick Advocaat. Some wonderful managers to learn from. Graeme changed my game but I was only a very small part of the changes that were obvious throughout Scottish football as everyone sat up to take notice that day in 1986 when it was confirmed Graeme Souness was the new manager of Rangers Football Club. He turned our game in Scotland upside down.'

**Ian Ferguson: Rangers nine-in-a-row legend with ten league titles in total, 305 RFC appearances and 45 goals. Ian is now coaching in Perth, Western Australia**

## Significant Souness Landmarks

- Reversed the cross-border transfer trend and enticed top players from England to come to Scotland.
- Signed England captain Terry Butcher despite Manchester United and Tottenham wanting his services.
- Broke Rangers' transfer record with the club's first

## THE SIGNIFICANCE OF SOUNESS

seven-figure signing when Richard Gough joined.
- Brought Walter Smith to the club.
- He himself set a new record, when all at the same time he became the first-ever player–manager–director in British football.
- Souness scrapped the age-old Ibrox tradition of players wearing a shirt and tie every day to training.
- Souness sporting a beard himself confirmed that the previous Rangers rule of no facial hair for players was now very much obsolete.
- Won the Scottish title in his first season in charge, which was his own first season as a manager.
- Souness joining Rangers increased turnover and profits season-on-season, every season, until his departure.
- From Souness joining there was an unprecedented demand for season tickets to a level that a stadium-capacity review was initiated. Season tickets were not nearly so popular pre-Souness. It became almost the only way to guarantee admission.
- Commercial sales of replica strips etc., and corporate sponsorship set new records.
- Ally McCoist and Ian Durrant were given extended contracts to remain at Rangers despite serious transfer interest in both.
- Interest in Rangers at that time was so intense that the first-ever live Old Firm clash from Ibrox was broadcast on TV.
- Introduced future chairman David Murray to Rangers.
- Forced a UEFA rule change after narrowing the Ibrox pitch ahead of a European tie.

- Signed Rangers' first high-profile black player in Mark Walters.
- Signed Rangers' first high-profile Roman Catholic player in Maurice Johnston.
- Won the league title that set Rangers off for nine titles in a row.

# ADDENDUM: HONOURS

## GRAEME SOUNESS: honours as a player

Middlesbrough: 1 x Second Division League Championship
(1973–74) 35 appearances, 7 goals

Liverpool: 5 x First Division League Championships
(1978–79) 41 appearances, 8 goals
(1979–80) 41 appearances, 1 goal
(1981–82) 35 appearances, 5 goals
(1982–83) 41 appearances, 9 goals
(1983–84) 37 appearances, 7 goals

4 x League Cup Winner
(1980–81) 2–1 v West Ham (played first game, not replay)
(1981–82) 3–1 v Tottenham
(1982–83) 2–1 v Man Utd
(1983–84) 1–0 v Everton (played in both games)

3 x European Cup Winner
(1977–78) 1–0 v Club Brugge

(1980–81) 1–0 v Real Madrid
(1983–84) 1–1 v Roma (4–2 on pens)

Sampdoria: 1 x Coppa Italia
(1984–85) 3–1 agg v Milan (played in both games)

Rangers: 2 x Premier Division Championships
(1986–87) 25 appearances, 1 goal
(1988–89) 6 appearances

## GRAEME SOUNESS: honours as a manager

Rangers: 4 x Premier Division Championship

(1986–87) P–44 W–31 D–7 L–6 F–85 A–23 Pts–69
(1988–89) P–36 W–26 D–4 L–6 F–62 A–26 Pts–56
(1989–90) P–36 W–20 D–11 L–5 F–48 A–19 Pts–51
(1990–91) * P–32 W–21 D–7 L–4 F–58 A–20 Pts–49

4 x League Cup Winner
(1986–87) 2–1 v Celtic
(1987–88) 3–3 v Aberdeen (5–3 on pens)
(1988–89) 3–2 v Aberdeen
(1990–91) 2–1 v Celtic

Liverpool: 1 x FA Cup Winner
(1991–92) 2–0 v Sunderland

# THE SIGNIFICANCE OF SOUNESS

Galatasaray: 1 x Turkish Cup
(1995–96) 1–0 v Fenerbahçe
1 x Turkish Super Cup
(1996) 3–0 v Fenerbahçe

Blackburn: 1 x League Cup
(2001–02) 2–1 v Tottenham

\* The Rangers title in 1990–91 is a bit of a tenuous one . . . Graeme Souness managed the team for 32 out of 36 games and Walter Smith for 4 out of 36, but most sources credit that title to Walter Smith and not Souness. Not sure why both can't be credited. I would certainly give credit to both.

In total Rangers played 36 games with Souness in charge for 32. Rangers in total won 24 – Drew 7 – Lost 5. Goals for 62 – Goals against 23 – Goal difference +39.
Rangers finished with 55 points.

\*\* A significant structural change to Scotland's top league was effected at the end of season 1987/88. Three teams were relegated: Falkirk, Dunfermline Athletic and Morton. Hamilton were promoted and that then established a top ten league rather than twelve. The clubs would play each other twice at home and twice away to reflect a 36-game programme compared to the 44-match style of previous.

# THE LAST WORD: ALLY McCOIST

Make no mistake, I had my run-ins with Graeme; and most of them, I suppose with hindsight, were pretty much justified. He had the most amazing presence and he still does. It was an education to work with him every day. He only wanted us to be the best we possibly could be and more importantly to be winners every time we took the field.

I have to thank him for taking my game to another level and making me part of his medal-hungry team. Graeme Souness came to the club at a time when we had maybe lost our way and needed help. He soon put that right. Graeme is due enormous credit for the part he played in getting Ibrox roaring again. He should be very proud of that achievement.

**Alistair McCoist OBE: nine-in-a-row hero, 581 Rangers appearances and 355 goals**

# ACKNOWLEDGEMENTS

Thanks to all the former Rangers players of the Souness era, and even before, for sharing some amazing memories.

Players and managers too of other clubs from 1986 and beyond, whose contributions are really appreciated and were a massive help to bring perspective and help complete the story.

To the many media legends from both print and broadcasting and others from within the game who all offered outstanding recollections of so many major events in the career of Graeme Souness.

Clearly Graeme Souness remains held in the highest esteem by all who contributed to *The Significance of Souness*.

Revisiting and chatting about Graeme's career was enlightening, enjoyable, engrossing and a genuine privilege.

I hope the reader enjoys the book as much as I enjoyed pulling it together.